Changing Higher Education in India

Bloomsbury Higher Education Research

Series Editor: Simon Marginson

The Bloomsbury Higher Education Research series provides the evidence-based academic output of the world's leading research centre on higher education, the ESRC/HEFCE Centre for Global Higher Education (CGHE) in the UK. The core focus of CGHE's work and of the Bloomsbury Higher Education Research series is higher education, especially the future of higher education in the changing global landscape. The emergence of CGHE reflects the remarkable growth in the role and importance of universities and other higher education institutions, and research and science, across the world. Corresponding to CGHE's projects, monographs in the series will consist of social science research on global, international, national and local aspects of higher education, drawing on methodologies in education, learning theory, sociology, economics, political science and policy studies. Monographs will be prepared so as to maximise worldwide readership and selected on the basis of their relevance to one or more of higher education policy, management, practice and theory. Topics will range from teaching and learning and technologies, to research and research impact in industry, national system design, the public good role of universities, social stratification and equity, institutional governance and management, and the cross-border mobility of people, institutions, programmes, ideas and knowledge. The Bloomsbury Higher Education Research series is at the cutting edge of world research on higher education.

Advisory Board:

Paul Blackmore, King's College London, UK; Brendan Cantwell, Michigan State University, USA; Gwilym Croucher, University of Melbourne, Australia; Carolina Guzman-Valenzuela, University of Chile, Chile; Glen Jones, University of Toronto, Canada; Barbara Kehm, University of Glasgow, UK; Jenny Lee, University of Arizona, USA; Ye Liu, King's College London, UK; Christine Musselin, Sciences Po, France; Alis Oancea, University of Oxford, UK; Imanol Ordorika, Universidad Nacional Autónoma de México, Mexico; Laura Perna, University of Pennsylvania, USA; Gary Rhoades, University of Arizona, USA; Susan Robertson, University of Cambridge, UK; Yang Rui, University of Hong Kong, Hong Kong; Pedro Teixeira, University of Porto, Portugal; Jussi Valimaa, University of Jyvaskyla, Finland; N. V. Varghese, National Institute of Educational Planning and Administration, India; Marijk van der Wende, University of Utrecht, The Netherlands; Po Yang, Peking University, China; Akiyoshi Yonezawa, Tohoku University, Japan

Also available in the series:

The Governance of British Higher Education: The Impact of Governmental, Financial and Market Pressures, Michael Shattock and Aniko Horvath

Changing Higher Education for a Changing World, edited by Claire Callender, William Locke and Simon Marginson

Forthcoming in the series:

Changing Higher Education in East Asia, edited by Simon Marginson and Xin Xu

Changing Higher Education in India

Edited by
Saumen Chattopadhyay,
Simon Marginson and N. V. Varghese

BLOOMSBURY ACADEMIC
LONDON • NEW YORK • OXFORD • NEW DELHI • SYDNEY

BLOOMSBURY ACADEMIC
Bloomsbury Publishing Plc
50 Bedford Square, London, WC1B 3DP, UK
1385 Broadway, New York, NY 10018, USA
29 Earlsfort Terrace, Dublin 2, Ireland

BLOOMSBURY, BLOOMSBURY ACADEMIC and the Diana logo are trademarks of
Bloomsbury Publishing Plc

First published in Great Britain 2022
This paperback edition published in 2023

Copyright © Saumen Chattopadhyay, Simon Marginson, N. V. Varghese
and Bloomsbury, 2022

Saumen Chattopadhyay, Simon Marginson, N. V. Varghese and Bloomsbury
have asserted their right under the Copyright, Designs and Patents Act, 1988, to be identified
as Author of this work.

For legal purposes the Acknowledgements on pp. xix–xx constitute an extension
of this copyright page.

Series design by Adriana Brioso
Cover image © Setthasith Wansuksri/EyeEm/Getty Images

All rights reserved. No part of this publication may be reproduced or transmitted in
any form or by any means, electronic or mechanical, including photocopying, recording,
or any information storage or retrieval system, without prior permission in writing
from the publishers.

Bloomsbury Publishing Plc does not have any control over, or responsibility for, any
third-party websites referred to or in this book. All internet addresses given in this book were correct at
the time of going to press. The author and publisher regret any inconvenience caused if addresses have
changed or sites have ceased to exist, but can accept no responsibility for any such changes.

A catalogue record for this book is available from the British Library.

Library of Congress Cataloging-in-Publication Data
Names: Chattopadhyay, Saumen, editor. | Marginson, Simon, 1951- editor. |
Varghese, N. V., editor.
Title: Changing higher education in India / Edited by Saumen
Chattopadhyay, Simon Marginson and N.V. Varghese.
Description: London; New York: Bloomsbury Academic, 2021. |
Series: Bloomsbury higher education research |
Includes bibliographical references and index.
Identifiers: LCCN 2021025493 (print) | LCCN 2021025494 (ebook) |
ISBN 9781350192379 (hardback) | ISBN 9781350192386 (ebook) |
ISBN 9781350192393 (epub)
Subjects: LCSH: Education, Higher–Aims and objectives–India. |
Education, Higher–India–Finance. | Education and state–India. |
Educational equalization–India.
Classification: LCC LA1153.C44 2021 (print) |
LCC LA1153 (ebook) | DDC 378.54–dc23
LC record available at https://lccn.loc.gov/2021025493
LC ebook record available at https://lccn.loc.gov/2021025494

ISBN: HB: 978-1-3501-9237-9
PB: 978-1-3501-9307-9
ePDF: 978-1-3501-9238-6
eBook: 978-1-3501-9239-3

Series: Bloomsbury Higher Education Research

Typeset by Newgen KnowledgeWorks Pvt. Ltd., Chennai, India

To find out more about our authors and books visit www.bloomsbury.com
and sign up for our newsletters.

Contents

List of Figures	viii
List of Tables	ix
Notes on Contributors	xii
Series Editor's Foreword	xiv
Acknowledgements	xix
List of Abbreviations	xxi

	Introduction: Changing Higher Education in India *Simon Marginson, N. V. Varghese and Saumen Chattopadhyay*	1
1	Directions of Change in Higher Education in India: From Massification to Universalization *N. V. Varghese*	23
2	Financing of Higher Education in India: Issues and Challenges *Saumen Chattopadhyay and Jinusha Panigrahi*	47
3	Equity in Higher Education for Inclusive Growth: Evidence from India *N. V. Varghese, Nidhi S. Sabharwal and C. M. Malish*	67
4	Privatization versus Private Sector in Higher Education in India *N. V. Varghese and Nivedita Sarkar*	95
5	The Dynamics of Union-State Relations and Higher Education in India *Anamika Srivastava and Saumen Chattopadhyay*	121
6	Changing Contours of Regulation in Indian Higher Education *Saumen Chattopadhyay and Emon Nandi*	143
7	Internationalization of Indian Higher Education: Issues and Challenges *Saumen Chattopadhyay*	165
8	Engineering Education in India *Jandhyala B. G. Tilak and Pradeep Kumar Choudhury*	187
9	Teachers and Students as Political Actors in Indian Higher Education *Aishna Sharma, Vanessa Chishti and Binay Kumar Pathak*	211

References	241
Index	263

Figures

0.1 Gross tertiary enrolment ratio (%), urban population as a proportion of total population (%), India and world, 2000–19   3

3.1 Subjects being studied by students as per their economic classes, 2014   85

5.1 Share of union and states/union territories' expenditure in the total expenditure on higher education (general and technical education, revenue account) between 2013–14 and 2017–18   128

5.2 Central government allocation on National Higher Education Mission (RUSA) (in million USD Purchasing Power Parity)   137

6.1 The proposed regulatory structure in National Education Policy 2020   156

6.2 Academic freedom and Burton Clark's triangle   159

8.1 Economic growth and number of engineering institutions (per 1 million population), 2018–19   193

8.2 Ratio of regional concentration of engineering institutions   197

8.3 Distribution of enrolments in engineering education, by household quintiles, India (%)   202

Tables

0.1	Five Selected World Top 100 Universities Compared to the Five Leading Research Producer Institutions in India, Three Indicators, 2020	9
1.1	Higher Education Expansion in India, 1950–51 to 2018–19	27
1.2	Stage-Wise Enrolment of Students, 2005 and 2019	28
1.3	Gross Enrolment Ratio in Higher Education in India, 2011–12 to 2018–19	33
1.4	Gender Parity Index in Higher Education in India, 2011–12 to 2018–19	34
2.1	Public Expenditure on Education as Percentage of GDP	54
2.2	Public Expenditure on Education by Education and Other Departments	55
2.3	Per Student Expenditure by Type of Institutions	57
3.1	Strategies to Improve Equity in Higher Education across Five Year Plans, 1951–6 to 2012–17	74
3.2a	Gross Enrolment Ratio by Social and Income Groups	82
3.2b	Gross Enrolment Ratio by Social Group and Gender, 2014	83
3.3	Subjects Being Studied by Students as per Social Groups, Gender and Location, 2014 (%)	84
3.4	Predicted Probabilities of Participation in Higher Education by Persons Aged 18–23, 1995 and 2014	86
3.5	Probability of Attending STEM (science, technology, engineering and mathematics) Subjects, 1995 and 2014	88
3.6	Unemployment Rates among Social Groups (Rural and Urban)	92
4.1	Higher Education Expansion: Institutions and Enrolments	102
4.2	Higher Education Enrolment by Management (%)	108
4.3	Distribution of Enrolment by Social Groups and Types of Institution	109
4.4	Distribution of Higher Education Students by Social Groups and Income	110
4.5	Enrolment by Gender and Type of Higher Education	111
4.6	Enrolment at the Undergraduate Level by Types of Education and Income	111
4.7	Per Student Expenditure by Type of Institutions	112

4.8	Per Student Higher Education across All States/Union Territories	113
4.9	Per Student Average Household Expenditure by Types of Institutions across All States/Union Territories	114
4.10	Per Student Average Household Expenditure on Private Coaching at Higher Secondary by Sex, Location and Social Group	115
4.11	Per Student Average Household Expenditure on Private Coaching at Higher Secondary by Expenditure Quintiles	115
4.12	Growth of Education Loans in India	118
4.13	Student Loan by Disciplines in India (in INR)	119
5.1	State-Wise Comparison of Net State Domestic Product Per Capita, Gross Enrolment Ratio and Private Higher Education Institutions, 2017–18	130
5.2	State-Wise Comparison of Deficit Indicators and Budget Allocation for Higher Education, 2017–18 (Budget Estimate)	131
5.3	A Comparison between States with and without State Higher Education Councils	137
5.4	A Comparison of High and Low Per Capita Income States and National Higher Education Mission (RUSA) Funds Allocation	138
6A.1	Methodology for University and College Teachers for Calculating Academic/Research Score	161
7.1	Top Six Countries by Research Output (All Publications Type), 2018–19	168
7.2	Proportion of Internationally Co-authored Publications	169
7.3	World Ranking of Indian Universities (Select) and Their National Ranking in National Institutional Ranking Framework, 2020	170
7.4	Outward and Inward Mobility for India	172
7.5	Gender-Wise and course-Wise Distribution of Foreign Students	174
7.6	International Branch Campuses: Home Country India	175
7A.1	Inward and Outward Student Mobility, India, 2018	185
8.1	Growth of Engineering Institutions and Enrolment in India	190
8.2	Private Engineering Institutions in India, 2018–19	192
8.3	Factors Influencing Growth of Engineering Institutions	194
8.4	Regional Concentration of Engineering Institutions and Intake in India, by Management, 2012–13 and 2018–19	196
8.5	State-Wise Engineering Institutions per 1 Million Population in India, 2018–19	198
8.6	Enrolment of Women in Higher and Engineering Education in India	200

8.7	Enrolments of Scheduled Castes and Scheduled Tribes in Engineering Education in India	201
8.8	Enrolment in Engineering (First Degree) Programmes, by Sub-Stream (%)	203
8.9	Growth in the Number of PhDs Awarded in Engineering/Technology and as a Proportion of Total Undergraduate Out-turn in India	206
8.10	Number of Vacant Student Places in Engineering/Technology Institutions in India	207
9.1	Interfaces of Teachers' Political Organizations and Emergence of Resistance	221

Contributors

Saumen Chattopadhyay is Professor at the Zakir Husain Centre for Educational Studies, Jawaharlal Nehru University, New Delhi, India. He teaches economics of education, and his research areas include higher education policy, governance and financing-related issues, corruption and the black economy.

Vanessa Chishti teaches history and politics at O.P. Jindal Global University in Sonipat, India. Her research is on the modern history of Kashmir, which she investigates as part of her interest in the economic and social history of capitalism.

Pradeep Kumar Choudhury is assistant professor in economics of education at the Zakir Husain Centre for Educational Studies, Jawaharlal Nehru University, New Delhi, India. His broad research areas include economics of education, education and health, education and labour markets, and applied development economics.

C. M. Malish is Assistant Professor in the Centre for Policy Research in Higher Education (CPRHE), National Institute of Educational Planning and Administration (NIEPA), New Delhi, India. His current research focuses on access, equity, student diversity, discrimination, student success, institutional culture and language of education in higher education.

Simon Marginson is professor of higher education at the University of Oxford, UK. He is also the director of the ESRC/OFSRE Centre for Global Higher Education, joint editor-in-chief of the journal *Higher Education*, a lead researcher with the Institute of Education at the Higher School of Economics in Moscow, Russia, and a professorial fellow of the University of Melbourne, Australia. His research interests primarily focus on global and international aspects of higher education.

Emon Nandi is a Fulbright Post-doctoral Fellow at the Centre for International Higher Education (CIHE) in Boston College, USA. She worked as an assistant professor at the Tata Institute of Social Sciences, Mumbai, India. Her current research focuses on quality, rankings and academic governance in higher education.

Jinusha Panigrahi is an assistant professor at the Centre for Policy Research in Higher Education at the NIEPA, New Delhi. Her research work lies in the areas of economics of education, financing, internationalization, privatization and private higher education.

Binay Kumar Pathak teaches Economics at Lalit Narayan Mithila University, Darbhanga, India. With an interest in the economics of education, his publications revolve around higher education, economics of information, choice and decision-making, teachers and students as actors, education policy and the social science research environment.

Nidhi S. Sabharwal is Associate Professor in the Centre for Policy Research in Higher Education (CPRHE), National Institute of Educational Planning and Administration (NIEPA), New Delhi, India. Her current research focuses on access, equity, student diversity, college readiness, student success and social inclusion in higher education.

Nivedita Sarkar is Assistant Professor at Ambedkar University, New Delhi, India. Her research focuses on the economics of education.

Aishna Sharma teaches economics of education, microeconomics and macroeconomics at Shiv Nadar University, Uttar Pradesh, India. She works in areas pertaining to education policy and governance of universities, with an interest in the construction of markets, academic freedom of faculty, funding of education, power relations in universities and corruption in the education sector.

Anamika Srivastava is Assistant Professor and Fellow at the International Institute for Higher Education Research and Capacity Building at the O.P. Jindal Global University, Sonipat, India. Her research interests include critical realism, marketization and quality in higher education.

Jandhyala B. G. Tilak is a former professor and vice-chancellor of the National University of Educational Planning and Administration, New Delhi, India. Currently he is ICSSR National Fellow and Distinguished Professor, Council for Social Development, New Delhi.

N. V. Varghese is Professor and Vice-Chancellor of the National Institute for Educational Administration and Planning in New Delhi, India. He was the founding director of the Centre for Policy Research in Higher Education (CPRHE), National Institute of Educational Planning and Administration (NIEPA), New Delhi, India, from 2013 to 2019, and head of Governance and Management in Education at the International Institute for Educational Planning (IIEP/UNESCO) from 2006 to 2013.

Series Editor's Foreword

Changing Higher Education in India is the third book to be published in the Bloomsbury Higher Education Research book series. This series brings to the public, government and universities across the world the new ideas and research evidence being generated by researchers from the ESRC/OFSRE Centre for Global Higher Education.[1] The Centre for Global Higher Education (CGHE), a partnership of researchers from ten UK and international universities, is the world's largest concentration of expertise in relation to higher education and its social contributions. The core focus of CGHE's work, and of the Bloomsbury Higher Education Research Series, is higher education, especially the future of higher education in the changing global landscape.

Each year this mega-topic of 'higher education' seems to take on greater importance for governments, business, civil organizations, students, families and the public at large. In higher education much is at stake. The role and impact of the sector is growing everywhere. More than 220 million students enrol at tertiary level across the world, four-fifths of them in degree programmes. Almost 40 per cent of school leavers now enter some kind of tertiary education each year, though resources and quality vary significantly. In North America and Europe, this ratio rises to four young people in every five. Universities and colleges are seen as the primary medium for personal opportunity, social mobility and the development of whole communities. About 2.5 million new science papers are published worldwide each year, and the role of research in industry and government continues to expand everywhere.

In short, there is much at stake in higher education. It has become central to social, economic and political life. One reason is that even while serving local society and national policy, the higher education and research sectors are especially globalized in character. Each year 6 million students change countries in order to enrol in their chosen study programme, and more than a quarter of all published research papers involve joint authorship across national borders.

---

[1] The initials ESRC/OFSRE stand for the Economic and Social Research Council/Office for Students and Research England. Part of the ESRC funding that supports the Centre for Global Higher Education's research work was sourced from the Higher Education Funding Council for England, the ancestor body to the OFS and RE.

In some countries, fee-based international education is a major source of export revenues, while this results in some other countries losing talent in net terms each year. Routine cross-border movements of students, academics and researchers, knowledge, information and money help to shape not only nations but the international order itself.

At the same time, the global higher education landscape is changing with compelling speed, reflecting larger economic, political and cultural shifts in the geo-strategic setting. Though research universities in the United States (especially) and UK remain strong in comparative terms, the worldwide map of power in higher education is becoming more plural. A larger range of higher education practices, including models of teaching/learning, delivery, institutional organization and system, will shape higher education in future. Anglo-American (and Western) norms and models will be less dominant, and will themselves evolve. Rising universities and emerging science systems in East Asia and Singapore are already reshaping the flow of knowledge and higher education. Latin America, South East Asia, India, Central Asia and the Arab nations have a growing global importance. The trajectories of education and research in Sub-Saharan Africa are crucial to state-building and community development.

All of this has led to a more intensive focus on how higher education systems and institutions function and their value, performance, effectiveness, openness and sustainability. This in turn has made research on higher education more significant – both because it provides us with insights into one important facet of the human condition and because it informs evidenced-based government policies and professional practices.

CGHE opened in late 2015 and is currently funded until October 2023. The centre investigates higher education using a range of social science disciplines including economics, sociology, political science and policy studies, psychology and anthropology, and it uses a portfolio of quantitative, qualitative and synthetic-historical research techniques. It currently maintains ten research projects, variously of between eighteen months and eight years' duration, as well as smaller projects, and involves about forty active affiliated individual researchers. Over its eight-year span, it is financed by about £10 million in funding from the UK Economic and Social Research Council, partner universities and other sources. Its UK researchers are drawn from the Universities of Oxford, Lancaster, Surrey, Bath and University College London (UCL). The headquarters of the centre are located at Oxford, and there are large concentrations of researchers at both Oxford and UCL. The current affiliated international researchers are from Hiroshima University in Japan, Shanghai Jiao Tong University in China, Lingnan University in Hong Kong, Cape Town University in South Africa, Virginia Tech in the United States and Technological University Dublin. CGHE also collaborates with researchers from many other universities across the world, in seminars, conferences and exchange of papers. It runs an active programme of global webinars.

The centre has a full agenda. The unprecedented growth of mass higher education, the striving for excellence and innovation in the research university sector, as well as the changing global landscape, pose many researchable problems for governments, societies and higher education institutions themselves. Some of these questions already figure in CGHE research projects. For example: What are the formative effects on societies and economies of the now much wider distribution of advanced levels of learning? How does it change individual graduates as people – and what does it mean when half or more of the workforce is higher educated and much more mobile, and when confident human agency has become widely distributed across civil and political society in nations with little state tradition, or where the main experience has been colonial or authoritarian rule? What does it mean when many more people are becoming steeped in the sciences, many others understand the world through the lenses of the social sciences or humanities while a third group is engaged in neither? What happens to those parts of the population left outside the formative effects of higher education? What is the larger public role and contribution of higher education, as distinct from the private benefits for and private effects on individual graduates? What does it mean when large and growing higher education institutions have become the major employers in many locations and help to sustain community and cultural life, almost like branches of local government while also being linked to global cities across the world? And what is the contribution of higher education, beyond helping to form the attributes of individual graduates, to the development of the emerging global society?

Likewise, the many practical problems associated with building higher education and science take on greater importance. How can scarce public budgets provide for the public role of higher education institutions, for a socially equitable system of individual access and for research excellence, all at the same time? What is the role for and limits of family financing and tuition loans systems? What is the potential contribution of private institutions, including for-profit colleges? In national systems, what is the best balance between research-intensive and primarily teaching institutions, and between academic and vocational education? What are the potentials for technological delivery in extending access? What is happening in graduate labour markets, where returns to degrees are becoming more dispersed between families with differing levels of income, different kinds of universities and different fields of study? Do larger education systems provide better for social mobility and income equality? How does the internationalization of universities contribute to national policy and local societies? Does mobile international education expand opportunity or further stratify societies? What are the implications of populist tensions between national and global goals, as manifest, for example, in the tensions over Brexit in the UK and the politics of the Trump era in the United States, for higher education and research? And always, what can national systems of higher education and science learn from each other, and how can they build stronger common ground?

In tackling these research challenges and bringing the research to all, we are very grateful to have the opportunity to work with such a high-quality publisher as Bloomsbury. In the book series, monographs are selected on the basis of their relevance to one or more of higher education policy, management, practice and theory. Topics range from teaching and learning and technologies, to research and its organization, the design parameters of national higher education systems, the public good role of higher education, social stratification and equity, institutional governance and management, and the cross-border mobility of people, programmes and ideas. Much of CGHE's work is global and comparative in scale, drawing lessons from higher education in many different countries, and the centre's cross-country and multi-project structure allows it to tap into the more plural higher education and research landscape that has emerged. The book series draws on authors from across the world and is prepared for relevance across the world.

CGHE places special emphasis on the relevance of its research, on communicating its findings and on maximizing the usefulness and impacts of those findings in higher education policy and practice. It has a relatively high public profile for an academic research centre and reaches out to engage higher education stakeholders, national and international organizations, policymakers, regulators and the broader public in the UK and across the world. These objectives are also central to the book series. Recognizing that the translation from research outputs to high-quality scholarly monographs is not always straightforward – while achieving impact in both academic and policy/practice circles is crucial – monographs in the book series are scrutinized critically before publication, for readability as well as quality. Texts are carefully written and edited to ensure that they have achieved the right combination of, on one hand intellectual depth and originality and, on the other hand, full accessibility for public, higher education and policy circles across the world.

Simon Marginson
Professor of Higher Education, University of Oxford, UK
Director, ESRC/OFSRE Centre for Global Higher Education

Acknowledgements

Changing Higher Education in India was developed in a small collaborative project funded by British Council, launched in 2017, led by the editors of this book and including a fruitful day-long seminar in New Delhi. The key driver and facilitator was Manjula Rao who worked for the British Council for most of the period of research and discussion. We express our respectful and heartfelt thanks to Manjula for her vision, deep commitment to cooperation, generosity and patience with the professors. We know that she will be delighted to find that we did get there in the end, and it was all worth it.

Saumen Chattopadhyay would like to thank his daughter Chandrima for her encouragement and endurance. He would also like to express his gratitude to his colleagues at the Zakir Husain Centre for Educational Studies for their support and understanding. He is also grateful to National Institute of Educational Planning and Administration (NIEPA) for ensuring sustained academic interaction between his centre and the NIEPA over the years.

Simon Marginson would like to thank his fellow editors for their warm collaboration under difficult conditions, intellectual insights and knowledge, and their many contributions throughout the text. He also thanks Lili Yang, for help with referencing and formatting of tables in the last stages prior to first submission to Bloomsbury, and Anna, for tolerating another publishing project with a deadline and for the life shared while this and much else was being done. And his son Sasha, and daughter Ana Rosa, who became friends with Chandrima while both were studying in Leiden.

The text was finalized in late January 2021 the midst of the COVID-19 pandemic and before vaccines were widely available, and then slightly revised in late April 2021 while India was undergoing a major crisis in which the flaring pandemic had vastly outpaced both vaccination and the capacity of the health system to cope. Our Delhi-based editors and contributors in different parts of the country were being called on continuously to assist with the care and survival of many others, giving care and hope without limit while dealing with their own losses. In the midst of this terrible tragedy, the challenges of putting a book together should not be overstated. Nevertheless, we deeply appreciate the work of our excellent collaborator-authors who sustained their commitment to scholarship amid all else, especially the doctoral students and early career scholars who have made such fine contributions to the pages that follow. The future of Indian higher education rests partly on your shoulders. We are also pleased to have had the opportunity to work with Professor Jandhyala B. G. Tilak during this project. His vast output of high-quality work has enriched and educated every one of us.

At Bloomsbury we benefited from the wise guidance of academic editors Alison Baker and Evangeline Stanford. We also appreciated the work of production editor Zeba Talkhani and designer Charlotte James.

New Delhi and Oxford, 30 April 2021

Abbreviations

ABC	Academic Bank of Credits
ABVP	Akhil Bhartiya Vidyarthi Parishad
AICTE	All India Council for Technical Education
AIFUCTO	All India Federation of University and College Teachers' Organisation
AISHE	All India Survey on Higher Education
AIU	Association of Indian Universities
AMU	Aligarh Muslim University
ARWU	Academic Ranking of World Universities
ASA	Ambedkar Students' Association
BE	Budgetary Estimate
BHU	Banaras Hindu University
BUCTU	Bombay University and College Teachers' Union
CAA	Citizenship Amendment Act
CABE	Central Advisory Board of Education
CBCS	Choice Based Credit System
CCTAD	Coordination Commission of Teachers' Association of Delhi
CGST	Central Goods and Services Tax
CPI	Cumulative Performance Indicator
CSR	Corporate Social Responsibility
CU	Central University
DNEP	Draft National Education Policy
DU	University of Delhi
DUTA	Delhi University Teachers' Association
ECB	External Commercial Borrowing
EOO	Equal Opportunity Office
EQA	External Quality Assurance
EWS	Economically Weaker Sections
FDI	Foreign Direct Investment
FEDCUTA	Federation of Central Universities Teachers' Association
FRBM	Fiscal Responsibility and Budget Management

FSA	Film and Television Institute of India (FTII) Students' Association
FTII	Film and Television Institute of India
FUTA	Federation of University Teachers' Association
GATS	General Agreement on Trade in Services
GEC	General Education Council
GER	Gross Enrolment Ratio
GFD	Gross Fiscal Deficit
GIAN	Global Initiative for Academic Network
GCSC	General Cultural Scholarship Scheme
GoI	Government of India
GPI	Gender Parity Index
GSDP	Gross State Domestic Product
HCU	Central University of Hyderabad
HECI	Higher Education Commission of India
HEERA	Higher Education Empowerment Regulatory Authority
HEFA	Higher Education Financing Agency
HEGC	Higher Education Grants Council
HEI	Higher Education Institution
ICCR	Indian Council of Cultural Research
ICL	Income-Contingent Loans
ICT	Information and Communication Technology
IDP	Institutional Developmental Plans
IHRDE	Institute of Human Resources Development in Electronics
IIIT	Indian Institute of Information Technology
IIM	Indian Institution of Management
IISc	Indian Institute of Science
IISER	Indian Institute of Science Education and Research
IIT	Indian Institution of Technology
INI	Institution of National Importance
IoE	Institutions of Eminence
IQAC	Internal Quality Assurance Cell
IRAHE	Independent Regulatory Authority for Higher Education
IT	Information and Technology
JEE	Joint Entrance Examination
JMI	Jamia Millia Islamia
JNU	Jawaharlal Nehru University
JNUSU	Jawaharlal Nehru University Students' Union

JNUTA	Jawaharlal Nehru University Teachers' Association
JRF	Junior Research Fellowship
MCI	Medical Council of India
MERU	Multidisciplinary Education and Research University
MHRD	Ministry of Human Resource Development
MoE	Ministry of Education (erstwhile MHRD)
MOOC	Massive Open Online Course
NAAC	National Assessment and Accreditation Council
NAC	National Accreditation Council
NBA	National Board of Accreditation
NBFC	Non-banking Financing Company
NCHER	National Council for Higher Education and Research
NE States	Northeast States
NEP 2020	National Education Policy 2020
NET	National Eligibility Test
NHEQF	National Higher Education Qualification Framework
NHERC	National Higher Education Regulatory Council
NIMS	Nizam's Institute of Medical Sciences
NIPER	National Institute of Pharmaceutical Education and Research
NIRF	National Institutional Ranking Framework
NIT	National Institute of Technology
NITI Aayog	National Institution for Transforming India
NKC	National Knowledge Commission
NPA	Non-performing Asset
NPE	National Policy on Education
NPM	New Public Management
NRC	National Register of Citizens
NRCE	National Resource Centre for Education
NRF	National Research Foundation
NSDP	Net State Domestic Product
NSQF	National Skills Qualification Framework
NSSO	National Sample Survey Office
NSUI	National Students' Union of India
OBC	Other Backward Class
PAB	Parliamentary Approval Board
PBAS	Performance-Based Appraisal System
PCI	Per Capita Income

PHEI	Private Higher Education Institution
PoA	Programme of Action
PMMMNMTT	Pandit Madan Mohan Malaviya National Mission on Teachers and Teaching
PHEI	Private Higher Education Institution
PPP	Public-Private Partnerships
PSSB	Professional Standard-Setting Body
PSU	Public Sector Undertaking
RBI	Reserve Bank of India
RD	Revenue Deficit
RISE	Revitalizing Infrastructure and Systems in Education
RUSA	Rashtriya Uchchatar Shiksha Abhiyan (National Higher Education Mission)
SAT	Scholastic Aptitude Test
SC	Scheduled Caste
SES	Socio-Economic Status
SET	State Eligibility Test
SGPGIMS	Sanjay Gandhi Postgraduate Institute of Medical Sciences
SHEC	State Higher Education Council
SPARC	Scheme for Promotion of Academic Research and Collaboration
SPU	State Private University
SPV	Special Purpose Vehicle
ST	Scheduled Tribe
STEM	Science, Technology, Engineering and Mathematics
SWAYAM	Study Web of Active Young Aspiring Minds
THE	Times Higher Education
UGC	University Grants Commission
UKIERI	UK-India Education and Research Initiative
USIEF	US-India Educational Foundation
UT	Union Territory
WCU	World Class University
YPC	Yash Pal Committee
1 lakh	100,000
1 crore	10 million

Introduction: Changing Higher Education in India

Simon Marginson, N. V. Varghese and Saumen Chattopadhyay

Introduction

The size and contribution of higher education is growing all over the world. Universities and colleges, like public administration and health care systems, have become central institutions of modern urban society everywhere, down to the level of medium-sized towns, though provision into rural areas is more uneven and incomplete. Higher education in every country carries out a remarkable range of social, economic and cultural functions, perhaps more functions than it can effectively handle without funding that few societies can afford.

Society's expectations of higher education are rarely met in full but its mission is at least partly met in almost every university, college and institute, regardless of the wealth of the country and the state, and the size and the resources of the institution. This mission is a multiple one. Higher education enhances the intellectual and social attributes of students and prepares them for lifelong learning. It helps people to form themselves. It prepares graduates for all professional occupations and many fields of skilled work, and it certifies them for work and further study. It does not guarantee employment – which depends on economic activity and policy – but helps graduates develop the necessary attributes and skills, including the capacity to respond effectively to changing requirements. It provides other essential conditions for economic activity in a fast-moving world, by developing and disseminating social networks, technological literacy, information and imagination. Higher education fosters the capacity to relate effectively to others, including openness and flexibility, tolerance and creatively working together. It encourages reasoned criticism and widespread civil discussion, and if it is doing its job properly, it implants a deep responsibility towards others. At best its graduates absorb citizenship, humanism, social justice and a passion for the common good, for sustainable communities and shared ecological survival. Teaching and learning are most important ways that higher education fulfils its mission, but faculty and research students also produce, organize and disseminate knowledge, and are sources of longer-term thinking, dispassionate truth and reasoned wisdom within a public discourse which is often confused and rife with shallow slogans and ideology. Through all these activities, higher education helps to build cities and communities and contributes markedly to global awareness and cooperation.

All universities, colleges and institutes carry out at least some of these functions while some carry out all of them. The COVID-19 pandemic, which has stopped economies in their tracks and dramatically reduced national and international mobility of persons, has not reduced the demand for higher education, though it has made higher education more difficult to provide, not just as face-to-face learning but also in the form of work experience in vocational programmes. Nevertheless, partly because there are few jobs for young people under pandemic conditions, demand for higher education has increased overall.

Higher Education and Modernization

Higher education's mission is the same in emerging countries as it is in North America, Western Europe and East Asia. Everywhere universities, colleges, skills-training and science have become front-rank policy matters. In South Korea and Taiwan, it is generally agreed that high-performing education and science have been integral elements in the successful journey of over sixty years from being a low-income country to one with a high level of economic and social development. China is on the same path. In Nordic Europe, universal high-quality higher education has long been one of the key contributing factors to societies that are outstanding in their prosperity, humanism and cohesion. But higher education policy faces especially difficult problems in India where the size and diversity of the country are immense, the majority of people still depend on agricultural work, many basic needs are unmet, infrastructure and trained personnel lag behind needs, and in many parts of the country the shared commitment that is essential to establishing higher education as a social project is only now becoming apparent.

Nowhere is the need for higher education greater than in India. Nowhere are the policy challenges larger and more complex or the problems more formidable.

Fortunately, nowhere is there a larger untapped reservoir of intelligence and energy that can be brought to bear on those challenges. As Amartya Sen (1999) argues in *Development as Freedom*, the essential keys to development are self-determining human capability and the democratic space in which agency is shared and expressed. Only the constructive energies of people operating on a large scale, on the basis of inclusion, without exception, can decisively change social conditions. The key to building democratic human agency is education. In turn, each advance in collective capability can be deployed to improving education itself, triggering a continuous feedback loop that brings the whole society forward. This is why the growth and improvement of higher education has become a core objective in most countries. It carries the potential for growth and improvement in all other social and economic sectors.

Drivers and Constraints of Participation Growth

Figure 0.1 indicates the dynamics of growth in India and the world as a whole since the year 2000. In 2019, just prior to the COVID-19 pandemic, the world's 40,000 or more tertiary education institutions enrolled 228 million students, four out of every five in the degree programmes customarily labelled 'higher education', of whom one in five, 45 million students, were in South Asia and

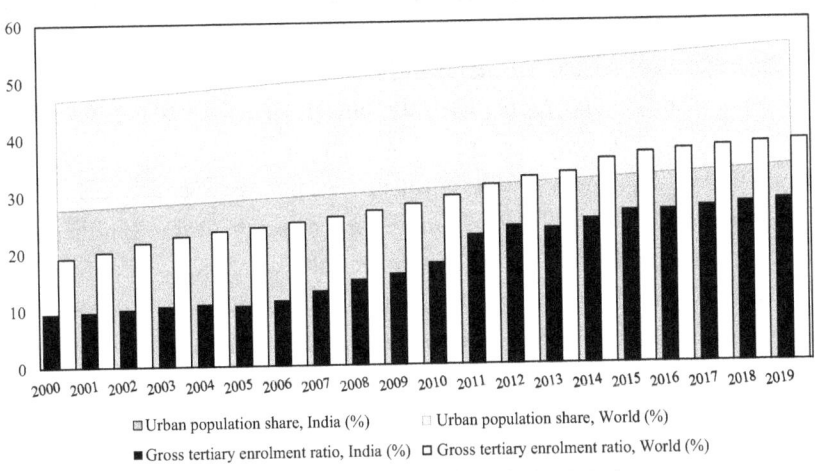

Figure 0.1 Gross tertiary enrolment ratio (%), urban population as a proportion of total population (%), India and world, 2000–19.
Source: Authors, drawing on World Bank (2021) data.

35 million in India (UNESCO 2021). As N. V. Varghese states in Chapter 1, India enrols the world's second largest number of students after China (47 million), though by no means do all students enrolled in India have the necessary facilities and access to adequate courses of study.

At world level, the enrolment of 228 million in 2019 represented 38.85 per cent of the age cohort that began in primary education more than a decade before. This number, tagged the 'gross tertiary enrolment ratio' (GTER) by statisticians, tells us how far access to post-school education has expanded and how far it has still to go before the opportunity to enter degree and diploma programmes is universal. As Figure 0.1 shows, India's GTER has grown from 9.51 per cent in the year 2000 to 28.53 per cent in 2019, from one young person in ten to more than one young person in four in only two decades. Figure 0.1 also shows that in proportional terms the gap between the world GTER and India's GTER is narrowing, even though average income per person in India is less than half of that of the world's population as a whole. Despite often severe problems of inadequate quality of provision in India, the number and proportion of enrolled students has kept on growing, with no end in sight.

What drives the growth of higher education in India and across the world? Why, despite recurring concerns about graduate unemployment in many countries, not just in India, do enrolments always seem to expand and not contract? Why do governments almost universally support growth and rarely impose a lid on the supply of places for long?

A worldwide study of the growth of participation, *High Participation Systems of Higher Education* (2018), which included twelve national case studies, found that the majority of tertiary education systems were expanding towards GTERs of 50 per cent and beyond. More than sixty countries had reached the 50 per cent mark already. Not all systems were on the high growth trajectory as yet – the take-off was yet to happen in most of the poorest quarter of countries in terms of income per head. Nevertheless, among a large majority of countries there was accelerated growth. It was striking how universal it was. These countries had a range of economic configurations, from manufacturing to services economies, at different levels of national wealth as measured by GDP per head, and at varying rates of economic growth.

The 2018 study concluded that the fundamental driver was not economic demand for skills. Neither was participation mediated by rates of graduate employment or unemployment. Nor was it determined primarily by government policy or the decisions of universities and colleges on the number of places they offer. The underlying driver of growth in higher education was the desire of families for a better life for their children, a desire which increases as higher education grows and other families are accessing opportunities. In this manner, the growth of higher education feeds on itself (Cantwell, Marginson and Smolentseva 2018: chapter 1). This was the same as the conclusion reached by Martin Trow (1973) in his path-breaking study in California at the beginning of the mass higher education era. While governments like to claim credit for opening up educational opportunities to more families while meeting the needs of the economy, in truth they have little choice. Middle classes are growing in size; almost every middle-class family wants to access higher education; the demand for higher education is moving also to lower-income families; and the accumulating desire for betterment through higher education aggregates into a continuous and growing pressure from below for opportunities.

In India, where government has marketized higher education as a means of managing the political pressures while minimizing the cost to itself, popular demand translates directly into the supply of more places by private providers. This is not a system design that is conducive to high-quality provision, especially given the lack of coordinated regulation of the private sector (see Chapter 4), but so far it has facilitated growth. Whether it can keep driving growth towards 50 per cent is another question.

Higher Education and Urban Development

The 2020 National Education Policy (NEP) announced the government's commitment to taking forward the growth of higher education. It established a national target of 50 per cent participation by 2035. While the government's policy coincides with growing popular demand for higher education, and educators want to extend and democratize opportunities to study, the target is not easy to achieve. This is because higher education is not only a contributor to the processes of modernization and development, it also partly depends on these processes. While it is a socially innovative sector in many respects, it cannot move too far in advance of the national resource base and the pace of modernization. There are two factors which mediate the capacity of higher education to expand. One is resources for higher education and the other is the extent of urban development in India.

Resources are a 'bottom line' condition of expansion to 50 per cent and beyond. Poorer families have a limited capacity to pay for tuition and the costs of student living support. In the absence of adequate public funding, with many poorer families forced into private education, the outcome is poor-quality institutional provision and the less than full-time character of many enrolments, while other families cannot participate at all.

The second factor is India's rate of urbanization. In India, the proportion of people living in cities is below that of the world as a whole (see the grey shading in Figure 0.1). This matters because in India, as in other countries, higher education is primarily an urban phenomenon. Universities and colleges are larger and more expensive to provide than primary schools and need more specialist staff. It is not cost effective to provide them in villages, and there is limited scope to provide them in towns. Cities enable economies of size and scope. In addition, in cities the demand from below for higher education becomes concentrated on a large scale. People can put effective pressure on governments to expand access, and market-based providers have large numbers of potential customers. Hence in every country, after a lag, the GTER tends to follow the urbanization curve on an upward trajectory. Urbanization means the proportion of the population living in cities. As societies modernize and economies develop, the GTER moves closer to the level of urbanization; the gap between the two starts to close. In the United States, the GTER curve is now slightly higher than the level of urbanization, at just under 90 per cent, meaning that tertiary opportunities are good even for some rural families. In China, the GTER curve has nearly intersected with the urbanization curve at just over 50 per cent. As Figure 0.1 shows, in India between 2000 and 2019 the GTER curve followed the urbanization curve upwards and the gap between them shrank significantly. Future city growth will enable the future growth of higher education. In 2015, India had 180 cities with a population of more than 300,000 people, led by Delhi (with over 26 million people), Mumbai, Kolkata and Bengaluru (UNDESA 2018). The cities will continue to draw more people from the countryside into the urban capitalist economy. As the cities grow, the effective demand for higher education will continue to expand.

Potential to Achieve the 50 Per Cent Target

Nevertheless, the majority of the national population are still outside the cities. Urban growth is steady and sustained but the urbanization share increases by only 0.3–0.5 per cent a year. At this rate India will not reach an urbanization ratio of 50 per cent until well after 2050. Given that, the national GTER is hardly likely to reach 50 per cent before that time. In short, it is very unlikely, if not impossible, that India will achieve the official target of a 50 per cent GTER by 2035, unless there is a truly extraordinary take-off of national development in the next decade.

Could the nation achieve the target by a major expansion of access in rural areas? Across the world, higher education has spread in an uneven manner to rural areas. Physical institutions are difficult to sustain at low levels of enrolment, especially when communities have prior needs for clean water, sustainable food supplies, ecological stabilization of the land and basic health care facilities. Online education is often seen by government as the most efficient way to expand rural access. Regrettably, it is not so simple. First, although online education can do some things well, it is less effective overall than good quality face-to-face learning, being less potent in socialization and cohort effects. On average, teaching is less engaging in this mode. The period of the pandemic has seen advances in online provision in every national system. At the same time, its educational limitations have been more clearly apparent, and when asked, students in most locations have emphasized an overwhelming preference for onsite education. Second and more fundamentally, as is well understood by educators in India, online education is everywhere constrained by the lack of bandwidth, reliable electricity supply and internet-receiving devices.

According to World Bank data, in India in 2018, a high 65.5 per cent of the population had no internet access (World Bank 2021). The ratio was much higher in rural areas. Even among *currently enrolled* students, according to the NSS 75th Round data for 2017–18, 32 per cent of students in urban areas and 58 per cent of students in rural areas had no internet access. Of the scheduled tribe (ST) and scheduled caste (SC) students, 58 per cent were without any internet access. Whereas 55 per cent of urban students did not possess a device adequate for online higher education, that ratio was 83 per cent in rural areas (Sarkar 2020). It is certain that the internet access ratio among families not currently enrolled in higher education would be worse.

Research

While the nation struggles to build its base level of participation and bring higher education to all corners of the country, there is a concurrent need to grow research to meet economic needs, underpin scientific, social and cultural development and connect the work of scientists and scholars effectively with global society.

Although India is, according to Scopus (NSB 2020), third nation in the world in the production of published science papers, relative to the size of the population and economy India is seriously underprovided with research capacity.

Government data show that in 2019–20, out of a total enrolment of 38.5 million students in higher education, only 202,550, of which 55 per cent were male, were enrolled in PhD and MPhil degrees (GoI 2021b), of whom 23,934 were enrolled in the MPhil programme. During the 2015–16 to 2019–20 period, the enrolment in the PhD programme witnessed an 8.5 per cent annual growth rate compared with 12.2 per cent for enrolment at postgraduate level (GoI 2021d: 44, Box 16). In 2019, 38,986 people were awarded PhD level degrees (GoI 2021d), of whom 55.3 per cent were male. Science and engineering predominate. In all, students enrolled in the PhD programme (excluding MPhil) as a proportion of enrolment in postgraduation was the highest for engineering and technology at 29.6 per cent, followed by 24.1 per cent for agriculture, 4.6 per cent for medical sciences, 7.8 per cent for sciences and 2.53 per cent for social sciences (GoI 2021d: Table 13, p. T-13).

The quality of research is of equal concern. India's share of world scientific publications is about 4.33 per cent, and 6.62 per cent of those in engineering (GoI 2020e). While expansion in the size of the higher education sector has increased the scope for doing research, because of limited funding and infrastructure the quantity is inhibited. In 2019, there were 1,416,299 teachers in colleges and universities who contributed to 187,432 research publications (International Facts and Figures 2020). That is thirteen publications for every 100 teachers, and although part of the college teaching force lacks any opportunity to do research, this is a low figure. The quality of research is also questionable. In terms of the aggregate citation index, India is twelfth in the world, well below its position in quantity of papers (Ramaswamy 2020).

In order to tackle the proliferation of fake journals and journals with little or no credibility, the University Grants Commission (UGC) has brought out a Consortium for Academic and Research Ethics (CARE) list of journals considered suitable for publications prepared by university and college teachers (GoI 2019c). This is a dynamic list under the constant monitoring of a team of experts. The UGC has also intervened to curb unfair practices in research and prevent plagiarism (GoI 2018b). This is in addition to the UGC regulations (GoI 2018c) which seeks to regulate research processes to ensure quality research.

The pattern of publications is also highly uneven within higher education. In the India Rankings 2020 (GoI 2020e), out of 955 higher education institutions considered for ranking, the top 100 accounted for 70.21 per cent of research

Table 0.1 Five Selected World Top 100 Universities Compared to the Five Leading Research Producer Institutions in India, Three Indicators, 2020

	ARWU ranks	HiCi	PUB	PCP
Harvard University	1	100	100	79.3
Stanford University	2	71.1	77.1	53.8
Peking University	49	29.7	78.1	24.4
UC, Santa Barbara	49	26.2	39.9	36.0
Fudan University	100	21.0	70.6	22.0
Indian Universities				
IISc Bengaluru	501–600	0	41.4	16.4
IIT Madras	601–700	0	32.5	12.8
University of Calcutta	601–700	0	20.1	10.0
University of Delhi	601–700	7.0	27.0	11.0
IIT Delhi	701–800	0	30.4	12.0

Note:
HiCi: the number of Highly Cited Researchers selected by Clarivate Analytics. Only the primary affiliations of Highly Cited researchers are considered (weightage 20%).
PUB: total number of papers indexed in science citation index (expanded) and social science citation index in 2019. Only publications of 'article' type is considered (weightage 20%).
PCP: Per capita academic performance of an institution (weightage 10%). Weighted scores of all five indicators-alumni, award, publication in Nature and Science (N&S), divided by the number of full-time equivalent academic staff.
UC = University of California. IISc = Indian Institute of Science. IIT = Indian Institute of Technology.
Source: Shanghai Ranking's ARWU (2020).

publications. Among the 273 universities considered for ranking, the top 100 universities account for 77.88 per cent of publications. If highly cited publications are a proxy for top quality publications, the top 100 institutions out of 955 account for 76.0 per cent and among the universities; the ratio is 80.0 per cent.

Table 0.1 compares research in the top Indian universities to some of the top universities in the world as listed in the Academic Ranking for World Universities (ARWU), using three of the ARWU indicators: highly cited researchers (HiCi), papers indexed in the science citation-index-expanded and social science citation index (PUB), and research performance per faculty (PCP). A group of selected universities from the ARWU range of 1–100 is placed alongside the top five Indian higher education institutions. Other than at the University of Delhi, India has no high-quality researchers (HiCi). In terms of the other two indicators, the selected world universities are far ahead of the top five universities of India. For PUB, the gap is somewhat smaller, but for PCP, it is significant.

The National Education Policy 2020 and Research

While diagnosing the state of affairs in research, the NEP 2020 notes 'lesser emphasis on research at most universities and colleges, and lack competitive peer reviewed research funding across disciplines' (GoI 2020c: Section 9.2 (g), 33). The NEP 2020 recognizes that investment in research and innovation in India is only 0.69 per cent of the GDP as compared to 2.8 per cent in the United States, and 4.2 per cent in the South Korea. The NEP 2020 recommends setting up of National Research Foundation (NRF) to channelize research funding for outstanding peer-reviewed research in universities and colleges (GoI 2020c: Section 9.3 (f), 34). It states that this will facilitate building a 'culture of research' across the universities. To ensure funding for research areas which are of immediate national interest, the NRF is expected to act as a liaison between the researchers located across the higher education institutions and relevant branches and ministries of the government as well as industry. This is expected to contribute to policymaking and its implementation.

The NEP has proposed categorization of universities into three groups, research-intensive universities, teaching universities and autonomous degree-granting colleges (GoI 2020c: Section 10.3). Though the boundaries are only indicative, and upward transition is possible and desirable, in practice it will be difficult to achieve. The necessary time and resources at the disposal of teaching-universities are likely to be inadequate to make the transition to Research-Intensive Universities. The NEP also suggests reorientation of the doctoral training programme: PhD students will be required to opt for credit-based courses in teaching pedagogy, and writing, as well as gaining teaching experiences.

Looking Forward

An inevitable outcome of the ongoing massification of Indian higher education, coupled with inadequate public funding, is poor quality of research in the majority of Indian higher education institutions. Another problem is the disconnect between teaching and research. The universities are no longer the primary sites of knowledge generation. The migration of research from the universities to the think-tanks, research institutes and national laboratories set up by the various ministries to conduct research in specialized areas of knowledge has led to the erosion of research capacities of the Indian universities, particularly their human resources (Raina 2015; Hatakenaka 2017). Research in science suffers the most given the absence of properly equipped laboratories. The weakening relationship between teaching and research has facilitated two developments. First, the government has set up Indian Institutes of Science, Education and Research (IISERs) in various parts of the country. The mandate of this new category of institutions explicitly combines teaching and research. Second, national research institutions and national laboratories entrusted with the task of doing research in specific areas began to offer PhD programmes by officially adopting the status of 'Deemed-to-be-Universities' (Raina 2015; Hatakenaka 2017). The policy measures mooted in the NEP, such as graded autonomy and setting up of Institutions of Eminence (see Chapter 6 on regulation), along with the proposed categorization of universities, suggest the concentration of research in the top-ranking universities at the expense of the middle and bottom tiers. Tendencies that weaken the unity of teaching and research end up enfeebling both.

The main concern is the great need for resources for doing research in the universities and colleges. In the post-COVID era, given the size of the higher education sector, it is likely that the budget for NRF will ever remain inadequate. The focus on national priorities for funding research may erode the autonomy of the researchers to decide on their research areas, including social science research that is critical of state policies, and research undertaken for the sake of knowledge generation rather than direct applications. But India needs all these kinds of inquiry, because fundamental research is the foundation of scientific and technological innovation, and critical research is key to taking society forward.

The Pandemic and Higher Education

As of 25 January 2021, as the main draft of this book was being completed, the COVID-19 pandemic had globally infected 100 million people and nearly 2.14 million people had lost their lives. India accounted for more than 10 per cent of the infections and a recorded 7 per cent of the deaths attributed to the pandemic. The pandemic has severely impaired economic growth and distorted the income distribution patterns in most countries.

According to the *Global Wealth Report* by Credit Suisse (2021), global household wealth fell by USD17.5 trillion in the first quarter of 2020 and the value of assets is likely to grow more slowly for the next couple of years. However, the effect of the slowdown and negative economic growth is very unevenly felt. For example, some tech companies have been performing well in business terms during the pandemic. The net worth of companies such as Facebook increased by more than 50 per cent in the first half of 2020. On the other hand, unemployment reached new heights, throwing more than 200 million people out of jobs worldwide. Working from home is an option more for high-end job holders than for those holding middle and lower paid jobs. This reality has pushed the incidence of unemployment more completely onto to the relatively vulnerable households.

In education, UNESCO has estimated that more than 1.6 billion learners worldwide have been affected by school and university closures. The lockdown in India declared on 25 March 2020 affected the lives and livelihood of many millions of people across the country, while the closure of schools and colleges has affected education of millions of children and young people. How has COVID-19 affected the higher education sector?

Transition from Face-to-Face to Online Teaching and Learning

The most visible effect of the pandemic on education has been the closure of schools and colleges and the transition from face-to-face mode to an online mode of learning. In many cases, this shift was smooth and successful. However, such a transition poses challenges in countries such as India for several reasons. The technological divide has been apparent on several counts. First, technological infrastructure in the institutions has been poor and insufficient. Many of the institutions engaged in undergraduate teaching have found it most difficult to cope with the constraints imposed by technology. Second, many students and teachers have not had easy access to technology. A high proportion of teaching has been facilitated through mobile phones rather than through laptops. Third, even when technology has been available, many teachers have found it difficult to adapt to online teaching. Lack of experience in managing technology and competences in remote learning pedagogies have made the transition more difficult. Fourth, online student assessment has proven more difficult than online teaching. In the first year of the pandemic, the final examination results were delayed and the students found it difficult to seek admission to courses in the next stage of education within the same universities or in other institutions.

Private schools and private universities have been better placed in facilitating the transition from face-to-face learning to online learning, partly because on average their students come from households in higher-income brackets than is the case with public institutions, and these households could afford to buy the technological devices relied on for online learning.

Decline in Economic Growth

Most economists forecast that the years 2020 and 2021 will be lost years for growth. The global economy will contract by 5.2 per cent in 2020, and the economy will not return to pre-COVID-19 levels before 2022. The likeliest long-term scenario for advanced economies is one of low growth, low inflation and high levels of debt. Slow economic growth will bring down government revenue and the capacity to invest. On the other hand, government spending is on the increase because the health crisis created by the pandemic response has generated stimulus packages. This suggests that in the coming years public financing will be characterized by reduced overall revenues and increased public spending on health.

Developing countries such as India may face an additional difficulty because of reduced aid flows. Because the pandemic has affected the economies of the aid-giving countries, their capacity to continue providing existing levels of aid may be impaired. All of these factors taken together suggest that the likely scenario in most countries will be reduced or stagnating public spending on education. The decline in public spending on education may lead to a freeze on appointment of teachers. Such a situation could create very severe problems in India since a large number of teaching positions in higher education institutions are lying vacant. Another implication of declining public revenue might be a reduction in capital investment and on infrastructure and facilities.

The pandemic has also triggered a decline in the incomes of many households, because of the loss of jobs. The loss of cross-border migrant employees' jobs leads to the reduction or elimination of late remittances. Declining incomes from job loss and the reduction of remittances may force many households to shift their children from private fee-paying institutions to subsidized public institutions. This in turn would place additional pressure on the underfunded public educational institutions.

Cross-Border Student Mobility

Cross-border student mobility has declined as a result of the pandemic. Two factors have reduced cross-border student mobility: the restrictions on international travel and loss of household incomes both reduced demand for cross-border education. Many institutions have moved from face-to-face to online modes of international education. However, resistance by international students to pay the same amount of fees for online as for face-to-face classes has posed problems in many education hubs, in sustaining revenues and hence maintaining staff and facilities.

As noted, online education minimizes the benefits of the interaction and socialization that a student is exposed to in face-to-face mode. Student interactions with teachers and among peer groups are important sources of learning. This aspect of learning is largely nullified in the online mode. It seems that some of the pandemic-induced changes in teaching and learning will continue even after the pandemic period is over. However, it may be important to treat online as an add-on to face-to-face interactions, not a substitute.

Public Good and Political Culture

As the problem of creating rural access indicates, and as all the chapters of *Changing Higher Education in India* make clear, the policy challenges in India are formidable. This does not mean the challenges are impossible. The old idea of world-systems theory (Wallerstein 1974), that countries on the 'periphery' are trapped in permanent underdevelopment, has been exploded by the uplift of many middle-income and lower-income countries (Marginson and Xu, 2021) and the dynamism of economic and social development in India itself. Nevertheless, in higher education the task is onerous, and solutions require time.

Consider the size of India's population and the great diversity of regions and cultures; the urban poverty and rural underdevelopment that despite progress are still very high in world-terms; the poisonous inheritances of colonialism, including caste and gender discrimination and the ongoing conflict with Pakistan; the growing economic inequality in the country, worsening during the pandemic; and a polity which essentially has been fractured since partition but has become more tense in recent years. There is also the absence of a strong endogenous tradition of higher education. The colonial era still casts its long shadow. In one respect this is surprising, given the vast cultural resources and capabilities of India, whose people contribute in large numbers to science, universities, corporations, governments and the arts all over the world. However, it is readily explained, given national poverty and the lack of resources for higher education, not to mention the continued hold of Anglo-American universities in the Indian (and world) imagination, as seemingly confirmed in global rankings – rankings systems that have been designed precisely to sustain the old neo-imperial supremacy in global higher education (Marginson and Xu, 2021).

Because of these inheritances and conditions, more than seventy years after independence, though India has the third largest GDP in purchasing power parity (PPP) terms (World Bank 2021) and according to Scopus is the third largest producer of published science (NSB 2020), the country has yet to build a coordinated national higher education system grounded in robust institutions with a mix of comprehensive and specialist missions, supported by honest and effective cultures of institutional management and professional academic labour. Nor has higher education policy in India yet found a way to compensate effectively for inequalities between the states in economic capacity, so that provision is highly uneven across India's regions.

A strong effective endogenous national higher education system can be conceived and designed only on the basis of the national political culture. It cannot be achieved by borrowing one or another international blueprint for 'World Class University performance', such as those suggested by the Times Higher Education World University Rankings or QS World University rankings. In any case, rankings drive the leading Indian institutions into a global competition they cannot win at this stage of economic and educational development, while encouraging those same institutions to cut loose from supporting the rest of the system.

Still less can a strong endogenous system be derived from the 'stimulus' of foreign providers within India. Universities that establish branch campuses rarely bring their A game to the foreign country. At best, foreign providers can provide competent teaching institutions, learn for themselves about cross-cultural problems and establish a pipeline into their main campus in the home country for selected Indian families. While there is nothing intrinsically wrong with inviting foreign campuses, this should not be presented as a quality driver, or as the proxy for a strategy of reform, and still less as a source of local ideas, or a solution for local gaps. Indian higher education policymakers and institutional leaders have many better ways to observe international models of provision than by inviting in foreign providers.

An overarching question that underlies the chapters in the book, one that affects all of the issues and problems discussed, is *what are the necessary components of the national political culture in higher education?* The term 'political culture' refers to the compound of words, ideas, policies, institutions, regulatory structures, resource configurations and behavioural norms that together constitute the role of collective public authorities to social order. In higher education policy, this goes to the issue of the mission of higher education in creating collective public and common goods of value to the whole of Indian society.

Public good and public goods are referenced in most of the chapters of the book. That frequent referencing in itself reflects a shared unease – a sense that the government, the organs of public opinion in the media and civil society, and leaders in higher education itself lack a common set of assumptions about higher education's contribution to the public good – a framework sufficiently practical to guide policies, outcomes and behaviours. Yet without such normative guidance, we cannot expect higher education to spontaneously evolve so as to create the kind of future education system and society that is needed. Still less can market forces be expected to solve the problem of higher education's contribution to the public good. Leaving the resolution of fundamental values to the workings of competition between individuals and between institutions may be adequate to run a bond market, but cannot be optimal for the provision of higher education, teaching, equitable social access as well as research and science; neither can it guide the contribution of higher education to economic activity, cities, local communities and the democratic 'public sphere' in higher education (Chapter 9).

Market-Based Public Goods?

In market-based societies, the policy conversation about public good or goods in higher education has become narrowly focused on Samuelson's (1954) influential economic argument about public and private goods (Marginson 2016, 2018). Samuelson establishes a minimalist definition of public goods based on non-rivalry and non-excludability. Goods produced under both of these conditions are subject to market failure, and if their provision is desired, they must be financed by the state or philanthropy. All other goods are private goods in whole or in part. They can be produced or part produced in competitive markets. As is well known, higher education fulfils the first condition, non-rivalry, but not the second, non-excludability. Access is rationed and places in elite universities have private value. Hence higher education is a Samuelson mixed good and might be funded on a mixed public/private basis (see Chapters 2 and 4). Samuelson's argument about market failure is useful for policymakers because it identifies a category of goods that must be supported, for example basic research, and socially equitable access for students who cannot self-finance their education.

However, it is basically a funding formula (and a normative argument for the maximum extension of market capitalism) rather than a wholistic basis for a policy on the combined public good. It is thin as a basis for an endogenous social philosophy in higher education.

Samuelson pushes policymakers towards the idea that even public goods should be understood as individualized spill-overs from market transactions. Hence in a Samuelson framework, outcomes such as tolerance or political connectedness acquired in higher education become seen not as the combined relational qualities that they are, but as portable goods carried by individuals, parallel to private human capital. These individualized public goods are even given shadow price values (McMahon 2009). They are only characterized as 'public goods' because they are not directly rewarded in labour markets and so they are subject to market failure, in danger of being under-provided in a market system of higher education. The point is that they are defined as individual benefits rather than collective benefits. This misses the main point about public goods in higher education. The real issue is how to enhance the collective goods generated by this sector.

The nature of collective goods is partly policy determined. For example, societies can decide to provide free universal primary education of good quality because that helps to build the kind of community they want. Nordic societies do this. At that point, primary education becomes a public good in Samuelson's sense. Likewise, the government can decide on the appropriate mix of public and private institutions, and public and private financing, on the basis of the social outcomes that the society wants to achieve from education.

However, with such policy-determined public goods there is a danger to be avoided. History has repeatedly shown that even free public goods are readily captured by powerful social groups' interests, and their shared character is often stymied in distribution (Marginson 2016). For example, access to elite universities is free or low cost in many countries but they are nevertheless largely occupied by students from the affluent middle class, no different from the situation in market systems; for example, in countries such as the United States where high fees are levied. Abolishing status distinctions between institutions, as with universal primary education of good quality, might help, but is unlikely to happen. This shows that providing higher education places as nominal public goods in the Samuelson sense does not necessarily regulate the sector's contribution to the combined public good. A deeper policy is needed, rather than just shifting the balance between public and private costs – a policy that focuses on the desired kind of society, and on the political culture that can achieve it. Here the ultimate challenges of higher education policy in India become apparent.

Common Goods and Moral Frameworks

What might be the possible content of such a policy? One way to think about this is to move from the American economic idea of Samuelson public goods to the grassroots Western European communitarian idea of 'common goods' which has been adapted by UNESCO (Locatelli 2018). 'Common goods' introduces new strands into the discussion. Common goods are broadly beneficial by definition, and subject to democratic processes of determination, which diminish the potential for capture of elite social groups.

Common goods are goods that contribute to sociable human agency, shared social welfare and relations of solidarity, inclusion, tolerance, universal freedoms, equality, human rights and the acquisition of individual capability on a democratic basis. Equality of opportunity in education is one example. The British National Health Service is an example of common goods provision. It provides universal health care that is free of charge to all, while adopting the principle of priority for people in greatest need because of serious illness or accident, regardless of their individual social position. Common goods are collective non-market goods, but they are not necessarily provided by government. Because 'common' is defined by the content of the activity, both government and non-government organizations, including voluntary local cooperation (Ostrom 1990) and private corporations, can contribute to common goods. However, 'some kinds of private participation are more defensible than others' (Locatelli 2018: 8), and state funding and ('public') regulation of the private sector may be needed to ensure that commonality is uppermost (Locatelli 2018: 13).

This then has two implications for higher education policy in India. First, UNESCO's concept indicates that non-state institutions can contribute to socially common goods in higher education. Second, as noted in several chapters of this book, it is necessary to regulate the private sector in higher education more closely to ensure its contribution to a common policy of equitable higher education of adequate quality to all students in all communities. Here one useful example is the regulatory framework used in South Korea and Japan. Both countries, partly under US influence in the post-Second World War period, established majority private sectors in higher education. These private sectors are largely self-funding and subject to market forces. Large numbers of private colleges close during periods of demographic downturn, as at present. However, unlike the situation in the United States, Korea and Japan closely regulate quality in private universities and colleges and these institutions contribute to the high overall quality of both education systems at all levels, as indicated by the performance of each education system in the OECD's regular PISA tests.

Could regulation in India carry out such a policy effectively? That goes to the question of political culture. Like some Western European countries, the East Asian jurisdictions are notable for their commitment to policy goals and to continuous improvement towards those goals. That is, policy is treated as authentic. Targets are real, transparent and actually achieved – something that does not happen in every country across the world. These systems of government, whether the economy is capitalist or communist, are also vigilant in policing corruption in government. Officials are caught pursuing their self-interest illegally in Korea, Japan and China, and such cases often receive extensive national and international publicity. This might be a healthy sign, indicating that a clear moral framework is operating. In contrast, in an atmosphere in which officials and educational institutions operate on the basis not simply of organizational self-interest but personal self-interest, and where corruption of rules, laws and core mission and values is normal, the good of students and the public is routinely pushed aside.

In the long run, the challenge for India is to establish a new normative climate in which the common good is genuinely uppermost in policy implementation and administration. This is ultimately a problem of moral order, especially in government, though moral order must also become embedded in local communities. In higher education top-down government and institutional leaders as well as bottom-up teaching faculty and students (Chapter 10) have equal contributions to make, in establishing a common good moral order in the sector. Likewise, evidence-based policy-related research on higher education, such as that contained in this book, seeks to contribute to the moral framework of authentic public and institutional policy and their implementation.

Chapters of the Book

There are signs that a better higher education system can be built in India. As Chapter 1 argues, in some respects the NEP 2020 is pointing in the right direction and it has been well received. Nevertheless, more detailed prescriptions are needed, and more important than the words in policy is the implementation of policy. India has had a disappointing history of well-led and well-intentioned agencies in higher education, with good policy ideas, that have been unable to gain enough traction in practice to kick-start a process of transformation. This suggests that more fundamental issues need to be diagnosed, measured and addressed.

That is what *Changing Higher Education in India* sets out to do. It is not a blueprint. As the contributors to this book see it, we are not at the stage of blueprints. We are at the stage of defining problems, researching them sharply and building a consensus on them so that we can move forward from the present situation, at both state and union levels. Chapter 1 sets down the main policy issues. The succeeding chapters provide depth in key aspects of existing provision: governance and regulation, financing, inequalities, union-state relations, the private sector, internationalization and the internal political life of the sector.

These are expert chapters. They have been prepared by social scientists who work or have previously worked at the National Institute for Educational Planning and Administration (NIEPA) or Jawaharlal Nehru University in Delhi, and who are grounded in years of research. India has a strong policy research culture in higher education, partly centred on NIEPA and its advisory role to government. This policy culture is evidence-based, practically minded and as directly productive as its equivalents in any other country. This book is an outcome of that culture.

In Chapter 1, 'Directions of Change in Higher Education in India: From Massification to Universalization', which is also the introduction to the main themes of the book, N. V. Varghese discusses the continuing expansion of higher education in India, sanctioned by the NEP; the key role of the private sector in that process; and factors that are likely to align with future developments, including more flexible and technologically based structures and learning programmes, institutional reorganization and new modes of quality assurance. Governance, equity, coordination and quality present large ongoing challenges.

Chapter 2 by Saumen Chattopadhyay and Jinusha Panigrahi, 'Financing of Higher Education in India: Issues and Challenges', examines the emerging trends in public funding of higher education and reflect on the possible implications for the objectives of expansion, inclusion and excellence. Data on allocations and mechanisms are provided, and the chapter introduces the institutional reconfiguration of Indian higher education as proposed in the 2020 NEP.

In 'Equity in Higher Education for Inclusive Growth: Evidence from India', Chapter 3, N. V. Varghese, Nidhi S. Sabharwal and C. M. Malish outline the purposes of equity policy and strategies to promote equity in higher education, and they discuss empirical evidence on persisting inequalities within the context of massification, including factors affecting particular social groups.

Chapter 4, 'Privatization versus Private Sector in Higher Education in India', by N. V. Varghese and Nivedita Sarkar focuses on private higher education in India. It reviews issues related to the public good nature of higher education, and discusses privatization and the private sector in India and around the world. The chapter reviews the features of the sector and discusses issues related to regulatory measures and mechanisms.

In Chapter 5, 'The Dynamics of Union-State Relations and Higher Education in India', Anamika Srivastava and Saumen Chattopadhyay explore the complex federal higher education system in India and the paradox of a union-heavy regulatory structure in which the main responsibility falls on state governments. The chapter also notes disparities in the fiscal capacity of different states and the limitations this imposes in financing, the likelihood this has favoured private sector development and the role of central government allocation on National Higher Education Mission (Rashtriya Uchchatar Shiksha Abhiyan, RUSA) in tackling imbalances.

In Chapter 6 by Saumen Chattopadhyay and Emon Nandi, 'Changing Contours of Regulation in Indian Higher Education', the authors provide an account of the existing regulatory framework, and identify the major dilemmas and conflicts as policymakers negotiate the trade-offs between public and the private, centre and the states, and general and professional education. The chapter also examines recent reforms to regulation.

'Internationalization of Indian Higher Education: Issues and Challenges', Chapter 7, by Saumen Chattopadhyay takes stock of major trends, developments and policy initiatives in relation to the internationalization of Indian higher education. It talks about how a key issue is to strike the right balance between national and global compulsions. The chapter also discusses programme mobility, student mobility, institutional mobility and movement of skilled persons from India.

Chapter 8, 'Engineering Education in India', by Jandhyala B. G. Tilak and Pradeep Kumar Choudhury, addresses the growth of engineering and technology education, while noting the unevenness in regional provision, and examines the status and prospects of the field. The chapter discusses how the private sector has grown much faster than the public sector, thus widening inequalities in access to different socioeconomic groups thereby exacerbating concerns relating to declining quality.

The final chapter in the book, Chapter 9 by Aishna Sharma, Vanessa Chishti and Binay Kumar Pathak, is titled 'Teachers and Students as Political Actors in

Indian Higher Education'. The chapter discusses about how a university is not only a space for teaching and research but also the site where young people are shaped as affective subjects and as bearers of civic and political sensibilities. The authors address the implications of recent policy measures to curb the publicness of higher education, the academic freedom of faculty and organized political dissent among teachers and students. They note that it is essential that teachers and students are free of fear, and their energy and commitment is welcomed, if they are to fulfil the responsibilities of higher education to social improvement, as a passive higher education sector is one that must fall short of its potential for the nation.

1

Directions of Change in Higher Education in India: From Massification to Universalization

N. V. Varghese

1. Introduction

Universities are institutions relied on for generation and transmission of knowledge. While living in the present, universities pass on the inheritance of past to the next generations and generate knowledge that shape the future of nations. The post-war reconstruction phase in Europe and post-liberation stage in developing countries relied on higher education graduates for designing development and providing professional support for national development efforts. In most newly independent countries, higher education remained a source of self-reliant national development to replace expatriates on the one hand and to promote public sector-led development strategies on the other. The political interest and public support for higher education were forthcoming during this period. Consequently, public funding and state control of higher education became a common practice in most countries of the world.

Ever since knowledge has replaced other resources as the main driver of economic growth, investing in knowledge became profitable and corporate interest in institutions producing knowledge grew. The public policy, the private interest and the household aspirations contributed to increasing social demand resulting in fast expansion of the sector in this century. The social demand for higher education, very often, surpassed the fiscal capacity of the state to finance the sector. The market-friendly reforms in the form of privatization of public institutions and fast growth of private institutions fuelled expansion of the sector. The massification of the sector in many countries is driven by private institutions and non-state funding. Interestingly, markets were relied to massify higher education in the less-developed market economies, and public institutions were relied on to massify and eventually universalize higher education in the developed market economies (Varghese 2013). Higher education continues to be a major contributor to the public and common good, across the range of economic and social development tasks, but private as well as public institutions make that contribution.

The higher education developments in India followed a pattern similar to these global trends in the sector. This chapter analyses the trends in the development of higher education in India. It shows that the higher education development in the recent decades has moved away from its initial framework of public funding and state control to market-friendly reforms and non-state funding. This transition helped transform higher education from a slow-growing low-enrolment sector to a fast-growing massified sector with diversification of institutions, study programmes, sources of funding and student bodies. The National Education Policy of 2020 (NEP 2020) (GoI 2020c) targets further accelerated growth of the sector to reach a stage of universalization by the year 2035. Managing quality and equity in a market-mediated massifying system will remain a major challenge in the development of higher education in India in the coming years.

The plan of this chapter is as follows. The next section discusses the stages of evolution of the sector from a slow-growing to a fast-expanding sector to reach a stage of massification. Section 3 shows the role of private institutions in massifying higher education in India. Section 4 analyses issues related to equity and inclusion in a market-mediated massification. Section 5 deals with challenges of assuring quality in an expanding system followed by a discussion on governance and management of higher education in India in Section 6. Section 7 discusses issues related to financing and Section 8 focuses on the new directions of NEP 2020 and the final section draws some conclusions from the analysis made in the chapter.

2. Transition from Low Enrolment to Massification

According to Martin Trow's classification of stages of development of higher education (Trow 2006), India with a gross enrolment ratio (GER) of 27.1 per cent in 2019–20 is in a stage of massification with around 38.5 million students, 1.5 million teachers and more than 42,000 colleges in 2019–20 (GoI 2021d). There are 988 universities of which 429 are state universities, 125 deemed-to-be universities, 54 Central Universities and 380 private universities (GoI 2021c). India has surpassed the United States to become the second largest higher education sector in the world. In the first fifty years of planned development (between1951 and 2001) when public universities were the major institutional arrangement for pursuing higher studies, the growth of the sector was slow and GERs were low. The country achieved an enrolment level of 8.8 million and a GER of 8.4 per cent in the first fifty years (1951–2001) of planned development (Table 1.1).

The expansion of the sector accelerated from the turn of this century. The enrolment increased from 8.8 million in 2001–2 to 37.4 million in 2018–19. The first decade of the present century experienced an annual addition of nearly 2.0 million students making it the largest expansion ever experienced by the sector in any decade. The annual additions in enrolment, despite a decline, still continues to be high at around 1.2 million students during the period from 2011–12 to 2018–19 (Table 1.1). The NEP (GoI 2020c) has set a target of a GER of 50 per cent by 2035. The fast expansion of the sector is also attributed to the contributions by the private institutions. At present, private institutions account for a major share in the total number of institutions and in student enrolment.

The higher education development in India during the post-independence period can broadly be categorized into three stages: (1) a period of expansion to support self-reliant development (1950–70); (2) a stage of declining growth and public support (1970–2000) and (3) a stage of revival and massive expansion of the sector in this century.

Expansion to Support Self-Reliant Development (1950–70)

Independent India accorded high priority to higher education. The first commission on education (Radhakrishnan Commission) established in independent India was on higher education. The recommendations of the first commission laid the foundation for higher education development in India. Following the recommendations of the commission, India established national regulatory bodies such as the University Grants Commission (UGC) and other similar bodies to regulate and maintain overall quality and standards in higher education. The initial priority concerns for higher education development in India seemed to be on (1) linking higher education with development; (2) expanding access with equity and (3) ensuring quality.

India, like many developing countries, adopted a public-sector led strategy of development during the post-independence period. It adopted a planning framework and formulated five-year plans to direct self-reliant economic and social development. India made serious efforts to link higher education with the country's aspirations for self-reliant development. The initial priorities of the sector focused on economic growth relying on agriculture, industrial growth relying on technological advancement as well as ensuring health security and social equity. India established agricultural universities, medical colleges and specialized institutions – such as Indian Institutes of Technology (IITs), Indian Institutes of Management (IIMs) and National Institutes of Technology (NITs) – to support economic development and several institutions of higher education to expand higher education with equity. As a result of these initiatives, the enrolment in higher education institutions increased by ten times (from 0.2 to 2.0 million) in the first two decades of planned development in India (Table 1.1), although the GER remained low at 4.2 per cent.

A Stage of Declining Growth and Public Support (1970–2000)

The 1970s and 1980s experienced declining rates of growth of institutions and enrolment in higher education. While many private institutions became public in the 1950s, private colleges (the recurring expenditure mostly met by the government) increased in number in the 1970s. 'Private colleges that were legally private but publicly financed dominated the higher education landscape until 1980' (Agarwal 2009: 72). From the 1980s, cost recovery measures were introduced in many public institutions, and private self-financing colleges in professional and technical subject areas came into existence. In other words privatization of public institutions and promotion of private institutions became common features of higher education development in India (Varghese 2013). The private self-financing institutions popularly known as 'capitation fee' colleges (Tilak 1994) became popular and high in demand in the areas of technical and professional education in the 1990s.

The committees appointed by the UGC in the 1990s (the Punnayya Committee of 1992–3) and All India Council for Technical Education (AICTE) (Dr Swaminathan Panel 1992) recommended privatization of public institutions through reduced subsidies and increased cost recovery from students. The Birla-Ambani Committee (2000) went one step further when it recommended establishment of private universities and full cost recovery from students.

Revival and Massification of Higher Education

The next stage in the development of higher education is marked by a revival and fast expansion of the sector. A revival of the system implied increase in

Table 1.1 Higher Education Expansion in India, 1950–51 to 2018–19

Year	Central universities	State universities	Deemed-to-be Universities	Institutes of national importance	Private universities	Total	Colleges	Enrolments (in millions)	GER (%)
1950–1	3	24	–	–	–	27	578	0.2	1.5
1960–1	4	41	2	2	–	49	1819	0.6	4.2
1970–1	5	79	9	9	–	102	3277	2.0	4.7
1980–1	7	105	11	9	–	132	4577	2.8	5.9
1990–1	10	137	29	9	–	185	6627	4.4	8.1
2001–2	18	178	52	12	–	260	11146	8.8	11.6
2005–6	18	205	95	18	7	343	17625	11.6	19.4
2011–12	42	299	40	59	178	621[a]	34908	28.5	24.5
2015–16	44	342	122	75	198	799[b]	39071	34.6	26.3
2018–19	47	385	124	127	305	993[b]	39931	37.4	

Notes:
[a] This figure includes others category.
[b] This figure includes others category and Institute under State Legislature Act.

Source: Author, from Varghese (2015a); MHRD (2019).

the number of institutions, student numbers and resource availability in the sector. Between the 2001 and 2019, the number of universities increased by 660 (mostly private universities), the number of colleges increased by nearly four times, enrolment by more than four times and GER by more than three times (Table 1.1). This massive expansion helped India enter a stage of massification of higher education (Varghese 2015a).

The massification of the sector is also because of the growth in private universities. India has made efforts to permit opening and operation of private universities from the 1990s onwards. Since a bill on private universities could not be passed in the national Parliament, many state governments legislated to establish private universities in the 2000s. Private universities were established in many states, and they proliferated in numbers. Between 2002 and 2019, around 305 private universities were established in India (Table 1.1). The open learning systems – open universities, distance learning in traditional universities and the Indian massive open online course (MOOC) platforms – also helped massifying higher education in India. They account for around 10–12 per cent of the total enrolment in higher education.

Higher education in India is mainly undergraduate education leading to the first university degree (bachelor's). Although its share in total enrolment declined from 89 per cent in 2005 to nearly 80 per cent in 2019, it continues to be the dominant segment of higher education in India. There was a corresponding increase in enrolments in diploma programmes during the same period (Table 1.2). The major shift in demand for higher education seems to take place at the undergraduate level from choosing degree courses to diploma programmes. This change in the choice of course reflects the changing orientation of the diverse group of students entering institutions of higher education in a stage of massification in India.

Table 1.2 Stage-Wise Enrolment of Students, 2005 and 2019

Stage	2005 (%)	2019 (%)
Undergraduate	89.0	79.8
Postgraduate	9.2	10.8
Research	0.6	0.45
Diploma/Certificate	1.0	7.2
Others	0.2	1.8
Grand total (millions)	10.0	37.4

Source: Author, derived from MHRD (2005a; 2019).

The enrolment in master's courses is low at 10.8 per cent. The enrolment in research programmes (Doctoral studies) is not only low but also declined from 0.66 per cent in 2005 to 0.45 per cent in 2019. The low enrolment in postgraduate programmes acts as a severe constraint on the system to produce qualified teachers for the higher education sector and knowledge producers for the economy. More number of teachers are required when the system moves from a stage of massification to a stage of universalization as envisaged in the new policy on education. Similarly, to provide a strong human capital base for the expansion of the knowledge economy and for improving the national competitiveness in a globalized economy, the country needs to expand its intake in graduate and research study programmes.

There has been faster growth of enrolment in professional courses such as engineering, medicine, management, law and other vocational courses from the 1980s. This, at times, led to 'disciplinary distortions' (Anandakrishnan 2010) primarily due to the increasing share of private institutions which majorly offer employment-oriented technical and professional courses. Some of these courses are significantly more expensive than general courses – sometimes up to ten times more expensive (British Council 2014). However, parents are willing to invest in such courses because of the expected high employability of such graduates and their higher salary expectations. The most recent trend is that of lack of social demand for these courses in the private institutions.

3. Market Influence on Massification of Higher Education in India

While public universities were the most common institutional framework to provide higher education until the 1980s, market influence became common thereafter. The public universities became entrepreneurial (Clarke 1998) with diversified sources of funding in the developed countries, and private higher education institutions became common in the developing countries. India too moved from a public sector-led growth to a market-mediated private sector-dominated sector of higher education.

The evolution of the private sector in higher education in India is an interesting story (Varghese 2013). Immediately after independence, the private institutions were made public-funded institutions. In the 1970s, public-funded private higher education institutions were established through the grants-in-aid system. In the 1980s, the non-state-funded self-financing private institutions most commonly called 'capitation fee colleges' emerged (Tilak 1994). The capitation fee colleges were mostly for-profit private institutions offering courses in the subject areas of engineering, medicine, and management (Agarwal 2007b), and they proliferated especially in the southern states of India. These colleges were mostly teaching institutions affiliated to public universities, and their degrees were awarded by the parent universities.

The private capitation fee colleges were subjected to several court cases in the 1990s. Their differential fee policies were challenged in the Karnataka court (*Mohini Jain v. the State of Karnataka* case in 1992). In fact, the Supreme Court banned the capitation fee in a 1992 ruling which said that the capitation fee colleges 'are poisonous weeds in the fields of education and are financial adventurers without morals and scruples and characterized them as pirates in high seas of education' (Gupta 2008: 250). No doubt, the reckless growth of self-financing private colleges has resulted in establishing institutions with poor infrastructure, less-qualified faculty members, and such institutions provided poor-quality higher education.

The next stage was the emergence of deemed-to-be-universities in the private sector in India in the 1990s. The deemed universities were authorized to offer courses and award degrees, and the private sector saw this as a safety valve to free them from academic supervision and controls by the public universities. The Birla-Ambani Report of 2000 (GoI 2000) recommended the establishment of private universities in India. Although the federal Parliament could not legislate on the Private Universities Act, many of the state legislatures passed the act and private universities became a new feature of development in higher education. The UGC brought out regulations, *Establishment of and Maintenance of Standards in Private Universities*, in 2003 (UGC 2003b); following these regulations and policy support, private universities proliferated in India as shown in Table 1.1.

Some of the private universities offer high-quality education and are identified as Institutions of Eminence (IoEs). However, a majority of the private universities have been offering poor-quality education, and the court intervened to close down some of them. For example, the Supreme Court in 2005 in one of the cases (*Yashpal Sharma and Others v. the State of Chhattisgarh*) ruled that all private universities established by the Chhattisgarh state as null and void leading to closure of 117 private universities. Another trend emerging recently is the closing down of many private technical and professional colleges due to declining enrolment, questionable quality of education imparted and high cost of pursuing education.

4. Massification, Equity and Challenges of Inclusion

How did massification affect equity and quality of higher education in India? It is believed, in general, that the fairness and inclusion in access are the basis for ensuring equality of opportunity (Marginson 2011) in any democratic framework. Universities and colleges are an essential part of the infrastructure of democracy. The polls between 2015 and 2018 indicate a decline in public confidence in and support for colleges and universities in the United States (Peterson 2020). The empirical evidence on access to higher education shows that when the value of the indicator of inequality is increasing in an expanding system, the privileged benefits; when it is stable, the privileged and the less-privileged benefit equally and when it is declining, the poor benefits (Shavit and Gamoran 2007).

India made serious efforts to ensure social justice in all sectors including education. The initial step to formulate equity policies was to set criteria to identify the disadvantaged to develop targeted programmes. The Constitution of India recognized the scheduled castes (SC) and the scheduled tribes (ST) as the two most backward groups in 1951 and guaranteed 15 per cent reservation in admissions to higher education and in employment for the SCs and 7.5 per cent for the STs. In 1987, an additional quota of 27 per cent was extended to other backward classes (OBCs) in jobs and in higher education institutions. The Constitutional Amendment Act 2019 extended a quota of 10 per cent to the economically weaker sections (EWS) within the general category.

Taken together, the reservation or the quota of seats covers nearly 59.5 per cent of the admissions in institutions of higher education in India. It needs to be added that some of the state governments follow quota systems in admissions to higher education institutions which exceeds this level. In addition, the disadvantaged groups, especially the SCs and STs, are given hostel facilities in the universities. Some of the universities and colleges have separate hostels for the disadvantaged. Since the STs live in remote rural areas, the central government established tribal universities in some of the states to promote their education.

Have these initiatives helped to develop an equitable and inclusive higher education in India? This question may be analysed in terms of disparities in terms of regions, social groups, gender, economic categories and language groups.

Regional Disparities

The regional inequalities in the distribution of higher education facilities and enrolment have widened in the recent past. In 2018–19 the number of colleges per 100,000 population varied from seven in Bihar and eight in Jharkhand to fifty-three in some of the states such as Karnataka and fifty in Telangana. The states with larger share of private institutions experienced higher concentration of higher education institutions. The regional concentration of institutions also resulted in the widening of regional disparities in enrolment (Varghese 2019). For example, between 2001–2 and 2018–19, the GER increased by three times in some states, two times in others while it was too low in other states. The states with high concentration of institutions and private universities experienced faster growth and expansion of higher education.

An analysis will reveal that the market process has contributed to the widening of the regional disparities in the distribution of higher education institutions and enrolment in India. Further, the same process has widened rural-urban disparities. The private sector establishes institutions mostly in the urban, suburban and semi-urban areas which can attract larger number of fee-paying students leading to increasing rural-urban divide. It is interesting to note that the market process widens the regional disparities despite public policies to reduce regional inequalities by establishing new public institutions in the rural areas.

Social Group Disparities

While massification benefited all social groups, the social inequalities in access to higher education continue to persist. Some of the disadvantaged remain far behind others. In 2018–19, the GER at the all India level was 26.3 per cent while that for SC was 23.0 per cent and that for ST was 17.2 per cent (Table 1.3). Although the disparities in enrolment continue, there are signs of catch-up by the SC and ST groups and a faster growth in enrolment of the OBC categories, at times at the cost of general category students. For example, the OBCs increased their share in enrolment from 32.9 per cent in 2014–15 to 36.3 per cent in 2018–19, and the share of the general category students in enrolment decreased from 48.8 per cent to 43.3 per cent. It seems that the single group that benefited the most from massification of higher education in India is the OBC category (Varghese 2019).

The disadvantaged groups are progressing at a faster speed than those among the general categories, and the evidence gives scope for optimism to narrow down these differences in the future. One of the constraints is that the disparities in the higher education sector are extensions of those in the school education sector. Therefore, unless school enrolments are universalized, even a high transition rate from secondary to higher education may not increase GER in higher education.

Table 1.3 Gross Enrolment Ratio in Higher Education in India, 2011–12 to 2018–19

Year	ALL			SC			ST		
	Both	Male	Female	Both	Male	Female	Both	Male	Female
1	2	3	4	5	6	7	8	9	10
2011–12	20.8	22.1	19.4	14.9	15.8	13.9	11.0	12.4	9.7
2012–13	21.5	22.7	20.1	16.0	16.9	15.0	11.1	12.4	9.8
2013–14	23.0	23.9	22.0	17.1	17.7	16.4	11.3	12.5	10.2
2014–15	24.3	25.3	23.2	19.1	20.0	18.2	13.7	15.2	12.3
2015–16	24.5	25.4	23.5	19.9	20.8	19.0	14.2	15.6	12.9
2016–17	25.2	26.0	24.5	21.1	21.8	20.2	15.4	16.7	14.2
2017–18	25.8	26.3	25.4	21.8	22.2	21.4	15.9	17.0	14.9
2018–19	26.3	26.3	26.4	23.0	22.7	23.3	17.2	17.9	16.5

Source: Author, based on MHRD (2019).

Gender Disparities

The gender inequalities are narrowing down in higher education in India. One of the unique features of higher education is that, unlike school education, gender parity is achieved at lower levels of GER in higher education than in school education. In most of the developed countries, the GER of females surpasses that of males. India has not yet reached that stage, although in some of the states the female GER is higher than that of the males. The variations in GER between sexes are the lowest among the general category students. In 2018–19, the GER of general category women was almost 60 per cent higher than that of ST women and 13 per cent higher than the GER of SC women (Table 1.3).

The gender parity index (GPI) at the national level was 1.0 in 2018–19. Although traditionally women have been lagging behind men in terms of enrolment in higher education among all social groups, this trend has changed. For example, the GPI is 1.0 among all the caste groups while it is 1.03 in case of SC groups and 0.92 among ST groups (Table 1.4). These changes are due to the faster progress in enrolment of girls than boys, as can be seen from Table 1.3.

The gender parity has another dimension if one looks at the choice of courses by women. At all levels of studies – undergraduate, graduate and postgraduate – the largest share of women enrol in arts and humanities programmes (Chanana 2012; Sabharwal and Malish 2018). For example, the share of men and women are almost equal in commerce study programmes. More women than men join study programmes in social sciences, medical sciences, languages and education.

Table 1.4 Gender Parity Index in Higher Education in India, 2011–12 to 2018–19

Year	All	SC	ST
2011–12	0.88	0.88	0.78
2012–13	0.89	0.89	0.79
2013–14	0.92	0.92	0.81
2014–15	0.92	0.91	0.81
2015–16	0.92	0.91	0.83
2016–17	0.94	0.93	0.85
2017–18	0.97	0.96	0.87
2018–19	1.00	1.02	0.92

Source: Author, based on MHRD (2019).

The share of men in engineering courses is almost double that of women. These trends have remained more or less similar in the past several years.

Disparities among Economic Groups

The economic inequalities in access to higher education have been consistently high. There seems to exist a positive association between income levels and GER in higher education. A major share of the children from higher-income groups attend higher education institutions while the figures from the lower-income groups is low. This trend is consistent over time. For example, in 2007, the GER of children belonging to the poorest group in the lowest quintile (lowest 20 per cent) was around 4 per cent while that among the privileged belonging to the highest quintile (highest 20 per cent) was 47.6 per cent. The corresponding figures for the year 2014 were 9.9 per cent and 73.8 per cent, respectively. This shows that, despite the fast expansion, the disparities in access have widened among economic groups, and this can be attributed to the dominance of private institutions in accelerating growth rates in enrolment. It shows that the market process systematically excludes the poor from entry into institutions of higher education. Policies targeting the poor in the form of student support systems become a necessary condition to progress towards a more inclusive higher education in India.

Medium of Instruction and Disparities

Another source of exclusion in India is the medium of instruction. English language is seen to be the language of the elite and is the most preferred language in the universities. According to the National Sample Survey of 2014, nearly

72 per cent of the students in unaided private schools followed English as the medium of instruction while the corresponding share in government institutions is only 34 per cent. More importantly, the share of students following English as a medium of instruction has increased in the unaided private sector while it remained the same in government institutions. Hence students from private English-medium schools have a disproportionately high share in higher education enrolment.

There seems to be an interesting pathway to higher education in India. The students from private English-medium schools account for a disproportionately higher share in enrolment in the universities and elite institutions. An interesting trend seems to be that parents tend to prefer elite English-medium private institutions at the school education level and elite public institutions at the higher education level. This pattern reinforces the elite nature and exclusionary pattern of higher education development in India irrespective of the state or market provision.

The Indian experience shows that the affirmative policies have helped in bringing more children belonging to the disadvantaged groups to institutions of higher education. A more formidable challenge India faces is in terms of translating these achievements to improve learning outcomes and developing inclusive campuses. Many students from the disadvantaged groups do not perform well in their studies even in elite institutions. The limited cultural capital the students bring along with them, the lack of English language proficiency and poor college preparedness are some of the factors affecting their academic integration in the classrooms and social inclusion in the campuses (Sabharwal and Malish 2018). In the absence of supportive policies for academic integration, disadvantaged students face high dropout rates and lower levels of academic success and poor learning outcomes.

The higher education outcome in terms of employment opportunities also reflect the need for more public policy interventions. The graduate unemployment rate among different social groups indicate that it is highest at 10.5 per cent among SC followed by 8.9 per cent among ST, 8.2 per cent among OBC and 6.4 per cent among the non-disadvantaged category. In other words, the incidence of unemployment is higher among the higher education graduates belonging to the disadvantaged groups (Varghese 2019).

5. The Challenges of Quality Assurance in a Massifying System

The fast expansion and massification has put tremendous pressure on quality of provisions and outcomes of higher education. Indian universities do not appear in the top positions in the world university rankings, which is a matter of serious concern in the country. The Indian response to world ranking results was two-fold: (1) initiate efforts to establish world class universities/IoEs and (2) introduce its own national rankings. India has initiated steps to establish twenty IoEs (ten private universities and ten public universities. The National Institutional Ranking Framework (NIRF) helped the launching of a national ranking exercise in India in 2015. The ranking results are published in the month of April every year. A close look at some of the trends in the results indicate that mostly the public institutions attain top positions in the NIRF rankings.

Rankings cover only limited number of institutions and, therefore, may not be relied upon for improving the overall quality of the higher education sector. Countries have been relying on external quality assurance (EQA) mechanisms to carry out accreditation and quality audit to ensure quality of higher education. The EQA can ensure a threshold level of quality across institutions and can strengthen accountability in terms of learning outcomes in higher education.

India established EQA agencies in the 1990s. The National Assessment and Accreditation Council (NAAC) was set up by the UGC in 1994 to accredit universities and institutions of general higher education and the National Board of Accreditation (NBA) was established by the AICTE to accredit programmes in technical education. The NAAC accredits institutions and certifies for educational quality of the institution based on seven criteria: (1) curricular aspects; (2) teaching-learning and evaluation; (3) research, consultancy and extension; (4) infrastructure and learning resources; (5) student support and progression; (6) organization and management and (7) healthy and innovative practices.

Accreditation by the NAAC is voluntary and is valid for five years. The progress in accrediting institutions is very slow in India. It seems that only about one-third of the universities and about one-fifth of the colleges have been accredited in the past twenty-seven years of existence of the NAAC. Higher education institutions in India have also established internal quality assurance assurance cells (IQAC). It seems these cells mostly collect data on various aspects related to teaching learning and prepare reports. The effectiveness of these cells (IQAC) in monitoring and improving quality needs to be studied systematically.

Several quality improvement initiatives created through a new scheme called Pandit Madan Mohan Malaviya National Mission on Teachers and Teaching (PMMMNMTT) was launched in the previous decade. Many universities have established schools of education to research on pedagogical aspects and to improve teaching learning processes and learning outcomes in higher education in India. The National Resource Centres for Education (NRCEs) under the same scheme extends teacher support through providing learning materials and research references to teachers.

India has made serious efforts to enhance entry level qualifications and salary levels of teachers in higher education and has introduced screening at national and state levels to ensure that only good quality scholars enter the teaching profession. The number of teaching staff with doctoral degrees has increased in India. Further, entry into the teaching profession also requires competing and succeeding in national eligibility tests (NETs) or its equivalent at the state level.

Have these efforts resulted in quality improvement in higher education? The answer may not be conclusive. Variations among institutions exist in terms of basic facilities, teacher qualifications and competencies, and student profiles, and they have implications for both learning outcomes and the quality of higher education. India has a small share of high-quality institutions but a large share of low-quality higher education institutions in both public and private sector institutions. The difference is that many of the poor-quality institutions in the private sector, especially in the professional and technical domains, are closing down while similar institutions in the public sector continue to survive. The closing down of private institutions for lack of demand shows that quality has become a non-negotiable element for the survival of the market-mediated higher education process in India.

6. Governance and Management of Higher Education

The first set of universities were established in India in 1857. There existed no regulatory bodies for decades. India established the Central Advisory Board of Education (CABE) in 1921 to bring consensus among provincial governments on policy matters pertaining to education. The first regulatory body in higher education in India was, perhaps, the Medical Council of India (MCI) which was established in 1934. MCI had the authority to lay down norms and standards as well as recognize or derecognize courses and institutions.

When India became independent, education became a state subject as per the Constitution. In 1976, education was transferred to the concurrent list making it a joint responsibility of the central and state governments. It was felt that the sector needs regulation to ensure planned and coordinated development, quality of education, equity and social justice (quotas and other affirmative policies) and to prevent unfair practices (Ayyar 2013). The areas which require closer examination and regulation from this point of view are granting permission for the following: to open an institution; to operate the institution; to decide on the intake of students and introduction of courses; and to monitor its overall performance including issues related to governance and management and levels of student learning.

The first education commission of India (Radhakrishnan Commission, 1948) recommended giving autonomy to universities. The commission proposed the establishment of a legislative framework for universities to operate independently as well as a strong governing body with external members, thereby allowing universities to be free from external interference. Universities were supposed to be self-regulating entities and expected to voluntarily adhere to standards determined by the UGC. The recommendations of the commission led to the establishment of bodies such as AICTE and UGC, and it helped shift the regulatory authority to the central government (Carnoy and Dossani 2011). Thus, centralized regulation became the norm. In other words, public policy, state funding and state control became the features of higher education development in India during the initial periods after independence.

The UGC came into existence on 28 December 1953 and became a statutory organization of the government of India by an act of Parliament in 1956, for the coordination, determination and maintenance of standards of teaching, examination and research in university education.[1] Unlike the MCI, the UGC does not have authority to derecognize a university or its degree, and it remains a recommendatory entity (Singh 2004), although some of the committees appointed by the UGC have proposed closure of certain institutions, especially deemed to be universities. Although, UGC is the main regulatory body, several regulatory bodies in higher education exist in India. Since higher education is organized by several ministries, each ministry has its own body to regulate. There are nearly sixteen regulatory bodies functioning in higher education.

There have been discussions to establish a single regulatory body to ensure coordinated development of higher education. The National Policy on Education (NPE) (1986) and the Plan of Action (1992) proposed the establishment of a national apex body. The National Knowledge Commission in 2006 recommended setting up of an Independent Regulatory Authority for Higher Education (IRAHE). The Yash Pal Committee of 2011 also recommended the creation of an apex body – National Council for Higher Education and Research (NCHER) – to regulate the higher education sector. It envisaged increased

---

[1] https://www.ugc.ac.in/ (accessed on 29 June 2021).

state funding for higher education, more regulation of the private sector and increased institutional autonomy. The committee was against commercialization of education and discouraged for-profit private institutions while encouraging partnership with non-profit private organizations in higher education. It was expected that the regulatory body would guard against fast expansion of for-profit institutions providing education of questionable quality.

Another institutional arrangement that influences the management of higher education at the state level is the setting up of state higher education councils (SHECs) which were established following the recommendations of the NPE of 1986. The SHECs are expected to carry out the planning and coordination functions which include initiatives to improve the standard of higher education; to advice state governments on various issues relating to development of higher education in the state; to monitor and release grant-in-aid from state governments to universities and colleges; to promote cooperation and coordination of higher education institutions among themselves; to explore the scope for interaction with industry and other related establishments; to propose guidelines for establishment of new institutions; and to suggest ways to augment resources to the sector.

Academic functions include the promotion of innovations and restructuring of courses, improvement of standards of examinations, promotion of programmes of academic cooperation, interactions between colleges and university departments and academic staff training. Advisory functions include determining block maintenance grants, laying down the basis for such grants and setting up of a state research board. Unfortunately, many of the SHECs do not have regular faculty members which constrains their capacity to effectively intervene in the planning and management of higher education at the state level.

The major issue is that of autonomy of higher education institutions. It may not be incorrect to argue that institutional autonomy in the 1950s was with guaranteed funding. Today autonomy is posed as an alternative to public funding. Many public higher education institutions are starving for funds, and resource allocations do not meet even the salary budgets of the institutions. India has also introduced a process of staggered autonomy – institutions getting high scores in accreditation have greater independence and those obtaining low scores are subject to more controls. One of the studies by Centre for Policy Research in Higher Education (CPRHE) also indicated that the central universities enjoy better funding and autonomy while the state universities are getting low levels of funding and are subjected to higher levels of control (Malik 2020).

7. Financing of an Expanding Higher Education Sector in India

Public institutions, public funding and state control were important characteristics of development of higher education in India in the initial decades after independence. The share of education in the GDP continued to be low in the initial decades. Following the international commitment, the NPE of 1968 recommended allocating 6 per cent of the GDP for education. The 1986 policy on education reiterated the national commitment of investing 6 per cent of the GDP on education. The Jomtien Statement of 2011 reiterated the need to invest at least 6 per cent of their GDP and 20 per cent of their public expenditure on education.

The expenditure on education as a share of GDP has been increasing in India from 0.64 in 1950–1 to reach a share of 4.07 per cent of the GDP and nearly 10 per cent of the public expenditure on education in the year 2016–17. The CABE Committee of 2005 recommended that at least 1.5 per cent of the GDP needs to be allocated to higher education – 1 per cent to university and higher education and 0.5 per cent to technical education. These allocations continue to fall short of the allocation targets both for the education sector and for the higher education sub-sector.

The budget estimates of the Ministry of Human Resource Development (MHRD) for 2019–20 indicated the allocation of resources between school and higher education. It is observed that nearly 60 per cent of the public expenditure on education is on school education and nearly 40 per cent is in the higher education sector. Nearly twenty states allocated less than 15 per cent of their education allocation to higher education. Public expenditure on higher education is low in some states partly due to the presence of private providers.

The dominant role of the government in financing the higher education sector has come to an end and at present expansion of the sector does not rely heavily on public funds. Some of the committees appointed by the government in the 1990s (Punnayya Committee and Swaminathan Committee) noted that the fee levels in India are very low, and they recommended cost recovery of 15 per cent initially and 25 per cent (Punnayya Committee) eventually. In the past decades many universities have introduced fees or enhanced the then existing levels of tuition fees. The amount of fees to be levied in the universities and their equity implications have been an area of debate in India (Bhushan 2010; Chattopadhyay 2007; Tilak 2004).

The government of India set up a Higher Education Financing Agency (HEFA) in 2017 to mobilize funds from the market for the centrally funded higher educational institutions. HEFA is a non-profit, non-banking financing company (NBFC) for mobilizing extra-budgetary resources for building crucial infrastructure in the higher educational institutions. The central budget of 2018–19 called for increased investments in research and related infrastructure in premier educational institutions. The launch of Revitalizing Infrastructure and Systems in Education (RISE) with a total investment of INR 1000,000 million in next four years is a step in that direction. The funds mobilized through HEFA will be used to finance quality infrastructure, research labs and other facilities in centrally funded institutions such as Indian Institutes of Technology (IITs), National Institutes of Technology (NITs), Indian Institutes of Information Technology (IIITs), Indian Institutes of Science Education and Research (IISERs) and central universities. The NEP 2020 envisages setting up a National Research Foundation (NRF) with funding from the federal government to promote research in higher education institutions in India.

Several forms of cost recovery measures and student loans are becoming new strategies for financing higher education institutions in India (Panigrahi 2019). Student loans are becoming very popular in India and are availed for studies both within the country and abroad. In 2000–1 the total number of loans taken was 0.112 million, and it increased to 2.59 million in 2013–14. The education loan amount increased from INR 1.03 billion to 7.03 billion in 2013–14, which was more than the total central allocation to higher and technical education (Rani 2016). The increase in student loans is also a reflection of the expansion of private higher education where students rely on loans to pay relatively high fees.

8. Internationalization of Higher Education in India

Higher education in India has greatly benefited from international collaborations. The first three universities established during the colonial period were modelled after the University of London. Several missionary institutions of higher education were functioning in India during the colonial period. These collaborations continued even after independence when international cooperation and collaborations were relied on for the establishment of top-ranking technical and professional institutions in India, especially the IITs and IIMs, development of laboratory facilities for science research and training of higher education teachers. The first-generation professors in many of India's higher education institutions were either of foreign origin or trained abroad.

Even today, a good number of professors in most of the top-ranking higher education institutions in India are trained abroad (Varghese 2020a).

India is a beneficiary of the scholarship programmes extended by USAID and the Fulbright programme, Colombo Plan, British Council and Commonwealth scholarship program, and the German Academic Exchange Service (Deutscher Akademischer Austauschdienst, DAAD). India is one of the largest sources of international students and it sends more than 0.3 million students abroad for studies. The United States, UK and Australia are favourite destinations for Indian students. Indian students form the second largest group after China among the cross-border students and among those enrolled in MOOCs programmes after the United States.

The flow of cross-border students to India is low. In 2018–19, India hosted 49,348 foreign students (GoI 2021d). Most of them came from South Asian countries led by Nepal and African countries. An overwhelming majority of the foreign students in India came for undergraduate studies mostly in technology (BTech.), commerce (BCom.) and medical sciences.

Institutional mobility is not permitted as yet, and hence India has more institutional collaborations than operation of branch campuses. According to the Association of Indian Universities survey (AIU 2012), nearly 631 foreign institutions, mostly from UK, Canada and the United States were collaborating with Indian universities. The NEP 2020 plans to permit opening of branch campuses by foreign institutions in India, while Indian institutions have already been establishing branch campuses abroad in countries such as Mauritius, Dubai, Malaysia and Singapore.

A programme – Global Initiative for Academic Network (GIAN) – was launched in 2017–18 to attract foreign faculty members to teach for short durations in Indian universities. It attracted around 1800 scholars from fifty-six countries to offer courses in 2017–18 and 2018–19. In its next phase, GIAN II, the government intends to promote mobility of Indian faculty members to teach in universities abroad. Another programme called the Scheme for Promotion of Academic Research and Collaboration (SPARC) was launched in 2018 to promote research collaboration between Indian institutions and reputed institutions abroad. India hopes to enrol 500,000 international students in Indian institutions by the year 2024. The government is also planning to expand the number of student scholarships to 50,000 by the year 2024.

Such new initiatives, including the recommendations in the NEP 2020, help open up new avenues for international collaborations in research and cross-border mobility of institutions, programmes, students and teachers.

9. Directions of Change: National Education Policy 2020 and Higher Education Development

More than three decades after the education policy of 1986, India announced a new policy – NEP 2020 (GoI 2020c) – which will guide education development in the country in the coming decades. The NEP 2020 expects to universalize higher education, facilitate institutional consolidation and encourage flexible pathways to higher learning to take advantage of the technological developments and introduce new governance structures. The major focus is on improving quality of higher education and improving learning outcomes to enhance India's standing and role in the global education landscape.

From Massification to Universalization

The NEP 2020 (GoI 2020c) provides a long-term perspective, as it recognizes the importance of public policy and funding on the one hand and the role of the market in the provision of education and employment on the other. Unlike the previous policies of 1968 and 1986, NEP 2020 makes a welcome recommendation for the expansion of the higher education sector and its eventual universalization by 2035. It implies almost a doubling of the GER from the current level of 26.3 per cent to 50 per cent within the next fifteen years. Some of the states are already close to achieving this target while others lag far behind the national average, which makes it difficult for them to reach the target of 50 per cent GER by 2035. The transition rate from secondary to higher education level is high even in educationally backward states and therefore, unless school education is sufficiently expanded in the educationally less-developed states the national goal of universalization of higher education may not be realized. The direction of change in higher education is to make the sector reach the levels reached by developed (e.g. Organisation for Economic Co-operation and Development [OECD]) countries.

Institutional Consolidation

The NEP 2020 proposes the transformation of existing institutions into multidisciplinary institutions – such as research universities, teaching universities and multidisciplinary autonomous colleges – to develop world class multidisciplinary education and research universities (MERUs). It will also put an end to the system of affiliated colleges over a period of next fifteen years.

The NEP promotes flexible pathways to higher learning through several initiatives. The policy proposes developing three- or four-year undergraduate degree programmes and one- or two-year master's programmes as well as enabling credit transfers between universities and between online courses and face-to-face courses. The flexibility of curricular choice shall be an important element in restructuring the pedagogy.

Another related recommendation of the NEP 2020 is to phase out small colleges and ensure a minimum of 3000-student enrolment in any college. As of 2019, nearly 6.5 per cent of the colleges have an enrolment of fewer than 500 students; nearly 92 per cent of the colleges have fewer than 2000 students; and only 4 per cent of the colleges have more than 3000 students (GoI 2019). The reason why several small-sized colleges exist is two-fold. First, the government encouraged a policy of establishing higher education institutions in the rural areas to improve access, especially for girls. Second, there are many single discipline institutions and most of them are in the private sector. While it may be easy to consolidate colleges under the same management in the urban areas, it is more difficult to consolidate or merge institutions under different managements. More importantly, such consolidation effort in the rural areas may lead to increasing inequalities in access to higher education.

New Accreditation Arrangements for Quality Enhancement

The NEP 2020 accords high priority to enhancing the quality of higher education outcomes. As noted in earlier paragraphs, Indian universities do not appear in the top positions in the global rankings. Quality assurance efforts have also not succeeded in accrediting a majority of institutions. The NEP 2020 considers setting up of a meta-accreditation agency called the National Accreditation Council (NAC). The NAC attempts to create a set of accreditors at the regional level and will accredit the accreditors (the decentralized or regional accreditation agencies) to create a pool or an ecosystem of accreditors. These decentralized efforts for provision of accreditation facilities may increase the number of institutions accredited in the future years.

New Governance of Higher Education

The NEP has segregated the functions of standard-setting, funding, accreditation and regulation by allocating each of these functions to separate agencies. The policy proposes transforming the governance system by setting up a single regulator as Higher Education Commission of India (HECI) with four verticals for: (1) regulation (National Higher Education Regulatory Council, NHERC); (2) accreditation (National Accreditation Council, NAC); (3) funding (Higher Education Grants Council, HEGC); and (4) managing academic standards (General Education Council, GEC). The standard-setting functions will be performed by the professional standard-setting bodies (PSSBs) under the GEC.

The idea of creating a single regulator is to facilitate 'light but tight' regulation by mitigating the problems of over-regulation in higher education. All professional bodies, except medicine and law education, will be under the HECI. Private and public sector institutions of higher education will have the same set of regulations.

NEP 2020 envisions university as an autonomous structure with an empowered structure of governance at the institutional level. The idea of institutional autonomy within the framework of graded autonomy is one of the governance reforms recommended. The policy proposes an empowered structure of board of governors for each higher education institution. In other words, future growth of the sector will rely less on public authorities and state controls. However, the policy is less pronounced when it comes to the issue of funding of education. NEP 2020 does not provide any new promises other than reiteration of the recommendations of earlier education policies of 1968 and 1986.

10. Conclusion

The analysis presented in this chapter shows that higher education in India has been expanding at an accelerated rate in recent decades. While expansion of the sector until the 1980s depended largely on the fiscal capacity of the state, the expansion in the present context does not rely heavily on state funding. The market influence has accelerated the growth of higher education institutions and student enrolment. In other words, unlike in the developed countries where massification was facilitated through public institutions, India has experienced a market-mediated process of massification. This shift in the policy from public-funded to private/household-financed higher education has implications for affordability, equity and inclusion. Unless equity policies are in place and are effectively implemented, this model of development may have implications for creating an egalitarian society within a democratic framework.

The NEP 2020 indicates that the pressure to expand the sector will continue to reach a stage of universalization. India's demographic dividend and the success of HEFA programmes may help the efforts to universalize higher education. However, given the past experience, the question of quality will remain a major challenge in Indian higher education. A new trend is that household demand is for quality higher education. Unless quality is guaranteed, households are not willing to invest their resources. For example, many private higher education institutions have been closed in the recent past for lack of adequate demand and student enrolment. It can be argued that unless quality initiatives are not effectively implemented, the expansion of the sector is uncertain.

The policy does not give scope for increased public funding for higher education. It reiterates the commitment made in earlier polices of allocating 6 per cent of the GDP and 20 per cent of public expenditure to education. Even if these financing targets are met, they will remain grossly inadequate for the expansion requirements of the sector. More than two-thirds of the students and 75 per cent of the institutions of higher education are in the private sector. Therefore, regulation of the market process to ensuring equity and quality becomes an important step in the development of higher education in India. Further, limited public funding needs to be better targeted for equity programmes and quality enhancement measures. In other words, increasing public allocations and better targeting the allocations as per the national priorities become necessary conditions for an equitable and balanced development of higher education in India.

2

Financing of Higher Education in India: Issues and Challenges

Saumen Chattopadhyay and Jinusha Panigrahi

1. Introduction

Inadequate growth in public financing of higher education has been considered to be a major factor behind suboptimal functioning of Indian higher education institutions (HEIs), increasing concern for poor quality and forcing a compromise with inclusiveness of expansion of the higher education sector. The policymakers have long been goading the public-funded HEIs to recover a larger portion of the costs of operation so as to reduce dependence on public funding and diversify revenue sources. In a federal country with pressing needs for health and physical infrastructure, the resource constraint is likely to become more acute in the era of post-pandemic. The policymakers have also evinced keen interest in using public funding as a policy instrument for fixing accountability and improving quality while safeguarding the interest of the needy and the deserving sections of the society. The emerging scenario in financing of higher education makes a clear statement for shifting responsibility to the HEIs to mobilize resources and borrow rather than depending heavily on public funding. Students too are increasingly resorting to loans to pursue their higher studies. The policymakers have been trying to institutionalize this shifting of responsibility.

The objective of this chapter is to examine the emerging trends in public funding of higher education and reflect on the possible implications for the objectives of higher education, namely expansion, inclusion and achieving excellence. We begin with a brief discussion on the issues related to who should fund higher education and how, as university functioning is a complex affair. This is followed by a brief review of the present context of financing of the sector focusing on the role of the government, and then we move on to discuss the possible implications of the policy measures. We present the emerging situation in shifting responsibilities for funding higher education from the state, to the market and the households. The chapter ends with an introduction to the institutional reconfiguration of the Indian higher education as proposed in the National Education Policy (NEP) 2020.

2. Funding Higher Education: Conceptual Issues

We need to set the context by addressing the questions of adequacy of public funding and mode of funding at the conceptual level though this terrain has been well explored in the literature (e.g. Jongbloed 2007; Marginson 2016).

Higher Education as a Quasi-public Good

The debate on the issue of adequacy of public funding of higher education and the associated issue of cost sharing is linked with that on the very nature of higher education as a good (or a service), whether it is a public good or a private good or even a blend of this two, a quasi-public good. We need to consider two different dimensions of higher education: access to the HEIs for the purpose of pursuing higher studies and conduct of research for the production of knowledge.[1]

In terms of the traditional definition of public good (Samuelson 1954), a public good is non-rival in consumption and it is non-excludable. Strictly speaking, higher education is not a public good as access to higher education is rival as the number of seats in a HEI is limited, which makes it excludable too. However, higher education has a public character because the transformed graduates churned out by the universities contribute to the nation building in various ways which help maintain social and political order by the concerned and responsible citizens (Marginson 2016). These, what are called externalities, entail that the delivery of higher education should be financed by the public subsidies so that costs borne by the students are reduced to help attain the social optimum. It also means that the private element of higher education which manifest in terms of earnings of the students during their working life period attributable specifically to the augmented level of human capital embodied should be borne by the students themselves. As pointed out by Chapman, Dearden and Doan

---

[1] This is not to deny the overlapping between the two activities, teaching and research, and mutually reinforcing tendencies between the two.

(2020), this is an equity issue as tax financing of higher education is argued to be regressive because taxpayers, who all do not pursue higher studies, end up funding higher studies of mainly the privileged section of the society. However, we need to take note of two main issues. One, the taxpaying population gain from the externalities generated by the graduates irrespective of their levels of awareness of the contributions made by the graduates, directly and indirectly, knowingly and unknowingly. Two, the needy as well as the meritorious students who have high opportunity costs of pursuing higher studies because of high propensities to join job market should have to be supported financially to help them continue their studies in the interest of nation building.[2] In view of the differentiatedness of a higher education system, equalization of opportunities to access higher education is only a first step. The HEIs cannot and should not run on cost recovery mode as exclusion of the meritorious and the needy can result in compromising the quality and the very of purpose of education. The advocacy for income-contingent loans (ICLs) is appealing because it allows for abolition of tuition fees but recovery from the graduates employed only if their income exceeds a threshold level (Chapman, Dearden and Doan 2020). Higher education being a blend of both private and public elements can be characterized as a mixed good or a quasi-public good. However, Marginson (2020a) argues for invoking the concept of common goods to fully appreciate the social contributions of higher education in a political and cultural context to emphasize the political processes of participation, the role of civil society and the extent of solidarity that a community desires and values. He points out that the binary between state and non-state or market and non-market is conceptually limiting.

The other crucial aspect of higher education is the production of knowledge which is in the nature of a pure public good, and therefore, it should be ideally be funded by the government (Marginson 2016). It is here the definition of public good offered by Samuelson is found inadequate and deficient (Marginson 2016). Publicness of a public good is not derived on the basis of its technical features but it is a policy decision or, to put it differently, the degree of excludability is a sociopolitical and economic construct decided by the policymakers and the context. Even if it is a quasi-good, the important issue of public-private divide remains unaddressed as externalities and contribution towards common good character of higher education cannot be quantified precisely.

[2] Becker (1993) in his demand-supply model, the case for subsidizing the meritorious students is brought out very clearly.

It is also imperative to distinguish between positive and normative with reference to public good. Higher education is more like a private good in the positive sense as the growing private participation indicates. However, the policymakers should foster publicness of higher education by suitable policymaking to encourage mobility and sociability while attaining humane growth.

The second emerging aspect in the policy discourse is whether public goods are to be necessarily funded by the government. The neoliberal approach to funding argues that it need not be. With focus on market construction and governance reform, public funding can be so channelized that a market evolves with the financial empowerment of the students thereby bestowing them with sovereignty in their choice-making, as in the case of school voucher (Friedman 1962). In the process, this would generate competition which is expected to have a salutary effect on quality.

The Mode of Funding a University Is a Bit Tricky

The university, which is often referred to as a multi-product firm, does not face a market in the popular sense as the university deliverables are not quantifiable and saleable, strictly speaking. There does not exist any market unless a market is created which remains riddled with imperfections. A university follows a customer-input technology as students are both the inputs as well as the customers. Since students are the embodiments of human capital, the universities always look forward to selecting the best by levying lower fees and giving them scholarships. In absence of full public funding, the universities need to balance cost recovery and student support. Construction of a market which treats students as consumers is inimical to the rigour of scholarship and quality. Degrees are not sold because learning outcomes are co-constructed by the students and the teachers. Teachers are the most critical inputs who are supposed to be intrinsically motivated; however they too behave typically as self-optimizing agents. This typicality of university as an institution makes modes of funding it tricky and challenging. Funding, costing and pricing in the context of university finances are not grounded on rigour and objectivity but on intention, judgements and subjectivities.

3. Higher Education as a Public Good in Policy Discourse

The extent of public funding for higher education depends, albeit theoretically and arguably, on the quasi-ness of higher education as a public good. With the introduction of the new economic policy in the early 1990s, the government of India took stock of the extent of subsidization of various goods and services as well as the rationales behind it (Srivastava et al. 1997). In a white paper entitled 'Central Government Subsidies in India' tabled in the Parliament in 2004 (GoI 2004) by the Ministry of Finance, education other than elementary was described as 'Merit-II good', which implied that the extent of subsidization should be pitched at a lower level than that of 'Merit-I good'.

Tilak (2004) argues that cost recovery in Indian higher education was already high, and India was not spending adequately on higher education compared to the developed countries. In fact, higher education had ceased to be regressive with democratization of higher education participation, and therefore the rationale for budget cuts for higher education being regressive was no longer tenable, he argues. Based on a study of several universities, Tilak and Rani (2000) inferred that on an average the extent of dependence on grants was 80 per cent. With several universities, the support was much less implying a cost recovery to the tune of 20 per cent or more. The possible reason was to encourage technical education which has a clear link with economic growth while the link between non-technical education and growth was argued to be fuzzy and unclear. This is a typical problem in the context of the debate that externalities and collective goods produced by higher education which hold the society and the polity together remain undermined and unrecognized by the policymakers and the people in general. In fact, contribution to the public sphere to generate discussion and debate regarding the state of affairs is expectedly not to the liking by the state even in a democratic country such as India. Inadequate public support for non-technical education undermines public good research carried out in this sector, including research in hard sciences. Without public support for fundamental research, applied research cannot flourish. Funding of social sciences, arts and humanities plays a crucial role in the self-formation of the students which is a precursor to the generation of positive externalities.[3]

With the beginning of the era of new economic policy in 1991, the government gradually began to show signs of transitioning to a new system which focuses on the efficiency to be realized in the market in the presence of increased private participation. Punnayya Committee (1992–3) (GoI 1993) stressed on generation of own revenues and promotion of internal efficiency as negotiated mode of funding breeds inefficiency. The recommendation was to move towards

---

[3] Even at Indian Institutes of Technology (IITs), social sciences are taught because after all we are all accountable to the society and are expected to behave in a socially responsible manner.

a mix of input-based funding and student-based funding to be supported by education loans. This was expected to improve cost efficiency and generate competition among the HEIs. The Birla-Ambani Report laid stress on funding higher education based on user pay principle (GoI 2000) with safeguards for the underprivileged sections of the society.

The direction for reform that emerged from the policy documents indicated that the public-funded Indian HEIs would be veering towards adoption of cost recovery measures perforce, which would include offering of self-financing courses, hiking of student fees and promotion of education loans. Some of the recent policy changes for the institutions to avail loans for growth include the setting up of the Rashtriya Uchchatar Shiksha Abhiyan (RUSA or National Higher Education Mission), and the Higher Education Financing Agency (HEFA), and partnering with private parties in the form of public-private partnerships (PPPs) (GoI 2013). Both the central and state governments have encouraged the institutions perforce to rely on various cost-saving or cost-cutting methods and explore income-generating activities in the form of collecting user charges, renting out of institutional infrastructure, outsourcing of institutional activities, starting new short-term courses, conducting research projects, seeking alumni contributions and exploring contract farming opportunities (Panigrahi 2017; Varghese and Panigrahi 2019).

We find it heartening to note that the NEP recognizes higher education as a quasi-public good. The draft NEP proposes to enhance government budgetary support for the education sector as a whole by one percentage point every year to 20 per cent in a span of ten years (GoI 2019b: 406–7). The prevailing allocation on the education sector is 10 per cent of government expenditure.

Trends and Patterns of Financing Higher Education

In order to understand the trend and pattern of expenditure on higher education, we would like to begin with an overview of public expenditure on education incurred by both the centre and the states. Expenditure on education made by departments other than the education department is also considered in order to obtain a more complete picture. We begin with the education sector as a whole to situate funding for higher education in a context. The three levels of education need to be studied together because of their interdependencies. Based on empirical study, Dubey (2019) observes that low quality of elementary education affects both quantity and quality of the student cohort who can potentially access tertiary education. For high-income states, the forward linkages between elementary and higher education are good and hence in these states, public funding on higher education produces more effects than in others.

Though the public funding for higher education experienced remarkable growth post-independence, in real terms the growth looks unimpressive (Tilak 2004). In the 1990s, the budget for higher education faced a substantial cut both in terms of per-student expenditure as well as GDP. Chakrabarti and Joglekar (2006), based on a detailed empirical study of the states, observed that education expenditure on education for all levels fell after the introduction of the new economic policy in 1991. Privatization had a negative impact on public funding on higher education in select states with high private participation. During the first years after 1990, there was a compression in real terms which affected the quality in view of rising student enrolment (Chakrabarti and Joglekar 2006).

For the period 2000–1 to 2004–5, expenditure made by the states on the education sector fell from 2.74 per cent of GDP to 2.29 per cent in 2004–5 (Table 2.1). An increase by the centre in the share in GDP could not prevent the fall of total expenditure from 3.14 to 2.74 per cent. The rate of growth of centre's expenditure in nominal terms at 13.4 per cent was much higher than that of the states at 5.7 per cent.[4] During 2005–6 to 2009–10 period, the shares of public funding in GDP of both the states and the centre rose, which increased the total from 2.79 to 3.11 per cent. This is evident from the rate of growth of states and the centre at 18.3 per cent and 22.3 per cent, respectively.

Between 2010–11 and 2014–15, the rate of growth of states and the centre experienced a dip. The fall for the centre was steeper. The shares of the states and the centre in GDP declined too, consequently pulling down the growth in total expenditure to 2.9 from 3.22. For the period 2015–16 to 2017–18, both the states and the centre had registered low growth rates at 7.6 and 4.3 per cent, respectively. The states' share in GDP rose which compensated for the fall in the centre's share (see Tables 3.1 and 3.2).

If we add in the expenditure incurred by the other departments, which includes skill training, we observe that the shares in GDP was 4.43 per cent as per the budget estimate in 2017–18, to which the states contributed to the tune of 3.41 per cent while the figure was just above 1 per cent for the centre. The centre's share in total expenditure if inclusive of other departments was 23 per cent which was significantly higher than 15.7 per cent if we consider only the education department. In fact, the gap between the centre's share including other

---

[4] RoG is the compound growth rate calculated as g in the following growth equation: $Y_t = Y_1(1+g)^{t-1}$.

Table 2.1 Public Expenditure on Education as percentage of GDP

	Expenditure on education by the education department			Expenditure on education by education and other departments			Excl. other	Inc other
	States/UTs	Centre	Total	States/UTs	Centre	Total	Centre/Total	
2000–1	2.74	0.40	3.14	3.63	0.51	4.14	12.7	12.4
2001–2	2.62	0.37	2.99	3.03	0.65	3.68	12.4	17.7
2002–3	2.54	0.39	2.93	2.97	0.69	3.66	13.3	18.9
2003–4	2.40	0.39	2.79	2.74	0.65	3.40	13.9	19.2
2004–5	2.29	0.44	2.74	2.65	0.61	3.25	16.1	18.6
RoG	5.72	13.41	6.79	2.14	15.31	4.05		
2005–6	2.26	0.53	2.79	2.66	0.68	3.34	18.9	20.5
2006–7	2.19	0.60	2.79	2.61	0.87	3.48	21.6	24.9
2007–8	2.15	0.58	2.74	2.53	0.87	3.40	21.4	25.6
2008–9	2.23	0.65	2.88	2.66	0.90	3.56	22.5	25.4
2009–10	2.46	0.65	3.11	2.90	1.05	3.95	21.0	26.5
RoG	18.31	22.35	19.10	18.45	28.87	20.82		
2010–11	2.51	0.72	3.22	2.94	1.11	4.05	22.2	27.5
2011–12	2.40	0.69	3.09	2.84	0.99	3.82	22.3	25.8
2012–13	2.34	0.66	3.01	2.80	0.90	3.70	22.1	24.4
2013–14	2.33	0.64	2.97	2.83	1.00	3.84	21.5	26.1
2014–15	2.35	0.55	2.90	3.00	1.07	4.07	19.1	26.3
RoG	12.64	7.35	11.53	15.10	13.40	14.64		
2015–16	2.32	0.49	2.81	3.16	1.04	4.20	17.4	24.7
2016–17	2.39	0.48	2.87	3.33	0.99	4.32	16.6	23.0
2017–18	2.50	0.47	2.97	3.41	1.02	4.43	15.7	23.1
RoG	7.6	4.3	7.0	7.5	5.2	7.0		

Note: RoG is the compound growth rate calculated as g in the following growth equation:
$Y_t = Y_1 (1+g)^{t-1}$.

Source: Authors, derived from analysis of Budget Expenditure, various issues, MoE, GoI.

Table 2.2 Public Expenditure on Education by Education and Other Departments

	2013–14 Actual			2017–18 Budgetary estimate		
	States/UTs	Centre	Total	States/UTs	Centre	Total
Percentage of GDP						
Elementary	1.23	0.39	1.62	1.53	0.37	1.9
Secondary	0.85	0.11	0.95	0.95	0.13	1.08
University and higher education	0.44	0.23	0.67	0.47	0.2	0.67
Adult education	0	0	0.01	0	0	0.01
Technical education	0.32	0.26	0.58	0.45	0.32	0.77
Total	2.83	1.00	3.84	3.41	1.02	4.43
Percentage composition						
Elementary	43.5	39.0	42.2	44.9	36.3	42.9
Secondary	30.0	11.0	24.7	27.9	12.7	24.4
University and higher education	15.5	23.0	17.4	13.8	19.6	15.1
Adult education	0.0	0.0	0.3	0.0	0.0	0.2
Technical education	11.3	26.0	15.1	13.2	31.4	17.4
Total	100	100	100	100	100	100

Source: Authors, derived from analysis of budget expenditure, various issues, MoE, GoI.

departments and excluding other departments rose to more than 7 percentage points from virtually none in 2000–1. The centre's share is more than doubled from 0.47 to 1.02 per cent once we include other departments.

Out of total budget for higher education, university and higher education, and technical education, the share of university remained the same at 0.67 per cent of GDP out of the total allocation made by the centre in 2013–14, 23 per cent for university and 26 per cent for technical education. Within a span of four years, the share for university fell to 19.6 while that for the technical, rose significantly from 26.0 to 31.4 per cent.

We observe therefore (1) the centre's allocation for university and higher education has dipped in the recent years; (2), the share for technical education has gone up for both the states and the centre and it is more for the centre; and (3) expenditure by other departments on education has gone up at a steady rate. These expenditures are made mostly towards skill development and training.

What is worrisome is the intra-sectoral allocation of expenditure. In 2009–10, on an average, 85 per cent of the expenditure used to be kept aside for salaries and only 10 per cent for capital expenditure. The situation may not have changed much since then as with revision in teachers' salaries, it was rising faster than the aggregate budget for higher education. This is ominous because very little is left for other expenditures which are crucial for quality teaching-learning outcomes and research support (Tilak 2016 based on RUSA 2013).

Modalities of Allocation and Utilization of Resources

The University Grants Commission (UGC) is designated to be the major fund allocation body. Under Section 12(B) of the UGC Act, funds are allocated to the HEIs. Funding of universities is largely input-based and based on specific requests which makes it politically vulnerable (Panigrahi 2017: 6). While inadequate funding is a serious issue, allocation of funds and its utilization at the institutional level pose another layer of challenge. One common problem which acts as a disincentive for the mobilization of additional resources and resources saved by the HEIs is that any extra earnings are adjusted against maintenance grants payable by reducing the grants by the amount of extra earnings. The High Power Committee (AICTE 1994) recommended that universities should be allowed to retain additional earnings and resources saved as a way of reward instead of adjusting it against their maintenance grants. These funds can be kept in a separate fund for utilization towards attainment of university objectives. Low absorptive capacity of the institutions arises because of bureaucratic interference, restrictive bureaucratic processes and tardy decision making, all of which prevent the system from achieving optimum and timely utilization of funds (Panigrahi 2017).

Household Expenditure on Higher Education

Per student expenditure on higher education has increased in all states between 2007 and 2014. The increase has been to the tune of two times in 2014 as compared to 2007. For the states of Kerala, Karnataka, Haryana and Puducherry, household expenditure is much on the higher side. Expectedly, these states also have a higher share of private unaided institutions particularly in the professional and technical areas. If we examine the per student expenditure by type of institutions, private unaided is higher than that of private aided which in turn is significantly higher than that of government institutions (Table 2.3). For technical and professional institutions where fees are at higher levels, we see virtually no difference between private aided and private unaided but fees are higher than that of government institutions by two and half times.

Table 2.3 Per Student Expenditure by Type of Institutions

Type of higher education	Type of institution	Average expenditure (INR)		
		75th Round (2017–18)	71st Round (2014)	64th Round (2007–8)
General	Government	3135	10261	6451
	Private aided	14155	14612	7704
	Private unaided	17082	21371	11665
	Total	8331	13963	7518
Technical/Professional	Government	25433	40528	23960
	Private aided	60454	67094	38536
	Private unaided	61256	84133	45312
	Total	50307	70602	37573

Source: Authors, based on National Sample Survey (NSS) 71st and 75th Round unit level data (NSSO 2014b, 2018).

4. Designing Policies, Shifting Responsibilities

Public funding for higher education remains the driving force to determine how much the private sector is investing in setting up of private HEIs and how much the household sector is spending in accessing higher education. As pointed out above, the growth in public funding has not been commensurate in the face of the rising demand for higher education. The public-funded institutions have come under pressure to look for funds from alternative sources and even borrow for investing in infrastructure development. In the next section, we look at the sources of funding being opted for by the institutions to invest and sustain operations while the students and households look for education loans.

Responsibilizing Students, Promoting Education Loans

A scheme of interest free national loan scholarships was launched in 1963. It was reintroduced in 2001 in a revised form to ensure that all deserving students could continue with their studies without getting deterred by the cost of pursuing higher studies. It was revised again in 2004–5 to make it more liberal (Kapur and Mehta 2017). A loan guarantee authority was established to incentivize the system. The Income Tax Act provides for deducting loan repayment amount while calculating the taxable amount.

Education loan has witnessed a rapid growth from barely INR 3 billion (300 crore) at the beginning of decade to INR 40 billion (4000 crore) in 2005 with the outstanding amount now touching INR 600 billion (60,000 crore) (Krishnan 2017). The coverage in terms of geographical space and quality of HEIs has expanded. Krishnan (2017) argues that given the rising number students opting for higher education and rising cost of education, there is a scope for innovation in the education loan system to foster easier access by bringing in more flexibility in loan repayment with a concomitant reduction in financial commitment. He argues that, worldwide, for a successful loan programme, the governments should participate to ensure that deserving students get loans and reduce high risk of default due to the absence of collateral to encourage participation of the commercial banking sector. It is important for the government to stand as a guarantor by addressing systemic information asymmetries through rating of the institutions and by setting up a credit information bureau. But this is also inherently discriminatory as students from lower rated institutions are likely to be less favoured by the banks for granting loans.

In view of the worldwide trend in shifting towards ICLs (Chapman, Dearden and Doan 2020), Das and Ray (2019) argue for shifting towards ICLs in the Indian context. An interest subsidy scheme was introduced in 2009–10 to provide subsidy for the period of moratorium on the interest on loans borrowed from banks under the education loan scheme circulated by the Indian Bank Association for the students intending to pursue professional education. It was expected that a credit guarantee will reduce non-performing assets (NPA) and allow for easy availability of loans. It will also guarantee the repayment of education loans to the extent of 75 per cent for studies, even those availed by students who want to pursue higher studies abroad.

Nevertheless, these financing mechanisms of higher education do not appear to improve access and equity in the higher education system (Geetha Rani 2015).

While education loans are argued to be better than direct transfer of subsidies because they are both efficient and equitable, ICLs, if properly designed, are arguably still better because they make only those students who earn above a certain limit repay their loans. This eliminates the systemic job market uncertainty faced by the students. Students from economically weaker sections who are generally risk averse will face lesser uncertainty by opting for ICLs. For a country like India with a huge higher education sector, deficient infrastructure and a large share of the informal sector which is to the tune of nearly 85–90 per cent, the institutionalization of ICLs would require systemic planning for restructuring the financing mechanism of higher education to track and trace the graduates and their earnings. However, ICLs raise the larger issue as expenditure on education by the students is construed essentially as investment and not as a state's responsibility, which can make them feel less obligated to serve the nation beyond the call of their professions.

5. Bestowing Institutions with Financial Autonomy

The HEIs are now being nudged and pushed by explicit policy design to tap alternative sources of revenue generation. We discuss some of these alternative sources which have always been available with the universities and some recent policy thrust to push for a greater degree of financial autonomy. The issue is whether all HEIs are equally placed and equally capable of generating resources including alternative sources in a country like India which is experiencing massification with huge rural-urban differences to rely on alternative sources. The relationship between financial autonomy and academic autonomy is a bit tenuous as having the former does not guarantee the latter because the pursuit of academic activities remains circumscribed by the imperative of raising resources which generally come with strings attached. The total expenditure on higher education by the Union government went up by 15.7 per cent during 2018–19 and 2019–20 but it suffered a decline in the year 2020-1 as per the revised estimate, the year of the pandemic by 11 per cent (GoI 2020g; GoI 2021a). Though for 2021–2 the allocation for higher education is budgeted to rise by 16.6 per cent over 2020-1, there is a clear indication for a shift in the priorities as revealed by the budget estimates for 2021–2 (GoI 2021a). For the UGC, the budgeted rise is only 5.6 per cent and for the Central Universities, it is in fact, set to fall by 11.5 per cent. For the budget on Student Financial Aid, the rise is 2.7 times and for Digital e-learning, the rise is more than double. Out of the budget for Digital e-learning, the budget for National Mission in Education through ICT is set to go up by three times and for the MOOCs, it is budgeted to rise by 2.66 times. The year 2020-1 being the pandemic year, the budgetary allocation for Student Financial Aid and Digital e-learning fell by 41 per cent and 33 per cent respectively. The budgeted rise for 2021–2 for the IITs is barely 12 per cent whereas for the IISERs, it may fall by 5 per cent.

Self-Financing Courses

A majority of state universities depend on affiliation fees paid by the affiliating colleges and self-financing courses, short-term programmes, training and consultancy. The Punnayya Committee (GoI 1993) and the High Power

Committee (AICTE 1994) recommended for a reduction in subsidization of public HEIs and an increase in fees levied on the students for a larger cost recovery. To ensure greater cost recovery, the HEIs have increasingly been taking recourse to offer self-financing courses (Maitra 2019; Panigrahi 2017) which are mostly professionally designed to impart necessary skills keeping in mind the employability of the students. Consequently, given resource constraint, the traditional courses remain underfunded and undermined. Though this also allows for cross-subsidization of the courses which do not have high job prospects, access is compromised leading to distortions in choice making.

Tilak (2004: 283–4) noted that recovery through fees constituted 15 per cent of recurring costs of higher education in the early 1990s, which were comparable with the developing and developed countries including the United States. Hostel rents and electricity fees are subsidized to a large extent in the public-funded universities.

Charging different fees for different categories of students is not generally practised in the public-funded HEIs. Though this has limited potential, it can induce progressivity as long as it does not distort decision making by pushing students out of higher education. This can also take the form of charging uniform fees while some students are given scholarships (out of the fees collected) based on merit and need.[5] Fixing the fee structure at a certain proportion of cost of university operation would make the fee structure for similar courses widely varying across universities because of the variation in the cost structure. This may also potentially generate friction and discontentment among the student community as hiking fees would become a routine affair (Chattopadhyay 2007).

Public-Private Partnerships

It was felt that the public-funded higher education system is not sustainable in a globalized world, and there is a need to explore viable financing options including effective public-private partnerships (PPPs) in offering courses which have ample demand in the market and building partnerships with industries to promote research and training of manpower (GoI 2013). PPPs seek to combine the relative strengths of both private sector efficiency and enthusiasm in managing university affairs and public financial support for infrastructure and defray costs of operation, albeit partially, depending on the mutual agreements (Chattopadhyay 2016).

---

[5] This was found to be unsustainable as fees could not be hiked mainly because of the students' resistance but the scholarship had to be raised over the years. The deficit had to be met by the university's other sources of revenue. The UGC was reluctant to support this practice as it amounted to discrimination of other central universities which did not have such schemes.

The National Knowledge Commission (GoI 2009a), Yash Pal Committee Report (GoI 2009b) and Birla-Ambani Report (GoI 2000) all favoured private sector participation and PPPs to complement public sector effort in expanding the higher education sector and delivering quality. The Twelfth Five Year Plan had suggested PPPs for IITs and polytechnic colleges (GoI 2013: 101). The Twelfth Five Year Plan (GoI 2013) stated that taxes collected from 'for-profit' HEIs may be used for providing scholarships to the students (GoI 2013: 100). New types of PPPs should be explored to promote interdisciplinary research especially in technology-oriented fields to promote innovation. The Twelfth Five Year Plan also suggested that the public institutions which have been performing poorly could be supported through PPPs. The UGC constituted the K. B. Powar Committee to recommend possible modes of partnerships, legally termed as PPPs, in higher education in India. The recommended four models are as follows: (1) Basic Infrastructure Model, (2) Outsourcing Model, (3) Equity/Hybrid Model and (4) Reverse Outsourcing Model (GoI 2013). Chattopadhyay (2016) shows that in all PPP models there is an inevitable conflict between access and quality. The conflict arises because of a rise in fees due to a possible decline in public-funding support while maintaining quality which is a cost-intensive proposition given that the functioning of the institution remains unchanged.

Though RUSA notes the importance of sustained increase in public funding for higher education, there is an unmistakable emphasis on exploration of alternative sources of financing higher education. RUSA argues that up to 50 per cent of the resources required for funding higher education should ideally come from private sources in due course of time.

Higher Education Financing Agency

The setting up of the Higher Education Financing Agency (HEFA) in 2017 marks an important departure from the conventional ways of financing higher education in India. The HEFA was established as a non-profit joint venture company in the nature of a special purpose vehicle (SPV) by the Ministry of Education and Canara Bank for mobilizing extra-budgetary resources like corporate social responsibility (CSR) funds from public sector undertakings (PSUs) or corporates[6] for investment on crucial infrastructure in the centrally

---

[6] As required by the Corporate Income Tax Act, corporates are required to keep aside 5 per cent of their declared profits to spend on social causes.

funded HEIs. Since a large part of the public funds allocated to these HEIs are kept aside for maintenance and salary bills, there is generally very little left for expenditure on infrastructure for expansion to meet its growing demand. The HEFA was launched with an authorized capital of INR 20 billion (2000 crore). The government equity was INR 10 billion (1000 crore). It can leverage the equity to raise up to INR 200 billion (20,000 crore) for funding projects for infrastructure and development of world class labs in the IITs/Indian Institutes of Management (IIMs)/National Institutes of Technology (NITs) and such other institutions.

The HEFA extends a ten-year loan to finance the necessary planned infrastructure. The principal portion of the loan has to be repaid through the generation of 'internal accruals' (earned through the fee receipts, research earnings, etc.) of the institutions. The government would shoulder the responsibility for the interest costs. This requires the HEIs to escrow a specific amount from their internal accruals to the HEFA for a period of ten years. The Ministry of Finance has red-flagged concerns regarding the functioning of the HEFA based on a review (*The Economic Times* 2020). There is virtually no provision in the Union Budget for HEFA for 2021–2. It was drastically curtailed from INR 21 billion in 2019–20 to merely INR 2 billion in 2020–1.

Though interest burden will be borne by the government, pressure on cost recovery will be paramount as the commitment to repay the loans within a span of ten years will require the university to adopt cost recovery measures on a serious footing. This approach to financing HEIs narrows the gap between a business firm and a university. This would necessitate reorganizing academic activities comprising teaching-learning and research and offering market-oriented courses resulting in subsequent loss of autonomy of the institutes. A university has to evolve compulsorily to be entrepreneurial, strategic and competitive. Not all central universities are on the same level-playing field. The best ones will be able to take plunge and surge ahead in this highly competitive situation while the rest will find it difficult to compete and sustain.

Making Provisions for External Commercial Borrowings and Foreign Direct Investments

The Union Budget for 2020–1 (GoI 2020b: 11) announced that ECBs and FDIs will be encouraged in higher education. These sources may not constitute a significant source of revenue in the immediate future but the policy signals are indicative of encouraging private participation on cost recovery model. The finance minister stated thus: 'It is felt that our education system needs greater inflow of finance to attract talented teachers, innovate and build better labs. Therefore steps would be taken to enable sourcing External Commercial Borrowings and FDI so as to able to deliver higher quality education' (GoI 2020b: 11).

Signing Memorandum, Confirming Cost Recovery

In pursuance of pushing the HEIs to commit and adopt cost-recovery measures, the centre has signed MOUs with the central universities to ensure that all the new courses will be self-financing. The universities will now be required to recover 30 per cent of their costs of operations (Bhushan 2019).

Pricing Online Education, Unbundling and Differentiated Fee Structure

The rapid transition towards online teaching during the pandemic has brightened the prospect of augmenting revenue through the open distance learning. The top universities are being encouraged to offer courses and contribute to the massive open online courses (MOOCs) (GoI 2020a). Over time, there is likely to be a shrinkage in the faculty strength of the universities. Since the average cost per student for MOOCs is expected to be lower, offering courses online has the potential to fetch a good amount of revenue. But because of the very nature of the market, only the reputed ones will do well.

Tax Financing of Higher Education

It is reassuring that the NEP 2020 has argued for an increased budgetary support for higher education and education as a whole by raising it to 6 per cent of GDP. In fact, this has been in demand for long since the Kothari Commission (1964–5) recommended it. Fiscal constraint is construed to be binding for the centre and the states because of the imperative of compliance with the Fiscal Responsibility and Budget Management (FRBM) Act which requires that the fiscal deficit of the centre be kept at 3 per cent of GDP (or in terms of gross state domestic product (GSDP) for the states). The tax to GDP ratio in India is generally considered to be low mainly because of the large size of the black economy (Kumar 1999). A cess, an additional 3 per cent, is being levied on tax payable to enhance the budgetary allocations for primary, secondary and higher education.[7] Not only does the education sector have to compete with others for enhanced budgetary allocation, but within education, school and secondary education will be prioritized. After the COVID pandemic, all the states will reprioritize their budgetary allocations. Tax financing of higher education will continue to be opposed because the contributions of higher education to foster socioeconomic development are viewed from a limited economic perspective with overemphasis on narrow rate of returns which accrue to the graduates, albeit only to the successful ones.

6. Conclusion

Declining public funding in real terms has resulted in a clear shift from unconditional support to conditional support, from grants to loans, opted increasingly by both institutions and the students; this is a serious matter amid the need to widen access and improve quality. This indicates that contributions of higher education towards society, polity and the economy are being undermined. This shift has already started triggering changes in the essential character of what is meant by education and what is the purpose of a university from a broader perspective. The reason behind this shift is not only fiscal constraint but it is also to fix accountability to improve delivery of higher education, which is argued to have remained suboptimal. The question is whether this shift can help the HEIs address the larger concern of upholding the public good character of higher education. The resulting erosion of teacher autonomy and institutional autonomy have larger ramifications for creativity, innovativeness and diversity. The advocacy for teacher autonomy and institutional autonomy though adequately stressed by the NEP 2020 will have a very limited significance in the emerging context. In fact, the potential tension and conflict between the teacher and university will rise. Since the institutions are perforce moving towards greater cost recovery to compensate for the reduction in grants as more resources are earmarked for the Institutions of Eminence (IoEs) as per assurance, the remaining universities will find it tougher to function and grow. It is unlikely

---

[7] Cess is an additional tax levied on taxable income. Education cess consisted of primary, secondary and higher education to the tune of 3 per cent of tax payable. Initially education cess of 2 per cent was levied to garner additional resources for primary education. In 2007, an additional 1 per cent was added for funding higher education expansion necessitated by the policy to raise the student intake in the public-funded HEIs by 54 per cent.

that the budget for higher education will rise in the immediate future as fiscal health of both the centre and the states will remain under pressure in the post-pandemic years. The financial autonomy to the Category-I institutions comes at the cost of institutional autonomy. The proposed funding allocation mechanism in the NEP 2020 is likely to be competitive as funds allocated to a HEI will be based on the institutional development plan to be submitted by the individual HEIs to the Higher Education Grants Council (HEGC) (Chattopadhyay 2020). The process for availing research funds from the National Research Foundation (NRF) will also be tough and competitive; however the NEP assures that grant allocation will be equitable and based on peer-review. Overall, it will be a competitive scenario and not all HEIs will be able to participate on equal terms and succeed.

Expanding the coverage of education loans is not a solution for the students hailing from the economically challenged section of the society as they are more likely to be risk-averse in the face of rising graduate unemployment and are endowed with little social capital. However, given rising income and private rates of return, some extent of fee hikes could be possible as long as no distortion is caused and no student willing to pursue higher studies opts out of the system. Opting for an ICL may appear to be a good option but given India's socioeconomic structure, implementation challenges may prove to be daunting. The NEP rightly emphasizes that education is perhaps the best investment for a society (GoI 2019b: 399). Towards meeting this objective, the NEP (GoI 2020c) recommends that the public investment on education needs to be raised from 10 per cent of overall public expenditure to 20 per cent within a span of ten years. Enhancing public funding remains the most credible solution for creating a level-playing field among the HEIs before fund allocation is made more competitive, as competition both nationally and globally is likely to intensify. It is more a matter of political will rather than fiscal crunch and an unfair juxtaposition of higher education *vis-à-vis* other priority sectors. There is also an urgent need for students and teachers to reflect collectively and come together to find ways to minimize wastage and curb unethical practices to improve efficiency in the use of resources, human, financial and physical.

3

Equity in Higher Education for Inclusive Growth: Evidence from India

N. V. Varghese, Nidhi S. Sabharwal and C. M. Malish

1. Introduction

The idea of inclusive growth is based on the notion of equality of opportunity. Equality of opportunity demands that students from all social groups get sufficient opportunities for self-development, and no one is excluded in the process of development. The main bases of exclusion in India are region, religion, caste, gender, economic disparities and people with disabilities. The strategies for achieving inclusive growth necessarily need to include affirmative action policies targeting those who are excluded.

India has made considerable progress in reducing poverty and improving the quality of life of its people. There has been an increase in the per capita income levels and life expectancy, and a decline in fertility rates, infant mortality rates and in the share of people below the poverty line. Education has been one of the instrumental interventions for improving participation in economic activities and social well-being of the people. Access to education has improved at all levels, and most children born in this century are enrolled in schools. Ironically, however, these commendable achievements are accompanied by widening income inequalities and persisting social inequalities.

This chapter analyses the issues related to equity and inclusion in development of higher education. The main line of argument is as follows: while access to higher education has improved across all segments of the population, the disadvantaged groups continue to lag behind their counterparts in access to science, technology, engineering and mathematics (STEM) study programmes. Further, achievements in equity in access are overshadowed by the unfavourable conditions of progress faced and low rates of success experienced by students from the disadvantaged groups. It is argued that part of the reasons for uneven progress among social groups is the relative ineffectiveness of institutional mechanisms to address diversity and discrimination at the institutional level leading to low learning outcomes and poor labour market outcomes.

The plan for the chapter is as follows. The next section presents the imperative of equity in higher education and its role in facilitating a move towards an inclusive society. Section 3 presents strategies to promote equity in higher education in India. Section 4 examines the empirical evidence on expansion in access to higher education and the persisting inequalities within the context of massification. Section 5 identifies the determinants of access to higher education. Section 6 delineates the factors affecting equity in educational attainment by analysing learning and employment outcomes for students from the disadvantaged groups. The final section concludes the chapter by highlighting the nature of emerging inequalities in a stage of massification of higher education in India and the need for evolving new strategies to ensure inclusive higher education campuses and promote equality in educational attainment across student groups.

2. Equity and Democratic Societies

Development implies increased production and improved sharing of benefits of growth. The distribution becomes fairer under democratic regimes associated with more egalitarian policies. The idea of redistributive justice is a core theme in democracies to keep aspiration levels of the people high. Egalitarianism is a value promoted in the democratic frame of analysis and supported through legislative measures. While expansion of higher education is very often driven by economic agenda, the equity concerns are driven by social agenda and social justice. Since education is intimately related to income and wage, fostering equality in education is a powerful tool to decrease income inequality and, in this sense, equity in education supports social equity (OECD 2008). The question is not only of expansion of higher education but also of widening access to higher education to previously under-represented groups. Across the world, equity is seen as a central aspect of the role of higher education in furthering the public or common good.

Those excluded remain marginalized in the process of development. Marginality implies denial of right to resources in the present and opportunities to progress in the future. Marginalization is manifested involuntarily when groups are denied opportunities to partake in the productive activities in a society and poses a challenge to achieve the objective of inclusive development.

A faster progress of the deprived groups is necessary to level-off the differences among social groups. The advancement of the deprived groups is seen as an indicator of success of democracy. The egalitarian principles need to be seen not only at the entry level (equality of opportunities) but also at the outcome level. Many countries having limited number of people from the deprived groups holding high offices may not be a sign of extending democratic egalitarianism to all segments of population.

One of the challenges of promoting the idea of democratic egalitarianism is that the aspirations of the public outstrip the surplus generating capacity of the state. The group rights and a concern for the deprived groups at times slip into the domain of competitive populism resulting in discourses and dispensations focusing more on distribution than on growth and equitable distribution. The argument for indiscriminatory subsidies borders with competitive populism. Inequalities are 'the cumulative result of unjust policies and misguided priorities' (Stiglitz 2015: 3). Countries need committed public policy reforms to reverse the trend of economic inequality and promote conditions for broad-based prosperity.

There exists a positive correlation between economic status and access to educational opportunities on the one hand and between educational attainment and earnings on the other. The high and positive correlation between economic inequalities and education inequalities is a serious concern in all democratic countries. Education is an important factor influencing job entry and salaries of those recruited. In other words, education plays an important role in promoting growth in national income and an equally important role in the sharing (distribution) of national income through employment and earnings. When educational opportunities and attainment are unequally distributed, they become an important source of inequalities and it requires corrective public policies.

The question of equity in higher education needs to be looked at from two angles: (1) higher education as a factor of production and (2) higher education as a public good – national or global. When higher education is seen as a factor of production, investments in education may also come from the private sector or from the individuals who seek higher education. Firms like to appropriate the returns on their investment in knowledge and skills. If they cannot appropriate the returns, they will have limited incentives to invest in knowledge production or transmission. Many economies may not be in a position to ensure appropriation of returns by the firms investing in education. Consequently, market-mediated expansion of higher education may be in undersupply.

The public good nature of higher education demands an increased role of the state and greater public investment in the sector. In the absence of public intervention, higher education will be in insufficient supply. The global public good nature of knowledge and its production provides the rationale for global/international collective action (Samuelson 1954; Stiglitz 1999). The public good nature of higher education may be one of the reasons for continued state support to massify, and even universalize, higher education in developed market economies.

State policies play a significant role in promoting equity in access to higher education. Thus, progressive state policies under democracy will not tolerate unequal distribution of opportunities, income and wealth. The redistributive dimension of democracy stems from the belief that equality in the political arena will be translated into equality in the economic and social domains (Sirowy and Inkeles 1990), and this idea keeps the aspirations high among the poor.

Equity in higher education means that personal and social circumstances should not be an obstacle to reaching one's educational potential. It implies that access to and the outcomes of higher education do not depend on one's social background. Equity is an inclusive notion, and inclusion implies provision of a basic minimum standard of education for all (Santiago et al. 2008). Experience shows that countries where the poor perform well are those which have implemented programmes to promote equity in education.

Higher education in most countries has been traditionally offered through public institutions. The public institutions offered courses in a wide range of areas and followed equity-oriented admission policies aligned to state policies levying low or no fees. The deteriorating fiscal capacity of the state and the changing ideological orientation, especially from the mid-1980s, did not support an expansion of public institutions to accommodate the increasing social demand for higher education.

The access policy in higher education was dominated by three principles, namely, inherited merit, equality of rights and equality of opportunity (Clancy and Goastellec 2007). The concept of 'inherited merit' relates access to higher education to the circumstances of birth (being born to prosperous parents), and access to higher education becomes the preserve of favoured social groups (Roemer 1998). Under this framework, the higher education sector remained small with limited access to the non-privileged groups.

Social exclusion leads to several forms of disadvantages. Social exclusion leads to capability deprivation (Sen 1999) which is turn results in what is sometimes referred to as cumulative marginalization. Social exclusion denies access to resources, services and sharing of societal benefits. If people are excluded because of deliberate action on the part of others, it amounts to discrimination. Exclusion leads to uneven progress among groups and lies at the heart of inequality-generating processes (Tilly 2007). In the modern times, exclusion reflects those people living at the margins of society without access to the system of social security, social insurance and health services. In terms of public policy, exclusion implies the failure of traditional welfare state and its institutions promoting equity.

In the second half of the twentieth century, thanks to ideological orientations and political pressures, the idea of inherited merit was replaced by the notion of equality of rights (Goastellec 2006). This change reflected a friendly approach towards national diversity, extension of democratic principles and legitimacy of actions by the elected governments in any democracy. This policy helped in minimizing the adverse effects of formal barriers to entry to higher education of women, ethnic/racial and social groups as well as minorities.

The next phase in policy change is denoted by the notion of equality of opportunity which looks more closely into the variations in the opportunity structure. The talents are randomly distributed and the policy of equal opportunities places a responsibility on higher education institutions (HEIs) to widen their net to select talents from all social groups. The merit-based admission needs to be augmented by some form of affirmative action to ensure that national elite is drawn from all social classes. Most countries follow the policy of equality of opportunity in their student admissions to institutions of higher education.

Equality of opportunities and inclusion imply provision of a basic minimum standard of education for all (Santiago et al. 2008). Equal inputs need not always lead to equal outcomes in education. In fact, unequal inputs may be needed to achieve equity in outcomes in education. Students coming from different socioeconomic backgrounds may vary in their ability to compete. Those from privileged backgrounds may have an advantage over those from less-privileged backgrounds. The idea of providing additional resources to students from deprived groups is to equalize the conditions for competing and succeeding in the system. In other words, inequalities in inputs (in favour of deprived groups) are tolerated, since they produce advantages for the less-privileged groups and may help improve overall equity in education and eventually in all domains of human activity.

Inequalities in higher education are influenced by inequalities in the preceding levels of education. In a country where basic and secondary education facilities are not equally distributed, it is very difficult to attain equality of opportunity in higher education. Higher education will be offered to those who completed secondary level, and the existing inequalities in secondary education may be reflected in the higher education sector too. However, in countries where secondary education is universal, as is the case in most of the developed countries, equity in access to higher education may be more easily achieved.

The evidence on intergenerational mobility has highlighted the strong and persistent link between parents and children in their educational attainment (Black and Devereux 2010). It reveals that the opportunities are not evenly distributed and that life chances of individuals very often reflect factors for which they are not responsible. Therefore, fairness and inclusion in access are suggested to improve equity in higher education (OECD 2008). Fairness implies that personal and social circumstances, such as gender, socioeconomic status, ethnicity, region of residence, should not be an obstacle to educational access and success. Inclusion implies a minimum standard of education provided for all and has to do with whether overall levels of provision are sufficient and effective.

The countries with limited access to higher education tend to have low levels of income and a higher degree of inequality, while countries with expanded (massified or universalized) higher education have higher per capita income and lower inequalities (Varghese 2001). Disparities in earnings are inversely related to the levels of education and are less among university graduates. Access to higher education in most of the developing countries is still limited, and it may widen inequalities in these countries. Therefore, it is important to equalize the provision of higher education in order to promote economic and social equity.

Empirical studies (Arum, Gamoran and Shavi 2007) have shown that expansion does not reduce class inequalities until the advantaged groups reach a point of saturation. Expansion will contribute to reduction in inequalities beyond the point of saturation, since privileged groups cannot increase attendance rates any further (beyond 100 per cent). However, expansion with targeted state interventions in favour of deprived groups can improve equity even before the privileged groups reach a point of saturation in terms of their enrolment.

Given the positive association between the social background of students and their admission to the non-university sector of higher education, it is argued that differentiation is a process of diversion to channel working-class children to lower-status post-secondary education institutions and keep the elite in higher-status institutions. When the second-tier system expands, the first-tier system becomes more selective, increasing class inequalities in access to first-tier institutions. The differentiated system of education protects the status and privileges of the elite (Karabel 1999).

3. Strategies to Improve Equity in Higher Education in India

Many of the strategies to achieve equity are common across countries. The strategies, in general, include affirmative action or a quota system, supporting institutions to enrol students from disadvantaged groups and establishing specialized institutions. Some countries such as the UK introduced a programme – the Ethnic Minorities Achievement Programme – to address the issue of achievement disparities of children from minority ethnic groups (Bent et al. 2012). Other countries like Australia, Mexico and New Zealand set up specialized institutions for selected disadvantaged groups. India follows more of a policy of quota system in admissions than establishing special institutions of higher education for the disadvantaged groups.

The disparities in access to higher education are reflected in the widening of economic inequalities in India. Recent estimates for India (Chancel and Pikketty 2017) indicate that the top 1 per cent accounts for 22 per cent of the national income, the top 10 per cent accounts for 56 per cent and the bottom 50 per cent is left with around 16 per cent of the national income. This shows that the massification of higher education has not yet positively affected the inequality trends in income distribution. This may be partly due to the market-mediated massification where equity in access is not a priority concern. Although India, with more than 1,000 universities, over 42,000 colleges, and around 11,780 stand-alone institutions and 38.5 million students (GoI 2021d), is the second largest higher education system, inequalities continue to persist.

The public policies in India emphasized on equality of higher education opportunities. The Constitution guarantees provisions for equity. The National Policy on Education of 1968 (NPE 1968), National Policy on Education of 1986 (NPE 1986) and the Programme of Action (1992) have largely shaped the planning approach of the government to improve equity in terms of higher education opportunities (Thorat 2016). Table 3.1 shows a range of equity measures adopted in the planning process of higher education development (First Five Year Plan: 1951–6 to the Twelfth Five Year Plan: 2012–17) in India (Planning Commission 1952, 1956, 1961, 1969, 1976, 1981, 1985, 1992, 1997, 2002, 2008a, 2008b, 2008c, 2013a, 2013b).

Table 3.1 Strategies to Improve Equity in Higher Education across Five Year Plans, 1951–6 to 2012–17

Five Year Plans	Regional	Social	Gender
First Five Year Plan (1951–6)	Setting up of rural universities suited to the needs of the rural areas Providing special grants to backward states	Providing scholarship schemes	Expanding facilities for women's education, especially in the rural areas Providing free studentships and scholarships to encourage enrolment in HEIs
Second Five Year Plan (1956–61)	Setting up rural universities Organizing tutorials and seminars	Setting up special institutions (technical) in tribal dominated areas Setting up special institutions (technical and vocational: craft, trade and agricultural operations) for SCs Providing scholarships for SCs/STs Organizing tutorials and seminars	Setting up hostels and boarding facilities Introducing courses of special interest to women Organizing tutorials and seminars
Third Five Year Plan (1961–6)	Setting up rural universities	Setting up scholarships for SCs/STs/OBCs	Providing scholarships to improve enrolment assistance for women's colleges and hostels Introducing special courses for women
Fourth Five Year Plan (1969–74)		Setting up hostels and student study homes Providing post-matric scholarships Expanding hostel schemes Expanding pre-examination coaching	

Plan	Initiatives
Fifth Five Year Plan (1974–9)	Increasing scholarships for talented students from rural areas
Sixth Five year plan (1980–5)	Expanding facilities through evening colleges, correspondence courses and private study Setting up guidance and counselling services to facilitate proper selection of subjects at the time of entry into colleges and of remedial courses
Seventh Five Year Plan (1985–90)	Developing affirmative admission policies (providing access to existing institutions through appropriate reservation) Instituting scholarships Providing hostel facilities Promoting distance education Allocating special grants for institutions predominantly serving students for SC/ST/OBCs to improve student retention
Eight Five Year Plan (1992–7)	Developing distance education programmes Providing scholarships, loans and other financial assistance to SCs/STs and students below the poverty line Increasing scholarship amounts Diversifying HEIs in tribal areas (vocational institutes)
Ninth Five Year Plan (1997–2002)	Setting up new institutions in the underserved regions (northeast region) Allocating extra funds for institutions located in disadvantaged regions Diversifying HEIs in rural areas (polytechnics) Creating alternative admission pathways Providing hostels for boosting education programmes for women from backward classes

Five Year Plans	Regional	Social	Gender
Tenth Five Year Plan (2002–7)	Providing grant-in-aid for setting up new institutions, autonomous colleges and existing private colleges in underserved states Supporting activities of distance/open universities to increase access for northeastern and backward areas	Providing hostel facilities Providing access to counselling/study centres	Providing access to counselling/study centres and day care centres for children Setting up hostels
Eleventh Five Year Plan (2007–12)	Establishing 370 new degree colleges Establishing central universities in states with inadequate coverage Lending additional support to institutions in border, hilly, remote, small-town, and educationally backward areas	Lending additional support to institutions with larger student population of SCs, STs, OBCs, minorities and physically challenged students Providing special scholarships/fellowships and hostel facilities Establishing HEPSN and EOOs	
Twelfth Five Year Plan (2012–17)		Setting up scholarships Providing student loans with government guarantees for SES groups	Taking affirmative action for admissions in STEM subjects

Source: Authors, based on Planning Commission (various years).

While the financial mechanisms to support equity-related strategies in earlier plans were diffused with small outlays, in recent plans (Planning Commission 2013a, 2013b) budgetary support for equity-related measures have been targeted and integrated (Planning Commission 2013a, 2013b). The equity measures have favoured students from the socially disadvantaged groups, women as well as students from regions that have lagged behind in higher education development.

Strategies to Improve Access of Socially Disadvantaged Groups to Higher Education

The Constitution of India guarantees 15 per cent reservation of seats for the scheduled castes (SCs), 7.5 per cent for the scheduled tribes (STs) and 27 per cent for other backward classes (OBCs) in government and government-aided HEIs. Affirmative action in the admission policies vary at the state level. Top-ranking institutions in India such as the Jawaharlal Nehru University (JNU) in Delhi follow a unique policy of considering deprivation points for those from the disadvantaged regions and social groups (Sabharwal and Malish 2016). Apart from reservation, there is also relaxation in the minimum qualifying marks for admission for SC and ST candidates.

India has programmes for providing financial support to students in the form of subsidized tuition fees, scholarships and free-ships; in addition, affordable hostels are made available for students from poor background and from socially excluded groups in India as well as for women students. India extends student loans with government guarantees to students enrolled in the universities (Planning Commission 2013a). The government extends financial support to institutions predominantly serving students from the disadvantaged groups; it also provides special grants to students from the SC/ST/OBC social groups for their remedial teaching, preparatory training and special coaching as well as counselling services (Planning Commission 1981).

Diversification of the HEIs has been another strategy adopted in India to channel students from the disadvantaged social groups into various streams and specializations. Special institutions offering employment-oriented technical and vocational education (e.g. in craft, trade and agricultural operations) have been set up for the SCs and in tribal dominated rural areas. In addition, distance education facilities and diversification of study programmes and institutional differentiation have been good measures to attract large numbers of students and students from disadvantaged groups (Varghese 2011).

Strategies to Promote Gender Equity

To promote gender equity, the government has been establishing special universities and colleges, providing alternative admission pathways, introduction of courses of special interest for women (home science, music, drawing, painting, nursing) and encouraging institutions offering STEM subjects to practise affirmative action in admission policies. Provisions of hostels and boarding facilities have been made for improving access for women from the disadvantaged social groups and those residing in rural areas.

Strategies to Promote Regional Equity

Strategies to promote regional equity and encourage students from underserved disadvantaged regions include opening of HEIs in rural areas and educationally backward districts as well as allocating additional funds to educational institutions located in rural, hilly, remote, tribal and border areas. In addition, financial support has been extended to distance education programmes to increase access for students residing in northeastern and backward areas.

Strategies for Improving Learning and Employment Outcome

Indian policies of affirmative action have succeeded in improving access to the deprived groups. However, the major issue is what happens to students after they are enrolled in institutions of higher education. Considerable amount of empirical evidence shows that dropout rates are higher among disadvantaged social groups and that they face severe academic adjustment problems in the institutions. Public policies addressed these challenges in three ways: by providing learning support programmes, providing support for creating an inclusive campus environment, and promoting teachers and research.

Learning Support Programmes

Learning support strategies have been designed to include generic programmes and targeted learning support programmes which directly aim to facilitate learning of students. This includes organization of tutorials and seminars, book bank facilities, book grant facilities, remedial teaching, coaching for entry in services, NET/SET (National/State Eligibility Test for lectureship) coaching and preparatory courses. Tutorial programmes are developed with the aim of improving the overall quality of education, while other learning support programmes focus on disadvantaged social groups. Book bank programmes in professional colleges allocate funds for procuring books which are prescribed in the syllabus or essential readings in relevant disciplines. A separate section is earmarked for this scheme. Only SC and ST students are allowed to borrow books under this programme, and they can keep the book for longer time; book grants are given to students to buy books.

Three of the coaching schemes – remedial coaching, entry in services and NET/SET coaching – provide financial support to institutions to organize coaching classes as an additional learning input for students who wish to improve subject knowledge and prepare for competitive examinations for recruitment and tests for qualifying NET and JRF (Junior Research Fellowship). The preparatory course scheme in Indian Institutes of Technology (IITs) aims to improve student intake from SCs and STs. Students who fail to qualify in Joint Entrance Examination (JEE) are offered one-year residential training in basic science disciplines and English. Those who successfully complete the course are offered admission to BTech or dual-degree programmes depending upon the available vacant seats reserved for them. Pre-examination training provides coaching for students appearing for recruitment tests of government and of public sector undertakings (PSUs). This scheme also covers students outside college roles and is not confined to currently enrolled students. In order to facilitate learning of visually challenged SC students, funds are allotted for developing Braille books.

Support for Creating Inclusive Environments

Schemes for providing student study homes and student hostels have been established to provide housing and quality learning environment for disadvantaged students. Hostel and counselling centres are provided for girls in order to improve learning by creating a quality learning environment. Under girls' hostel scheme, funds are allocated to purchase equipment, furniture, utensils, books and periodicals. Both learning and infrastructure support programmes have been implemented during various five-year plan periods.

In addition to schemes for creating infrastructure, there are many other interventions to create institutional mechanisms to coordinate equity provisions for targeted groups. It includes establishment of SC/ST cell and Higher Education for Persons with Special Needs (HEPSN). In order to ensure better planning and coordination, an equal opportunity office (EOO) was envisaged in the Eleventh Five Year Plan period. According to the University Grants Commission (UGC), these are mandatory cells to be established in all colleges and universities. EOO was visualized as an umbrella organization which oversees various schemes targeted for promoting equity.

4. Inequalities in Access to Higher Education in India: The Empirical Evidence

As discussed, equity has been an important concern even in the context of massification of higher education in India (Varghese, Sabharwal and Malish 2018); nevertheless inequalities in access to higher education persists. Inequalities in access to higher education have three dimensions: regional inequalities, group inequalities and inequalities between sexes.

Regional Inequalities in Higher Education

Since HEIs have been traditionally established in urban areas, one may observe an urban bias in higher education development in India (Varghese, Panigrahi and Rohatgi 2018), and this bias has reinforced the elite nature of higher education development in India.

Based on analysis of data from the National Sample Survey Office (NSSO 2014b), Borooah (2017) shows that persons from rural areas attending higher education had to travel a longer distance when compared to urban students, and the gross enrolment ratio (GER) in rural areas remained low at 24 per cent as compared to the GER of 44 per cent in the urban areas.

The massification of higher education has not levelled off geographical inequalities in the distribution of higher education facilities in India primarily because the massification of higher education in India was led by the private sector. There is an urban bias in the establishment of private institutions in India stemming essentially from profitability considerations. This leads to polarization of access to higher education and varying rates of growth of higher education. For example, the GER in some of the states increased by three-fold, doubled in many major states and has been slower in other states. Empirical evidence indicated that the variations in GER between the highest and lowest states increased from 24.35 percentage points in 2002–3 to around 52 percentage points in 2015–16 (Varghese, Panigrahi and Rohatgi 2018).

Social Inequalities: Caste, Religion, Class and Gender

Unlike regional inequalities, social inequalities in access to higher education have not widened, though they continue to be high. During a period of two decades ending in 2014, the GER increased from 8.8 per cent in 1995 to 30.06 per cent in 2014 with all groups experiencing an improvement. The higher education GER for the socially disadvantaged groups such as the STs and SCs increased from 3.42 and 4.84 per cent, respectively, in 1995 to 17.19 and 22.31 per cent in 2014.

Social Group Inequalities

An individual's social group belonging[1] has a strong influence on access to higher education. For example, the GER of the higher castes was nearly twice that of the socially excluded groups such as the STs and 1.5 times that of the SCs. As one moves up in the caste hierarchy from the lower castes to the middle and upper castes, the GER also moves up. Another dimension of the disparities concerns religious groups. The GER was the lowest among Muslims, at 16.54 per cent, compared to a corresponding figure of 42 per cent for other minorities like Christians, Sikhs and Jains, and 32 per cent for Hindus.

The social and geographical disadvantages intersect. For example, students from the socially excluded groups such as STs from rural areas had a GER that was one-fourth that of the higher-caste urban students (NSSO 2014b). Many factors cumulatively lead to disadvantages for SC and ST students in accessing opportunities for higher education, including, hailing from low socioeconomic backgrounds, being first-generation learners and residing in rural areas that suffer from poor learning infrastructure.

Income Inequalities

Inequalities in access to higher education are also seen by income levels. For example, in 2014, the GER for the top quintile was seven times higher than that for the lowest monthly per capita expenditure quintile (0–20 per cent: Table 3.2a). The data thus indicate that economic status continues to have a significant bearing on the likelihood of gaining access to higher education.

Gender Inequalities

At the national level, access to higher education still favours men and the gender parity index is 0.86. Women among the lower-caste groups suffer more than those from other groups. For instance in 2014, the overall GER was 27.73 per cent for women – only 13.05 per cent among the ST women followed by 18.17

---

[1] According to the official classification, the Hindu population is classified into four social group categories – upper castes, OBCs, SCs and STs. While the upper castes occupy the top of the social hierarchy, OBCs are middle-level castes placed below the upper castes. The SCs or the erstwhile 'untouchable' castes are placed at the bottom of the caste hierarchy and have historically suffered from exclusion in social and economic life. The STs are aboriginal ethnic groups.

Table 3.2a Gross Enrolment Ratio by Social and Income Groups

Categories	1995	2007	2014
Gender			
Male	10.78	18.76	32.14
Female	6.76	14.72	27.73
Social groups			
ST	3.43	7.22	17.19
SC	4.84	11.35	22.31
OBC	NA	14.57	29.36
Others (higher castes)	NA	26.22	41.65
Others + OBC	10.53	19.44	34.13
Religion			
Hindu	NA	17.85	31.97
Muslim	NA	9.35	16.54
ORM[a]	NA	22.12	42.02
Income quintiles			
0–20	1.06	3.99	9.89
20–40	2.39	6.97	18.31
40–60	4.73	10.03	26.64
60–80	9.39	18.53	41.55
80–100	29.91	47.56	73.79
Total	8.82	16.83	30.06
Locational			
Rural	4.2	11.1	24
Urban	18.2	30.3	44

Note:
[a] Other religious minorities.
Source: Authors, derived from NSSO (1995, 2007–8, 2014b).

per cent among the SC women; 23.11 per cent for OBC women; and 35.39 per cent for the non-SC/ST/OBC women. Thus, the GER of higher-caste women was almost three times that of ST women. Similarly, the GER of higher-caste women was twice that of SC women (Table 3.2b).

5. Social Inequalities in Access to Science, Technology, Engineering and Mathematics Subjects and Elite Institutions

The under-representation of the socioeconomically disadvantaged learners in various fields of study is evident in India. Women remain under-represented

Table 3.2b Gross Enrolment Ratio by Social Group and Gender, 2014

Social group	Male	Female
ST	17.38	13.05
SC	21.94	18.17
OBC	29.64	23.11
Others	37.92	35.39

Source: Authors, based on NSSO (2014b).

in STEM subjects (Table 3.3) such as sciences, technology, engineering, management and chartered accountancy and over-represented in other subject areas such as medicine and education. For example, in 2014, the number of men studying engineering was three times that of the number of women, while the number of women enrolled in the field of education was twice that of men (Table 3.3).

It seems that STEM subjects are studied mostly by the privileged students, including men, those belonging to the higher castes and higher economic classes, and those residing in urban areas, whereas students from the socially excluded groups and those residing in rural locations study arts and humanities, social sciences and agriculture.

The access to STEM subjects was lower for the poor than for the rich (Figure 3.1). The participation of students from the disadvantaged socioeconomic groups in technical and professional courses such as engineering, medicine and chartered accountancy is lower than their share in the population (Table 3.3). Moreover studies (Sabharwal and Malish 2016) have also shown that socioeconomically advantaged students are over-represented in elite/prestigious institutions whereas the less-prestigious institutions primarily serve the underprivileged groups. This leads to ghettoization of the student population and results in low labour market returns to those who pursue studies in non-STEM subject areas.

What causes social inequalities? Using the method of inequality decomposition, Borooah (2017) computed the proportionate contribution of social groups to interpersonal inequality in the probabilities of eighteen- to twenty-two-year-olds in India. The study found that the largest contributor was social group and poverty, followed by location, with a very small contribution by gender. Various studies (Hurtado 1994; McDonough 1997) have shown that family attributes such as socioeconomic background and the educational level of parents are positively related to students' access to higher levels of education and

Table 3.3 Subjects being Studied by Students as per Social Groups, Gender and Location, 2014 (%)

Subjects being studied	Social groups				Gender		Location	
	Scheduled tribes	Scheduled castes	Other backward classes	Others	Male	Female	Rural	Urban
Humanities	8.9	20.3	38.1	32.6	51.4	48.6	70.9	29.1
Science	6.5	12.8	48.7	32.0	59.0	41.0	57.9	42.1
Commerce	5.7	13.5	37.8	43.1	57.3	42.7	42.7	57.3
Medicine	4.5	11.2	40.3	44.0	33.9	66.1	43.5	56.5
Engineering	2.7	9.9	47.6	39.7	74.4	25.6	32.9	67.1
Agriculture	11.6	20.9	37.7	29.7	62.8	37.2	53.7	46.3
Law	5.1	13.3	37.0	44.6	59.9	40.1	41.9	58.1
Management	1.9	8.6	39.9	49.6	58.9	41.1	28.3	71.7
Education	5.8	18.9	43.1	32.1	32.0	68.0	59.0	41.0
Chartered accountancy and similar courses	2.1	3.6	21.3	72.9	60.8	39.2	14.5	85.5
IT/Computer courses	4.5	10.9	37.0	47.5	59.2	40.8	40.2	59.8
Total	6.7	15.6	41.2	36.6	56.6	43.4	54.8	45.2

Source: Authors' own calculations from unit level data set of NSSO (2014b).

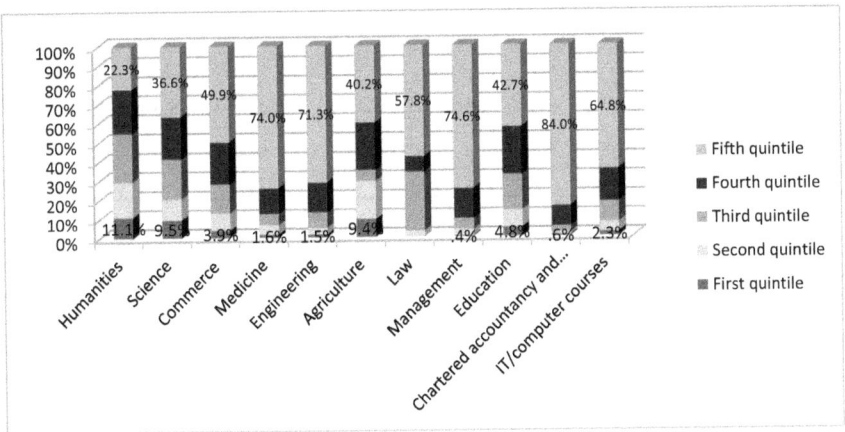

Figure 3.1 Subjects being studied by students as per their economic classes, 2014.
Source: Authors, prepared from unit level data sets of NSSO (2014b).

that cultural capital and habitus (tastes/preferences), which are influenced by the students' socioeconomic backgrounds, impact the college-related decision-making process for high school students.

In terms of social groups, the marginal probabilities of the disadvantaged social groups, irrespective of their significance, were lower than those for the reference group of the higher castes. The hierarchy by economic groups in access to higher education does not seem to have changed much over the years. In fact, the probability of accessing higher education for students from the poorest expenditure classes has declined between 1995 and 2014 (Table 3.4). Related to economic vulnerabilities, the predicted probability of individuals belonging to daily wage labour households accessing higher education was 6.3 per cent lower than that for regular salaried households.

The probability of accessing higher education in India is also significantly related to the state one resides in because the distribution of institutions of higher education is uneven among states, as has been analysed in the preceding section. The predicted probability of accessing higher education in the northeast was 23 per cent lower than that in the southern states. Varghese, Panigrahi and Rohatgi (2018) point to regional disparities in terms of number of institutions. Southern states such as Andhra Pradesh and Karnataka account for a considerably higher share of 37,862 institutions in India, at approximately 10 per cent of the total vis-à-vis states in the northeastern parts of India. For example, Mizoram, Meghalaya, Manipur, Nagaland and Tripura account for 0.2–0.3 per cent of the HEIs in the country. It is now widely recognized that in today's knowledge-based economy,

Table 3.4 Predicted Probabilities of Participation in Higher Education by Persons Aged 18–23, 1995 and 2014

Variables	NSS 71st Round (2014)		NSS 52nd Round (1995–6)	
Currently enrolled in higher education	Coef.	dy/dx	Coef.	dy/dx
Sex: Female	0.068*	0.023*	0.228***	0.020***
Rural	0.129***	0.043***	−0.093	−0.008
ST	−0.153**	−0.053**	0.430*	0.050*
SC	−0.089	−0.031	−0.010	−0.001
OBC	−0.002	−0.001		
q1	−0.525***	−0.195***	−0.428*	−0.026*
q2	−0.391***	−0.142***	−0.986***	−0.043***
q3	−0.171***	−0.060***	−0.558***	−0.034***
q4	−0.178***	−0.062***	−0.393***	−0.027***
Muslim	−0.220***	−0.078***		
North	−0.206***	−0.073***	0.316***	0.030***
East	−0.339***	−0.120***	0.221**	0.020**
Northeast	−0.618***	−0.233***	−0.461**	−0.027**
West	−0.361***	−0.130***	0.267***	0.025***
Casual	−0.179**	−0.063**		
Self-employed	0.035	0.012		
Constant	1.158***		−1.324***	
Log pseudolikelihood	−10602.511		−1701.2168	
Pseudo R2	0.0711		0.1037	
Number of obs.	18783		8754	

Notation for significance level: *** significant at 1 per cent level, ** significant at 5 per cent level, * significant at 10 per cent level.

Note: The classification of OBC and religion was not made during the 52nd Round of the National Sample Survey (NSS). dy/dx= marginal effect.

Source: Authors' own calculations from NSSO (2014b).

a region's growth prospects depend to a large extent on the skill levels of the regional labour force. The unequal distribution of institutions across regions leads to polarization of access to higher education, regional inequalities in the distribution of higher education opportunities and overall unequal regional economic development.

In terms of access of women to higher education, however, the picture is positive. The positive signs of the marginal probabilities of participation in higher education for women indicate that women were at an advantage relative to men in 2014: the predicted probability of women participating in higher education was 2.3 per cent higher than that for the reference group of men. The expansion of secondary education and the increase in the number of girls eligible for seeking admission to higher education, as more women cross the threshold of higher secondary education, contribute to an increase in their chances of participation in higher education. Similarly, the probability of participation in higher education by students residing in rural areas was 4 per cent higher than that for their urban counterparts, indicating that there has been an improvement in access to educational institutions in rural areas.

However, the predicted probabilities of women studying STEM subjects, those residing in rural areas and in the northeast have declined over two decades (Table 3.5). For example, in comparison to the reference group of men, the likelihood of women studying STEM subjects declined between 1995 and 2014 (-5 per cent in 1995; -10 per cent in 2014). Also, compared to the reference group of students residing in urban areas, those from rural areas were less likely to study STEM subjects in 2014 as compared to 1995 (-2.8 per cent in 1995; -4 per cent in 2014). Similarly, the predicted probability of students from lower-income groups studying STEM subjects was less than that for the higher-income groups. In other words, the results show that the challenges faced by these groups in accessing the STEM subjects have increased over the years.

Moreover, the results show that it is less likely that STEM subjects are studied in Hindi or a regional language, and more likely that English is the medium of instruction in STEM subjects. This becomes a disadvantage for students who have studied in Hindi or any regional language at the higher secondary level. A regional language being the medium of instruction poses a barrier to the writing of competitive examinations for higher studies. Furthermore, research (Sabharwal and Malish 2016) has shown that family background and pre-college credentials affect the choice of subjects. Students from the disadvantaged socioeconomic backgrounds and first-generation learners (who are more likely to be from government schools with a regional language as the medium of instruction) are most often tracked into less rigorous courses earlier in education, which then typically leads them to opt for less rigorous courses in higher education.

The probability of students studying STEM subjects in government institutions in comparison to private institutions has declined over the years. As shown in Table 3.5, the probability of studying STEM subjects in government institutions declined (-11 per cent). Most of the private HEIs were established to offer students the opportunity to study engineering and other STEM subjects. Since the poor overcrowd the public institutions, they have lower probability of accessing STEM subjects vis-à-vis those from the rich households. It seems the

Table 3.5 Probability of Attending STEM (science, technology, engineering and mathematics) subjects, 1995 and 2014

Variables	NSS 71st Round (2014)		NSS 52nd Round (1995-6)	
STEM	Coef.	dy/dx	Coef.	dy/dx
Sex: Female	-0.272***	-0.101***	-0.295***	-0.050***
Rural	-0.106***	-0.040***	-0.153**	-0.028**
ST	0.081	0.031	-0.424**	-0.061**
SC	0.020	0.007	0.083	0.016
OBC	0.223***	0.084***	–	–
q1	-0.133	-0.049	-0.665***	-0.084***
q2	-0.313***	-0.112***	-0.590***	-0.080***
q3	-0.166***	-0.061***	-0.533***	-0.078***
q4	-0.161***	-0.059***	-0.282***	-0.047***
Hindi	-1.186***	-0.400***	-0.751***	-0.125***
Regional language	-1.338***	-0.384***	-0.842***	-0.131***
North	0.525***	0.206***	0.109	0.021
East	0.000	0.000	-0.063	-0.011
Northeast	-0.757***	-0.234***	-0.560***	-0.075***
West	-0.080	-0.030	0.049	0.009
Govt.	-0.307***	-0.114***	0.245**	0.043**
Constant	0.535***	–	-0.477***	–
Log pseudolikelihood	-9875.0338		-3051.7671	
Pseudo R2	0.2148		0.1461	
Number of obs.	18783		8755	

Notation for significance level: *** significant at a 1 per cent level, ** significant at a 5 per cent level, * significant at a 10 per cent level.

Note: The OBC classification was not made during the 52nd Round of the National Sample Survey (NSS). dy/dx= marginal effect.

Source: Authors' own calculations from NSSO (2014b).

inequalities in access to prestigious programmes continue to reflect the inherited social privileges and contribute to the persistence of social inequalities.

Our results show that despite the expansion of higher education, students from privileged backgrounds still maintain their relative advantage and have greater access to opportunities for social and economic mobility offered by higher education. The affirmative policies and the incentive schemes seem to have attracted students to pursue higher studies and refrain from dropping out once they have secured admission in institutions of higher education. A study by Henry and Ferry (2017) demonstrated how the social and cultural capital stock of students from various social groups impacts their relative chances of securing admission in the IITs, which are elite HEIs. Qualifying in JEE alone does not ensure admission to the elite HEIs. Those who make realistic choices based on their JEE rankings have higher chances of getting admission in IITs even if their test scores are low. Therefore, well-informed students from the privileged social groups have a comparative advantage as compared to their ill-informed peers from the disadvantaged social groups. This trend of differentiation, which continues even after the admission, is discussed in the following section.

6. Inclusion and Equity in Educational Attainment

Many studies have generated empirical evidence on issues and problems faced by students from disadvantaged social groups in Indian universities and colleges (Sabharwal and Malish 2016; Ovichegan 2013; Deshpande and Zacharia 2013; Malish and Ilavarasan 2016; Sabharwal and Malish 2016). These studies show that the institutions have not responded positively to take account of the increasing student diversity in the classrooms and in the campuses. As a result, discriminatory and undemocratic values that exist in our society get reproduced in our campuses. Socially disadvantaged groups such as SCs and STs are major victims of these discriminatory practices. Non-supportive teachers, inadequate institutional mechanisms and non-inclusive pedagogical practices are some of the major factors of prevailing exclusion and discrimination faced by disadvantaged students and women. Nature and forms of discrimination practised in campuses that Sabharwal and Malish (2016) brought out demonstrate non-inclusive nature of campus spaces.

Equity in Outcomes

Educational outcome includes successful completion of programme of study and transition from higher education to employment. Successful completion refers to gaining required credits for completion of the course in prescribed period of time. Employment outcome refers to the extent to which higher education graduates get access to decent employment commensurate with the degree they possess.

Evidence indicates that among the dropouts, the larger share of students are from disadvantaged social groups (Sivasankaran and Raveendran 2004; Henry and Ferry 2017; Sabharwal et al. 2014). A student can also drop out due to social and academic reasons. Problems associated with social and emotional adjustment and 'academic integration' (Tinto 1975) contribute to a feeling of exclusion among the disadvantaged. Perceptions of teachers and institutional leaders indicate that they largely share negative perceptions about the academic abilities of disadvantaged students. Many factors contribute to academic non-integration of students from diverse backgrounds, including those related to the lack of pre-college preparation as well as to the academic environment and pedagogical practices in the institutions. While, there is a considerable gap in competency levels of students who enrol in colleges and universities, pedagogical practices to address these differences are relatively non-existent. As observed by Sabharwal and Malish (2016), non-existence of bridge courses and absence of foundational subject knowledge adds to cumulative academic disadvantage in classrooms.

Even when remedial coaching provisions exist, they are not effectively implemented in most HEIs. Medium of instruction is emerging as one of the major factors contributing to the lack of academic integration. As a larger share of students are more likely to have studied in schools with regional languages as the medium of instruction, the transition to English as a medium of instruction in HEIs poses a major academic challenge especially in the era of massification.

A study by Borooah and Sabharwal (2017) sheds light on the relationship between the medium of instruction and unequal educational opportunities. Nearly 49.4 per cent of the higher education students study with English as the medium of instruction. As a larger share of professional courses and elite institutions follow English as the medium of instruction, students from regional languages may face serious adjustment problems. It is also a fact that major textbooks in science and social science are available mostly in English language. Availability of e-resources which are mostly available in English poses further challenges for students from the schools that follow regional language as a medium of instruction. The overdominance of lecturing methods, lack of opportunity for peer learning and collaborative learning, as well as teacher shortage further aggravates the situation.

Cumulative effect of academic underpreparedness, language barriers and lack of diversity-oriented teaching-learning practices leads to academic vulnerability of the disadvantaged in classroom transactions. Students fail to comprehend basic subject concepts in their early days of college, which makes it difficult for them to follow subsequent parts of classroom teaching. As a result, their chances of failing or scoring lower grades are very high. Consequently, when they move to the next semester, they have to manage papers from the previous semester as well as papers of current semester. One of the reasons for students dropping out is their inability to manage this academic workload. This is what is called 'back paper syndrome' (Rajagopal 2012). The lack of peer-learning opportunities also severely impacts their capacity to overcome their academic difficulties.

Employment Outcomes

Studies on education-employment linkage provide valuable insights about dynamics of social inequality and social mobility. Estimates on unemployment rates among various social groups indicate that education-employment linkage is mediated by social group origin. As shown in Table 3.6, the comparatively higher rate of unemployment among educated SCs and STs indicates that there are many other mechanisms and processes in the labour market which systemically excludes disadvantaged groups in accessing employment. Education alone is not enough. A comprehensive study by Kannan (2019) demonstrate that during the post-reform period, SCs, STs and other disadvantaged groups lost ground in relation to all major indicators, except those specific to education. The authors also observed that the distribution of wage income among social groups provides evidence for the idea of persisting inequality, or durable inequality.

In relation to government jobs, policies of reservation and other positive discrimination are in place for the disadvantaged in government jobs. However, studies have shown that compared to lower-level jobs, representation of the disadvantaged is smaller in higher level jobs. Currently, the private sector, which provides employment to a majority of the educated youth, does necessarily follow the quota system. Number of studies have attempted to examine the process and mechanism by which certain social groups are excluded in recruitment process of the elite labour market which hires people with higher education qualification (Thorat and Attewell 2007; Upadhya 2007; Malish and Ilavarasan 2011). Identity-based discrimination may exclude people in early stages of recruitment, that is initial screening of applications (Thorat and Attewell 2007). Upadhya (2007) observes how caste influences candidate selection during interviews conducted by information and communication technology (ICT) companies as part of the campus placements. Evidence from India's premier institutions suggests that even with similar Cumulative Performance Indicator (CPI) levels, the SC, ST and OBC students are less likely to secure jobs than students of upper castes (Henry and Ferry 2017).

7. Conclusion

The empirical evidence and discussions examined in this chapter clearly indicate the prevalence of social group disparities among students in terms of retention as well as learning and labour market outcomes. The factors that contribute

Table 3.6 Unemployment Rates among Social Groups (Rural and Urban)

Social group	Not literate	Literate up to the primary level	Middle level	Secondary level	Higher secondary level	Diploma/ Certificate	Graduate	Postgraduate and above
STs	0.1	0.4	1.8	6.2	6.4	5.5	8.9	8.9
SCs	0.3	1.6	2.5	2.6	5.0	12	10.5	13.1
OBCs	0.4	0.8	2.1	2.7	4.0	10	8.2	8.3
Others	0.4	1.4	2	2.2	4.5	4.7	6.4	6.1
All	0.4	1.1	2	2.7	4.4	8.1	7.6	7.5

Source: Authors, based on 68th Round of the National Sample Survey (NSS) (NSSO 2014a).

to low levels of attainment in higher education include underpreparedness at the school level, English being the medium of instruction in HEIs, in addition to the lack of institutional support for academic integration and for creating a conducive learning environment. The HEIs are not adequately equipped as yet to address issues related to student diversity and hence fail to promote inclusion and create a positive learning environment. Given the fact that students from the disadvantaged social and income groups possess a lower stock of social and cultural capital, which is highly valued in the labour market, HEIs need to lay special emphasis on promoting both transferable and general competency skills among students along with their regular curricular studies.

4

Privatization versus Private Sector in Higher Education in India

N. V. Varghese and Nivedita Sarkar

1. Introduction

The growth and expansion of higher education in the post-world war period depended heavily on state funding and public institutions.[1] In this century, the sector relies more on non-state funding and private institutions for its expansion. This change resulted in shifting the financial burden of pursuing higher education from public to private sources, notably to households. The private sector has grown rapidly in many countries and has certainly increased its share in the total number of institutions and enrolments. Further, it remains a fast-growing segment of higher education in many developing countries. Experience shows that the matured market economies have relied more on public institutions and less on the market forces to massify higher education while the developing countries with poorly developed markets relied more on market forces and private institutions to massify their higher education sector. This chapter discusses about how India relied on private institutions and market processes to massify its higher education sector. The policy in practice in India seems to be one of relying on the public universities in core areas of research and development and on private institutions to meet the expanding social demand for higher education at the undergraduate level.

The plan of the chapter is as follows: The next section discusses issues related to the public good nature of higher education followed by a discussion on privatization and private sector in higher education in Section 3. Section 4 analyses the emerging typology of private higher education institutions.

---

[1] The views expressed in this chapter are of the authors and they should not necessarily be attributed to the organizations where they are employed.

Section 5 discusses the global surge and spread of private higher education. Section 6 talks about different phases in the evolution of private higher education in India. Section 7 profiles some of the features of private higher education in India. Section 8 highlights some of the issues related to the operation of private higher education institutions in India. And the final section underlines the need for regulatory measures and mechanisms.

2. Public Good and Public Investment in Higher Education

The arguments for or against public or private investment in higher education depends on the way the sector is viewed from economic and ideological points of view. While there is general agreement that knowledge is a public good (Samuelson 1954) or a global public good (Stiglitz 1999) and that public sector should invest in knowledge production, there is less agreement on whether or not institutions producing and transmitting knowledge should be treated as public goods.

A public good has two critical properties: non-rivalrous consumption and non-excludability in distribution (Samuelson 1954). A good becomes non-rivalrous when it can be consumed by any number of people without being depleted. The non-excludability in distribution implies that its provision cannot be restricted to a limited number of people. Only few goods can be classified as having these two characteristics in full measure. Many goods have one or other quality in part or full (Marginson 2011). The private goods are those which may not have any of the above two attributes.

It can be argued that higher education is more of a non-rival good than a non-excludable good. Its value may not diminish even when it becomes an item of mass consumption or when the sector is massified. However, its consumption can be restricted through pricing. In a situation of zero or close to zero public subsidy, access to higher education may be restricted to those who have the capacity to pay for it. Further, it is important to note that higher education has externalities since the benefits from it are not confined to students seeking higher education but also to society at large.

Cemmell (2002) notes that higher education is a merit good and the benefits from higher education are neither all public nor all private. It can be argued that in the absence of state investment, it will be underproduced and undersupplied since profits cannot be a criterion to decide the optimum amount of investment in a public good (Tilak 2008). The markets will not have incentives to produce it to the optimum levels and hence public investment in the sector needs to continue.

The argument in favour of dominant role of public investment in higher education was more appealing when state-led growth was the preferred strategy of development than during a period of market-led globalization. During the globalization stage, the private universities have been proliferating across globe, particularly in developing countries. Half a century ago, there were very few countries with private universities; at present, there are very few countries without them. Further, private institutions of higher education are growing faster thereby increasing their share in institutions and improving their share in student enrolments.

3. Privatization and the Private Sector in Higher Education

The state played an important role in the development strategy in the post-Second World War period. This model worked well during the reconstruction phase in Europe and during the postcolonial period in the developing countries. The public universities and state funding became the dominant feature of higher education development in most countries. The state-dominated model of higher education development was questioned in the 1980s by the changing ideological orientation and neoliberal thinking. The argument was for a reduced public investment in education in general, and a diversion of public investment from higher to primary education in developing countries in particular (World Bank 1986; Banya and Elu 2001). The emerging neoliberal reform measures manifested mostly through two phenomena: privatization of public institutions and promotion of private higher education institutions (Varghese 2004).

Privatization implies applying market principles in the functioning of public institutions of higher education. The ownership and management of the institutions remain with the public authorities while the operating principles centre around market ideology. Privatization is very often facilitated through transferring the governance to universities (autonomy) and many of them becoming public enterprises venturing into cost recovery, income generating, and for-profit activities (Kezar, Chambers and Burkhardt 2005). In the process, many public universities became managerial in their approach and entrepreneurial in their operations (Varghese 2013).

The higher education developments in Europe, notably in UK, and Australia are good examples of privatization of public institutions. Australia follows a policy of 'public privatization' wherein cost-recovery measures are introduced in public universities. The fee levels in UK are not only high but also comparable with that in the private institutions. The UK also follows a differential fee structure whereby non-EU students pay higher tuition than the EU students. The United States have one of the highest tuition fees among OECD countries and is the most expensive system with annual fees exceeding USD 8,000 a year in public universities and more than USD 20,000 in private institutions (OECD 2017). The student financing and student support systems, especially student loans, have become very common in many OECD countries. It can be argued that the OECD countries relied more on public institutions and privatization measures than private higher education institutions to massify and later to universalize higher education.

The private sector implies the non-state sector in higher education, in which institutions are owned and operated by private individuals or groups. In most cases, this sector does not receive funding from the government and in any case, they do not rely on state funding for its growth and expansion (Varghese 2004). Private higher education institutions can be universities or non-university institutions offering regular study programmes similar to those offered in public institutions, market-friendly courses or professional and management courses for which household demand continues to be high. Private universities offer courses leading to a degree, while courses offered in the non-university private higher education institutions, very often, lead to a certificate or a diploma.

Types of Private Higher Education Institutions

The private higher education institutions are of various types. One of the earliest and most commonly used classifications of private higher education institutions is categorizing them into elite, religious, and demand absorbing (Levy 1986). A more recent and modified categorization by Levy is in terms of elite and semi-elite, religious/cultural, and non-elite and demand absorbing (Bjarnason et al. 2009). Religious institutions are the fastest growing type of private higher education institution in almost every African country, perhaps, with the exception of South Africa (Varghese 2006; Karram 2011). While the Catholic Church dominated in the provision of private higher education in Latin America, Evangelical and Islamic faiths are common in Africa (Levy 2006).

Many of the religious-based private higher education institutions are not-for-profit, especially in Africa. While most of the private institutions are for-profit, some of the religious-based ones are not-for-profit. In fact some of them levy low tuition fees and at times provide financial support to students (Varghese 2008). Altbach (2005) terms the for-profit institutions as 'pseudo universities' since they do education as a business. It is also true that many private higher education institutions maintain a formal non-profit legal status while functioning like for-profit entities. They claim to produce 'surplus' which may not be taxable and claim not to produce 'profit' which is taxable.

There are many countries which have predominantly private higher education institutions. Countries in the South East Asian region traditionally have a high concentration of private higher education. Japan, Indonesia and Philippines have majority of institutions and students in the private institutions (Varghese 2015b). Private higher education existed for around half a century in Latin America. Countries such as Brazil, Chile, Costa Rica, El Salvador and Peru have more than 50 per cent of their students enrolled in private institutions. In fact, in Chile and Brazil more than three-fourths of the student enrolment is in private higher education institutions.

The private higher education institutions were established in Central and Eastern Europe during the post-Soviet era. The private sector is more common in countries such as Estonia, Georgia, Latvia and Poland (Slantcheva and Levy 2007). Sub-Saharan Africa is another example of fast growth and expansion of private higher education (Varghese 2006). Private higher education is an emerging sector in the Arab world where more than two-thirds of the universities founded since the 1990s are private. One notable feature of private higher education institutions in the gulf region is that many of them are branch campuses of foreign universities, notably from Australia, UK and the United States, which act as regional education hubs.

4. Global Spread of Private Higher Education

Private institutions can be for-profit and not-for-profit. The top-ranking universities in the United States such as Harvard, MIT, Yale, Pennsylvania, Chicago, and Columbia are elite not-for-profit private institutions. The United States also has some of the prominent for-profit institutions such as Phoenix, DeVry and Kaplan.

Many of the private higher education institutions in South Korea and Japan are elite whereas in Philippines many of them are non-elite. The private higher education institutions in Japan are engaged mostly in teaching and in the domains of humanities and social sciences at undergraduate levels while the public institutions are engaged in basic, applied and large-scale scientific research. In China, there are two types of private institutions – independent private institutions and private institutions affiliated to public universities which enrol students with low scores in entrance tests but at much higher tuition rates (Cao and Levy 2015).

In Poland, students who fail in university entrance examinations join 'evening' classes at the state universities or in private higher education institutions by paying high fees (Smolicz 1999). The former is an instance of privatization while the latter is a case of private higher education. Cambodia too has experienced privatization of public institutions and proliferation of private universities. The public institutions in Cambodia levy student fees and a good part of the revenue for the public institutions come from student fees. The government also gives scholarships to students and provides student loans.

Brazil has prominent private sector with liberal student loans. More than 70 per cent of the student fee cost can be met from student loans in Brazil. In Ukraine, there exists private institutions and profit-making branches of state institutions. Ukraine provides liberal financial support to students. Nearly half of the students receive state financing and the remaining 50 per cent pay tuition fees both in the public and private institutions.

The African region experienced a surge in private institutions in this century. Most of them are supported by religious groups (Levy 2005; Varghese 2006). Private universities in Kenya receives funds from tuition fees covering the total cost and they are run as 'not-for-profit' trusts. They do not receive any direct benefits from the government. The students in public universities can apply for loans and/or a bursary (Oketch 2004; Gudo 2014).

It can be seen from the above discussions that privatization of public institutions and proliferation of private institutions may coexist. Similarly, not-for-profit and for-profit private institutions coexist in many countries. Experience shows that both of them surged ahead and in the process 'private non-profit institutions became much more entrepreneurial in many respects like for-profit institutions' (Levy 2005: 35). The fast expansion of the for-profit institutions and commercialization of the sector have, especially in the cross-border segment, led to some undesirable influences, fraudulent practices and negative effects. Some of these providers are bogus offering a credential for payment and lack legal authority to operate although they offer study programmes and award degrees. In some instances these institutions become conduit for illegal migration (Middlehurst and Fielden 2011).

The discussions in the above paragraphs indicate a global trend of systematic shifting of the financial burden of expansion of higher education from public exchequer to households. This shift in the financial burden has taken two forms – privatization of public institutions and private sector in higher education. While matured market economies relied more on public institutions, the less-developed countries relied on private institutions to expand the system of higher education. The elite and non-elite, the for-profit and not-for-profit private institutions co-exist in many countries. Many instances show that the unregulated growth, especially of the for-profit private institutions, has led to commercialization and many undesirable practices in higher education.

5. Privatization and Private Higher Education in India

Massification of Higher Education

Although the first group of universities in India were established in 1857, the higher education sector remained an almost exclusive domain of the elites, and its expansion was very limited with only twenty-seven universities in 1951. The initial years of planned development saw high priority and larger share of plan allocations to higher education leading to fast expansion of the sector almost entirely through public institutions. The public investment and growth in public institutions declined from the 1970s and the growth in gross enrolment ratios (GERs) slowed down till the turn of this century (Table 4.1). After decades of slowdown in growth and expansion, the first decade of this century witnessed the fastest expansion leading to massification of higher education in India (Varghese 2015b). With more than 900 universities, 40,000 colleges, 36 million students and a GER of 25.8 per cent in 2017–18, the country has massified and became the second largest higher education system in the world after China.

The massive expansion and massification of the sector was due to the emergence and fast growth of private universities. Many states in India introduced laws to establish private universities from 2002 onwards. As can be seen from Table 4.1, the country had only seven private universities in 2005; this number has increased to 262 in 2017–18. The phenomenal growth in the number of private institutions promoted fast growth in enrolment resulting in the massive expansion of the system.

Privatization of Public Institutions in India

The government has been introducing cost-recovery measures in public institutions of higher education. Some of the elite institutions such as Indian

Table 4.1 Higher Education Expansion: Institutions and Enrolments

Year	Central Universities	State universities	Deemed-to-be universities	Institutes of national importance	Private universities	Total	Colleges	Enrolments (in millions)	GER %
1950–1	3	24	–	–	–	27	578	0.2	–
1960–1	4	41	2	2	–	49	1819	0.6	1.5
1970–1	5	79	9	9	–	102	3277	2	4.2
1980–1	7	105	11	9	–	132	4577	2.8	4.7
1990–1	10	137	29	9	–	185	6627	4.4	5.9
2001–2							11146	8.8	8.1
2005–6	18	205	95	18	7	343	17625	11.6	11.6
2011–12	43	299	128	59	105	634[a]	34852	29.2	20.8
2012–13	43	305	127	62	122	659[a]	35525	30.2	21.5
2013–14	43	322	127	68	154	714[a]	36634	32.3	23.0
2014–15	44	329	122	75	182	752	38498	34.2	24.3
2015–16	44	342	122	75	198	781	39071	34.6	24.5
2016–17	45	351	122	100	234	859	40026	35.7	25.2
2017–18	45	351	123	101	262	903	39050	36.6	25.8

Note:
[a] This figure includes 'Others' category.
Source: Authors, from Selected Educational Statistics MHRD 2005a, 2008, 2011b; All India Survey on Higher Education MHRD 2005b, 2011a, 2016, 2017, 2018, 2019, 2020.

Institutes of Technology (IITs) and Indian Institutes of Management (IIMs) which used to enjoy a high level of subsidy are now in the process of introducing fees and revising the fee rates. The IITs are revising the level of fees which was fixed when it was introduced in the past decade. The Ministry of Human Resources Development (MHRD) decided to increase the annual fee in IITs from INR 90,000 to INR 200,000. Over and above the increase by the MHRD, some of the IITs such as IIT Bombay decided to increase the fees charged under various heads. There was a 300 per cent hike in hostel rent; 167 per cent hike in gymkhana fees; 100 per cent hike in examination, registration and medical fees; and 30 to 50 per cent increase in other charges. According to an estimate, students staying in the campus had to pay an additional INR 22,000–INR 27,000 per annum towards hostel, mess, medical, gymkhana and other charges. The annual concessional tuition fees of INR 10,000 were reduced to INR 5000 (*Hindustan Times*, 1 June 2017).

The Karnataka state government decided to hike the fee for medical education (MBBS) courses in government and private medical colleges by 10 per cent a year over the next three academic years. For 2017–18 academic year, the MBBS course fees in government colleges and for students allotted government-quota seats in private colleges is expected to increase from INR 70,000 to INR 77,000. Similarly, the fee in private medical colleges increased from INR 5.75 lakh to INR 6.35 lakh (*Deccan Herald*, 26 September 2017). A Mumbai medical college (BKL Walawalkar Rural Medical College at Chiplun) announced a fee hike from INR 390,000 in 2016 to INR 725,000 in 2017. Similarly, in Sri Ramachandra University in Chennai, the annual tuition fee has nearly tripled from INR 650,000 in 2011 to INR 180,000 in 2017 and D. Y. Patil Deemed University's medical college has increased the tuition fees from INR 7.5 lakh in 2016 to INR 16.5 lakh in 2017. Other medical colleges also introduced higher fees.

Tamil Nadu government has announced a fee hike in engineering colleges for both government and management-quota seats in undergraduate courses. According to the revised fee structure, students admitted under government quota have to pay an additional INR 10,000 from 2017 for both non-accredited as well as accredited courses. The annual fee component under management quota has been hiked from INR 15,000 to INR 17,000 per year. Thus, students under management quota have to pay around INR 85,000 to INR 87,000 from 2017 (*The Hindu*, 1 July 2017).

6. Stages of Evolution of Private Higher Education in India

India, like many developing countries, relied on public sector for its economic and social development. The strategy of development became more market friendly in the 1990s. These changes are reflected in the provision of higher education.

Publicization of Private Institutions

India established mostly, if not entirely, public institutions in higher education in the 1950s and 1960s. In fact, in the 1950s, India nationalized many private institutions of higher education and transformed them into public institutions (Gnanam 2008). This was a stage of 'publicization' of private institutions.

Private Aided Sector

The next stage was the emergence of public-supported private higher education. The 1970s witnessed a growth in the private aided sector in higher education. The universities continued to be public entities but many of the colleges affiliated to the public universities were private aided and they received financial support from the state to cover a major share of their expenditure. The private aided colleges followed the same study programmes, offered the same courses and students appeared for the same examinations conducted by the public university to which these institutions were affiliated. The student fees in these private colleges were also fixed by the state governments. These colleges in general were functioning more like public institutions than like for-profit private higher education institutions.

Self-Financing Courses in the Public Institutions

The third stage in privatization of higher education is when self-financing courses were offered in public institutions. While some of the courses were self-financing, a majority of the courses continued to be in the traditional mode of public-funded study programmes. The committees appointed by University Grants Commission (UGC) and All India Council for Technical Education (AICTE) also recommended more for privatization than for promotion of private higher education. For example, the Punnayya Committee (1992–3) set up by the UGC suggested cost recovery and income generation to a level of 15 to 25 per cent of the annual recurrent expenditure of a university. Dr Swaminathan Panel (1992) set up by the AICTE also suggested cost recovery from students and the introduction of an education cess from industries.

Some of the state governments not only established self-financing courses in public institutions but also self-financing public institutions. Professor Gnanam (2008) notes that the policy of the government to empower public universities and colleges to offer 'self-financing courses' concurrently with public-funded programmes leaves one to wonder whether there are any more truly public institutions in the country. For example, to meet the growing demand for technical education and to arrest the outflow of students to other states seeking higher technical education, the government of Kerala decided to open institutions on a cost-recovery mode. The Institute of Human Resources Development in Electronics (IHRDE) is a case in point. The success of IHRDE led to the opening of self-financing public colleges supported by the government, and, later, many such colleges were established by the private sector (Varghese 2013).

Self-Financing Private Colleges

The fourth stage in the development of private higher education in India is denoted by the establishment and fast expansion of self-financing private higher education institutions. The self-financing colleges, which are commonly known as capitation fee colleges (Tilak 1994), are mostly for-profit private institutions. Most of these self-financing institutions were established in the subject areas of engineering, medicine and management (Agarwal 2007a). The southern states of Andhra Pradesh, Karnataka and Tamil Nadu and the western state of Maharashtra led the private higher education (self-financing colleges) revolution in India. A major part of India's private higher education surge came from proliferation of private self-financing colleges mostly in the technical and professional subject areas.

Private Deemed Universities

The fifth stage is the establishment of private deemed-to-be universities. In the 1990s, many private providers felt that the rules and regulations by the public authorities were very strict and severe. To escape from this and to attain the authority to award degrees, private institutions sought deemed-to-be university status; consequently, many private institutions became deemed universities (Agarwal 2007a).

Private Universities

The sixth stage is the establishment of private universities. A Private Universities Establishment and Regulations Bill was introduced in the Rajya Sabha (Upper House of the Parliament) in August 1995 with a view of providing for the establishment of self-financing private universities. The private providers were not happy with some of the provisions in the bill, especially those pertaining to endowment funds, regulation by government bodies and subsidized education for nearly one-third of the intake. Although the bill was not passed, discussions on the need for a private universities bill continued. In 2000, the Prime Minister's Council on Trade and Industry set up a committee (Birla-Ambani Committee 2000–1) that recommended entrusting the private sector with provision of higher education, promulgation of a private university bill, cost recovery from students, and loans and grants to economically and socially weaker sections.

Starting from the year 2002, several state governments have passed private university acts. Chhattisgarh took the lead in enacting a private universities act, and it has the distinction of having the first officially established private university in India (Shri Rawatpura Sarkar International University) in 2002. The state of Chhattisgarh established ninety-seven private universities in that same year. This was followed by many other state governments (Assam, Haryana, Himachal Pradesh, Gujarat, Odisha, Punjab, Uttar Pradesh, Uttaranchal, etc.) establishing private universities.

The private universities need to be established within the regulations stipulated by UGC (UGC 2003a). These regulations mandated that each private university should be established by a separate act, and it should conform to the provisions of the UGC Act of 1956. The private universities will be unitary in structure, but permitted to operate off-campus and off-shore campuses. The student admission procedures and fee structure shall be in accordance with the norms/guidelines prescribed by the UGC and other concerned statutory bodies. Some states established private universities before these regulations came into effect and, in some cases, before the Private Universities Act of 2002 was passed.

The pattern seems to be that some private colleges were deregulated by granting them an autonomous status. Some of them graduated to deemed-to-be universities status and further to private universities in later years (UGC 2003b). Others were new institutions established as private universities from the beginning. At present there are 380 private universities (GoI 2021c). The private sector accounts for 78 per cent of the higher education institutions including aided sector and more than 62 per cent of the total student enrolment in higher education.

There is another type of private institution where the university is public but it has privately managed affiliated institutions with free seats and payment seats. Fees for the free seats are decided by the university, while those for the payment seats are decided by the affiliated institution. The Guru Gobind Singh Indraprastha University (New Delhi) belongs to this category of private higher education institution. It has several self-financing courses in its affiliated institutions (Singh and Misra 2008). There are also non-university private institutions, for example, polytechnics, offering diplomas and certificates; in addition, there are also other types of private entities such as NIIT and APTECH group of institutions. Although they cannot grant degrees, a certification from these institutions is accepted by employers. Another type of private institution is coaching centres; however, these do not issue any certificates (Gnanam 2008).

It is argued that there is a declining signalling effect of higher education India. The best example is the replacement of university performance and certificate with competitive examinations for further studies and jobs (Kapur and Mehta 2004). Coaching for all competitive tests (for entrance to higher education institutions and jobs) has become very common in India. Parents and children willingly invest more money and time in coaching institutions for entrance examinations and competitive tests for jobs than as student fees in public institutions.

7. Empirical Evidence on the Growth and Expansion of Private Higher Education

The discussions in these sections are based on the National Sample Survey (NSS) data collected by the government of India and may not strictly correspond to the data relied on for the preceding paragraphs. According to the 52nd NSS round, the private share in total enrolment in general higher education in 1995–6 was 10.4 per cent and 21 per cent in professional and technical higher education, respectively. These shares have increased to 13.5 per cent in 2007 and further to 23 per cent in general higher education in 2014 (Table 4.2). The corresponding figures for technical education are 42.4 per cent in 2007 and 52.6 per cent in 2014. It is important to note some trends in the expansion of higher education. First, there is a decline in the share of enrolment in the government and private aided institutions both in the general as well as technical and professional higher education. Second, there is a corresponding increase in the share of enrolment in the private unaided sector. Third, over the period, the gap between the

Table 4.2 Higher Education Enrolment by Management (%)

Types of higher education	Percentage of currently attending students				
	Government	Private aided	Private unaided	Not Known	Total
71st Round (2014)					
General	50.79	25.63	23.24	0.34	100
Professional/ technical	22.15	24.21	52.58	1.07	100
64th Round (2007–8)					
General	55.44	29.63	13.49	1.45	100
Professional/ technical	25.52	30.59	42.37	1.52	100
52nd Round (1995–6)					
General	71.41	17.77	10.37	0.45	100
Professional/ technical	55.62	23.20	21.18	0.00	100

Source: Authors, based on NSS 71st Round unit level data.

relative share of enrolment in government sector and unaided private sector has widened in technical and professional subject areas, while it has narrowed down in general education indicating a better performance of the private sector than government institutions in enrolling relatively larger number of students in technical and professional subject areas.

An analysis of enrolment by social groups shows variations in the share of enrolment among the caste groups. Between 2007 and 2014, the share of ST enrolment in the government institutions continues to be high with marginal decline of less than 1 per cent (Table 4.3). However, substantial decline in the share of enrolment in the government and private aided institutions of the other social groups is observed. In case of other caste groups, the decline in the share of enrolment in aided private institutions is marginal. It can be seen that a majority of the scheduled tribes (STs) and scheduled castes (SCs) still rely on government institutions while the general category students and other backward class (OBC) category students rely on private institutions – private aided or unaided. Interestingly, all social groups have increased their share in unaided sector mostly at the cost of government and aided sectors. While the share of students in the aided sector remained relatively stable in case of ST and general category students, the share of SC and OBC categories of students experienced a sharp decline in the private aided sector.

Table 4.3 Distribution of Enrolment by Social Groups and Types of Institution

Type of institution	ST	SC	OBC	Others
71st Round (2014)				
Government	60.02	50.38	38.22	41.45
Private aided	21.16	22.64	24.96	27.42
Private unaided	18.82	26.98	36.82	31.13
Total	100	100	100	100
64th Round (2007–8)				
Government	59.52	54.27	44.67	49.76
Private aided	22.54	33.03	32.18	28.64
Private unaided	17.95	12.70	23.15	21.59
Total	100	100	100	100

Source: Authors, based on NSS 71st Round unit level data.

The distribution of enrolment by income levels shows considerable disparities in enrolment among income groups – across social groups and within the same social group (Table 4.4). A large share of students enrolled in higher education come from the fourth and fifth quintiles. The disparities in the share of students attending higher education institutions between income quintiles are more in the technical and professional subjects than in general higher education. The differences in enrolments between fourth and fifth quintile declined in the general education while they have increased in case of technical education (Table 4.4).

Gender disparities have been declining over a period of time. It seems that the larger share of females enrolled in general subjects are in government institutions while that in the technical and professional subject areas are in the private unaided institutions (Table 4.5). The general trend is that the enrolment share of both men and women students have increased in private unaided institutions, and correspondingly there is a decline in their share in government institutions.

The enrolment at the undergraduate level of study shows a pattern different from what we observed in the previous paragraphs. The disparities in the share of enrolment by income groups are less at the undergraduate level (Table 4.6). This trend is more applicable to enrolments in the government institutions. In the private aided and unaided sectors, the share of enrolment is positively associated with the levels of income – a larger share of students come from successive levels of income quintiles. Further, the differences in the share of enrolment from the first and fifth quintile is more than four times in the private aided sector and nearly five times in the private unaided sector.

Table 4.4 Distribution of Higher Education Students by Social Groups and Income

	MPCE	ST	SC	OBCs	Other
General					
71st Round (2014)					
	First quintile	7.7	11.6	7.8	4.1
	Second quintile	16.4	15.3	13.7	8.3
	Third quintile	29.0	24.7	21.9	18.8
	Fourth quintile	23.7	21.8	26.4	20.9
	Fifth quintile	23.2	26.6	30.1	48.0
	Total	100	100	100	100
Professional/ Technical	First quintile	7.5	6.1	1.6	0.7
	Second quintile	10.8	7.5	5.7	2.2
	Third quintile	10.9	16.1	11.2	4.8
	Fourth quintile	16.7	17.2	16.6	12.6
	Fifth quintile	54.0	53.1	64.8	79.7
	Total	100	100	100	100
64th Round (2007–8)					
General	First quintile	31.11	39.87	28.65	15.30
	Second quintile	26.08	30.46	28.65	26.30
	Third quintile	21.81	14.91	20.83	19.22
	Fourth quintile	16.58	10.86	14.28	22.95
	Fifth Quintile	4.42	3.89	7.59	16.23
	Total	100	100	100	100
Professional/ Technical	First quintile	9.24	6.69	4.32	6.18
	Second quintile	1.20	21.69	11.53	6.84
	Third quintile	9.87	35.17	11.23	10.65
	Fourth quintile	24.04	13.18	23.77	24.75
	Fifth quintile	55.65	23.27	49.15	51.58
	Total	100	100	100	100

Source: Authors, based on NSS 71st Round unit level data.

Another factor which favours the private higher education in India is the medium of instruction. English language is seen to be the language of the elite and most preferred language in the private universities. Students from the well-to-do families enrolled in English medium schools are attracted towards private universities.

The cost of private higher education varies. The average household expenditure per student by type of institution attended shows that the per student expenditure has increased over time. As expected, the per student expenditure in government institutions are lower than that in aided and unaided private institutions. In fact, the per student household expenditure in

Table 4.5 Enrolment by Gender and Type of Higher Education

Type of higher education	Type of institution	Male	Female
71st Round (2014)			
General	Government	53.57	48.09
	Private aided	23.47	28.2
	Private unaided	22.96	23.72
	Total	100	100
Professional/Technical	Government	22.19	22.71
	Private aided	24.75	24.0
	Private unaided	53.06	53.3
	Total	100	100
64th Round (2007–8)			
General	Government	59.67	58.34
	Private aided	28.22	28.00
	Private unaided	12.10	13.67
	Total	100	100
Professional/Technical	Government	19.61	35.70
	Private aided	37.09	21.71
	Private unaided	43.30	42.58
	Total	100	100

Source: Authors, based on NSS 71st Round unit level data.

Table 4.6 Enrolment at the Undergraduate Level by Types of Education and Income

MPCE quintiles	Government	Private aided	Private unaided	Total
71st Round (2014)				
First quintile	13.16	8.18	8.77	10.79
Second quintile	22.97	14.31	10.02	17.32
Third quintile	24.72	21.56	19.84	22.62
Fourth quintile	21.12	22.17	21.47	21.45
Fifth quintile	18.03	33.77	39.9	27.81
Total	100	100	100	100
64th Round (2007–8)				
First quintile	22.18	20.46	13.86	19.93
Second quintile	27.76	21.26	15.22	23.18
Third quintile	18.60	16.59	17.12	17.68
Fourth quintile	17.26	20.62	21.48	19.16
Fifth quintile	14.20	21.07	32.32	20.06
Total	100	100	100	100

Source: Authors, based on NSS 71st Round unit level data.

Table 4.7 Per Student Expenditure by Type of Institutions

Type of higher education	Type of institution	Average expenditure (INR)	
		71st Round (2014)	64th Round (2007–8)
General	Government	10261	6451
	Private aided	14612	7704
	Private unaided	21371	11665
	Total	13963	7518
Professional/ Technical	Government	40528	23960
	Private aided	67094	38536
	Private unaided	84133	45312
	Total	70602	37573

Source: Authors, based on NSS 71st Round unit level data.

unaided institutions is more than twice compared to per student household expenditure in government institutions (Table 4.7). The per student expenditure in aided private institutions lies in between that in government and private unaided institutions. Table 4.7 also indicates a tendency for a faster increase of per student expenditure in unaided sector, especially in the technical and professional education.

The per student expenditure on higher education varies among states in India (Table 4.8) and has increased in all states between 2007 and 2014. The increase in per student household expenditure is two to three times higher in 2014 when compared to the same in 2007. The states of Kerala, Karnataka, Haryana and Puducherry have the highest levels of per student expenditure. These states also have a higher share of private unaided institutions and that too in the professional and technical areas. This is further reinforced when we analyse the per student household expenditure by type of institutions (Table 4.9).

Another form of private education is private tuition classes. We find that private tuitions or shadow pricing in education is on the increase, and households invest considerable amount of money on this form of private education. In general households in the urban areas invest more than households in the rural areas in private tuition (Table 4.10). Private tuition is prevalent both at the secondary and higher education levels. It seems people in the higher-income groups spent more on private tuition than their lower-income counter parts. In 2014, those in the fifth income quintile spent around six times more than those in the first income quintile (Table 4.11).

Table 4.8 Per Student Higher Education across All States/Union Territories

States/UTs	Average expenditure (INR)	
	71st Round (2014)	64th Round (2007–8)
Jammu & Kashmir	26412	10790
Himachal Pradesh	36408	8078
Punjab	44774	30326
Chandigarh	59906	28330
Uttaranchal	17929	12808
Haryana	53381	11999
Delhi	34660	22077
Rajasthan	20704	13889
Uttar Pradesh	18722	8336
Bihar	24286	7745
Sikkim	49563	12011
Arunachal Pradesh	25510	7091
Nagaland	29907	10112
Manipur	30599	9686
Mizoram	34017	5527
Tripura	28086	9112
Meghalaya	25412	8042
Assam	17013	7960
West Bengal	25357	15356
Jharkhand	19675	6249
Orissa	29608	20357
Chhattisgarh	19924	11708
Madhya Pradesh	29061	11423
Gujarat	26707	10396
Daman & Diu	34916	5385
Dadra & Nagar Haveli	31980	10782
Maharashtra	39315	17110
Andhra Pradesh	35568	14102
Karnataka	33742	27364
Goa	18582	38829
Lakshadweep	28304	11900
Kerala	53150	15728
Tamil Nadu	54066	20604
Puducherry	54756	15209
Andaman & Nicobar Islands	29687	6805
Telangana	27970	–

Note:
ᵃ The state Telangana was formed only on 2014. Therefore, the household expenditure data is not available for 64th Round.
Source: Authors, based on NSS 71st Round unit level data.

Table 4.9 Per Student Average Household Expenditure by Types of Institutions across All States/Union Territories

States/UTs	71st Round (2014)			64th Round (2007–8)		
	Government	Private aided	Private unaided	Government	Private aided	Private unaided
Jammu & Kashmir	16986	38125	73340	9229	24373	35942
Himachal Pradesh	15967	35481	78341	6523	8474	20267
Punjab	24849	44051	52731	19033	41796	28877
Chandigarh	41589	88451	48560	24656	45099	33442
Uttaranchal	10618	19501	54133	4579	5317	56234
Haryana	21256	44859	89552	8607	11016	22431
Delhi	22809	65061	94425	13936	33445	84440
Rajasthan	10730	30138	30443	6960	20744	29696
Uttar Pradesh	11454	12848	31855	8070	8094	11489
Bihar	12719	36994	88961	4518	43513	22090
Sikkim	23597	96216	102850	7631	-	56264
Arunachal Pradesh	18044	46051	67778	6558	15750	-
Nagaland	21171	30536	35325	7830	12232	12842
Manipur	26786	27685	54504	8993	7955	22961
Mizoram	28355	103877	46240	5377	9100	5618
Meghalaya	21415	89019	119888	7858	5352	-
Assam	13811	16857	53329	7506	9161	14049
West Bengal	16265	35588	69987	10335	15734	49684
Jharkhand	10771	36187	60567	5360	8731	16803
Odisha	13862	25109	73018	14069	11283	46734
Chhattisgarh	9173	42303	65739	4795	31438	38192
Madhya Pradesh	14336	30580	48491	7348	19202	15305
Daman & Diu	7637	39318	123000	5484	3225	-
Dadra & Nagar Haveli	10172	32236	66103	7982	16280	-
Maharashtra	21448	34070	86297	11481	11581	39470
Andhra Pradesh	18364	30649	43105	5828	12771	20906
Karnataka	11754	35210	55100	5581	26093	48340
Goa	10995	21870	.	24269	16397	54679
Lakshadweep	21712	9745	44975	11900	-	-
Kerala	27003	34607	72907	9626	8782	23219
Tamil Nadu	17871	44791	73129	8212	23997	28722
Puducherry	23202	40985	78374	7366	14600	36572

States/UTs	71st Round (2014)			64th Round (2007–8)		
	Government	Private aided	Private unaided	Government	Private aided	Private unaided
Andaman & Nicobar Islands	12068	53971	31575	6825	-	-
Telangana	10137	27567	33059	-	-	-

Source: Authors, based on NSS 71st Round unit level data.

Table 4.10 Per Student Average Household Expenditure on Private Coaching at Higher Secondary by Sex, Location and Social Group

Social group	Male			Female			Total		
	Rural	Urban	Total	Rural	Urban	Total	Rural	Urban	Total
71st Round (2014)									
ST	1328	8009	3014	1319	6358	2275	1324	7381	2682
SC	2968	7973	4144	2567	5890	3339	2796	7086	3799
OBC	2866	7354	4145	1963	4684	2893	2501	6100	3613
Others	4142	12339	7815	3507	10419	6713	3866	11474	7328
Total	3153	9821	5371	2495	7566	4320	2874	8801	4916
64th Round (2007–8)									
ST	2433	4786	3431	1103	5631	3232	2009	5091	3364
SC	1769	4791	2690	2592	4719	3815	2003	4751	3134
OBC	2320	3947	2987	1832	3831	2770	2168	3905	2914
Others	2869	6977	5139	2651	6033	4668	2787	6580	4950
Total	2448	5708	3958	2281	5239	3906	2392	5513	3938

Source: Authors, based on NSS 71st Round unit level data.

Table 4.11 Per Student Average Household Expenditure on Private Coaching at Higher Secondary by Expenditure Quintiles

MPCE quintiles	71st Round (2014)	64th Round (2007–8)
First quintile	1674	1773
Second quintile	2514	1872
Third quintile	2762	2229
Fourth quintile	3745	2893
Fifth quintile	9592	5582
Total	4922	3938

Source: Authors, based on NSS 71st Round unit level data.

8. The Legal Challenges and Declining Enrolment in Private Institutions

India has experienced a fast growth of private higher education institutions, especially the unaided private institutions. Some of the recent evidence implicate that a reckless growth of self-financing private colleges in the domains of technical and professional education has resulted in establishment of institutions of questionable quality. Many private higher education institutions have very poor infrastructure, insufficient and unqualified faculty, and levy exorbitant fees from students. Questions are raised about the approval process adopted to grant permission for these institutions to operate. At times it is alleged that the process of granting permission to operate by the AICTE is not transparent and some of the AICTE officials were found guilty of corrupt practises (Misra 2011).

The student admission policies followed in the private unaided higher education institutions have not been fair at times, and they have been challenged in the courts of law. One such court decision that allowed increasing the number of paid seats in private professional colleges in Karnataka to 50 per cent contributed to proliferation of self-financing colleges in India. The self-financing or capitation fee colleges in the state of Karnataka followed a discriminatory pricing policy. The students from the state of Karnataka paid less fees and those from outside the state were levied a higher level of fees.

The discriminatory pricing policy was challenged in the court (*Mohini Jain v. the State of Karnataka* in 1992), and the Supreme Court banned the capitation fee as it did not agree with discriminatory fee structure, and declared the state notification to be null and void (Gupta 2005). In another case (*Unnikrishnan v. the State of Andhra Pradesh* in 1993), the Supreme Court came strongly against for-profit higher education institutions and noted that the capitation fee colleges are 'poisonous weeds' and are 'financial adventurers without morals and scruples' (as quoted in Gupta 2008: 250). The Supreme Court laid down a formula to bring about partnership between the public and private sectors and allowed state governments to administer and regulate admissions of private professional institutions.

In another instance, a court judgement in a case in 2005 (*Yashpal Sharma and Others v. the State of Chhattisgarh*), the Supreme Court ruled that all colleges established by the Chhattisgarh state under the Private Universities Act of 2002 as null and void since they did not follow the regulations stipulated by the UGC in 2003. This judgement implied closing down 117 private universities established by the state of Chhattisgarh between 2002 and 2005.

Quality is becoming a major concern affecting enrolments in private institutions. Many graduates from private institutions remain unemployed and even when employed they work in jobs with poor salaries. The high unemployment rate among the engineering graduates has led to low demand for these courses. It is estimated that more than 2.7 million seats in various engineering institutes across the country were lying vacant in 2016–17. During 2014–15 to 2017–18 period, about 410 private unaided engineering colleges across the country have opted for progressive closure. Further, the AICTE decided to close around 800 engineering colleges in the academic year 2018–19 since they have less than 30 per cent of seats filled in the past five years. Several colleges in the states of Telangana, Uttar Pradesh, Maharashtra, Andhra Pradesh, Rajasthan, Tamil Nadu, Haryana, Gujarat and Madhya Pradesh have sought progressive closure (*Times of India*, 2 September 2017). The situation in management courses is also similar.

9. Student Loans

The efforts to privatize public institutions and promote private institutions are also accompanied by extending student loan facilities. As is well known, student loan schemes is one of the alternative sources of financing higher education for the credit-constrained students; however, it may not fulfil the objective of social equity (Varghese 2011; Geetha Rani 2011). The National Loans Scholarship Scheme, which was started in 1963, distributed loans through the government channels to students in educational institutions (Tilak 1992). The new student loan scheme started in 2001 is different and is administered by scheduled commercial banks of India. It covers a wide range of courses at the post-matric levels including higher education and research studies. It is not an income contingent loan (ICL) and therefore, any student who secures admission in domestic/foreign educational institution is eligible to apply for this loan. Interest rate varies by loan slabs. It can be repaid in five to seven years, and repayment would commence one year after completion of the course or six months after getting employment, whichever is earlier. Interest is charged during the period of study and until the completion of repayment.

Table 4.12 shows that, since its inception, the number of education loans increased from 0.11 million, in 2000–1 to 2.59 million in 2013–14. The growth rate of loan accounted for 28.7 per cent, while growth in enrolment in higher education was around 12 per cent. Also, the amount of education loans released increased rapidly from INR 10,280 million in 2000–1 to INR 702,820 million

Table 4.12 Growth of Education Loans in India

Years	Education loans (in '000s)	% of students enrolled in higher and technical education	Education loans released (INR 10 millions)	Education loan as a % of government expenditure on higher and technical education
2000–1	112	1.3	1028	5.1
2001–2	157	1.8	1527	16
2002–3	239	2.5	2870	28.2
2003–4	347	3.5	4179	35.1
2004–5	470	4	6398	50.6
2005–6	641	4.5	10804	73.6
2006–7	1002	6.4	14012	84.5
2007–8	1215	7.1	19748	86.4
2008–9	1580	8.5	26913	104
2009–10	1911	9.2	35855	111.8
2010–11	2211	8.0	41341	96.9
2011–12	2373	8.3	46727	94.1
2012–13	2479	8.4	50927	86.7
2013–14	2590	7.8	70282	106.7
Growth rate	28.7	12.1	37.9	14.9

Source: Authors, derived from Geetha Rani (2016).

in 2013–14. The share of education loans constituted around 5.1 per cent in total government expenditure on higher and technical education in 2000–1; it increased to 84.5 per cent by 2006–7 and it exceeded government expenditures on higher and technical education from 2008 onwards. Table 4.13 provides data on student loans by discipline.

The trends indicate that education loans would be further increasing since the government funding is not keeping pace with demand for higher education. It is estimated by the Reserve Bank of India (RBI) that a 1 per cent increase in GDP growth is associated with 5 per cent increase in education loans (Chakrabarty 2010).

It is shown that the access to higher education, student loans and the interest subsidy schemes favour the rich, especially male students (Geetha Rani 2016).

10. Conclusion

The major focus of the chapter has been to provide an overview of private higher education in India. The discussions in the initial part tried to map out the trends

Table 4.13 Student Loan by Disciplines in India (in INR)

Course name	2009–10	2010–11	2011–12	2012–13
Medical	335077	326511	333370	344461
Architecture	291815	248745	313408	314137
Law	232654	181779	252480	278437
Fashion	271637	300749	297536	274430
Management	269925	261922	274918	259212
Nursing	231394	249507	239743	237839
Engineering	231024	225797	232726	234054
Pharmacy	228000	229268	233133	233495
Hospitality	225602	230876	226708	231271
Others	194762	190731	193005	205557
Physiotherapy	215592	99630	196133	205438
Science	178799	159277	176742	172293
BCA/MCA	157131	220669	155837	157227
Diploma	117078	145851	124348	125821
Commerce	115713	151124	99255	97502
Education	64860	66123	41776	45265
All	233949	229907	235692	238322

Source: Authors, derived from Geetha Rani (2016).

in the emergence and expansion of private higher education across countries. The chapter argued that while developed countries relied on public institutions to universalize higher education, developing countries such as India relied on private institutions and market processes to massify higher education.

The chapter elaborates on the evolution of private higher education. The discussions show that there was near state monopoly in higher education during the immediate period following independence. This was followed by public-funded private sector and later to self-financing private colleges and finally to private universities in this century. The growth and rapid expansion of private higher education is to be seen in the context of economic liberalization policies introduced in India in the early 1990s. The private sector expanded quickly and contributed substantially to the massification of the higher education sector in India. The country moved from a slow-growing low GER in higher education until the end 1990s to one of the fastest growing higher education sectors in this century. While the contribution of private higher education to expand the sector is very well received, private institutions do not rank very high in terms of academic prestige and quality. The unregulated growth of private higher education has invited criticisms on various counts.

Private sector in higher education, especially the capitation fee levying sector, comprises for-profit institutions promoting commercialization of the sector. Most private institutions offered courses in the technical, professional and management areas. This led to disciplinary distortions and overproduction of graduates who could not find rewarding employment opportunities despite heavy investment in their studies. The increasing unemployment led to a decline in the social demand for engineering education, resulting in many private sector institutions closing down.

International experience shows that unregulated growth of private higher education leads to unhealthy growth and practices. Studies show that (Hallak and Poisson 2007) fraudulent practices such as relaxed admission rules, distorted evaluation processes, faked examination results and fake degrees are prevalent in many countries. Therefore, to protect students this sector needs more regulations while establishing private institutions. The aim therefore is to ensure that an effective regulatory system is in place to prevent underqualified or fraudulent providers from trading higher education and from issuing worthless qualifications.

5

The Dynamics of Union-State Relations and Higher Education in India

Anamika Srivastava and Saumen Chattopadhyay

1. Introduction

The governance of higher education in India is the joint responsibility of both the Union and the states. However, the Union has been assigned the important task of coordinating and maintaining standards in higher education. While Indian federalism is often referred to as a Union-heavy system, the recent policy discourse in India aims to create an enabling space for efficient functioning of the Union and state governments, espousing the spirit of 'cooperative and competitive federalism'. However, higher education in India remains a highly differentiated space with interstate as well as Union-state disparities in the quality and funding of higher education institutions (HEIs). While elite higher educational institutions like the Indian Institutes of Technology (IITs) and Indian Institutes of Management (IIMs), established and funded by the Union government are few of the, relatively, richly endowed institutions in India, the core of the higher education lies at the state level where all the states are not equally placed in terms of funding as well as autonomy. Policy efforts have been made by the Union government to address interstate disparities in terms of regulatory space and funding requirements. However, it would be naïve to ignore the positional disadvantages that state governments may suffer vis-à-vis the Union as well as among themselves. Given this backdrop, this chapter aims to unravel the dynamics of Union-state relations in India, by focusing on their struggle and negotiations in implementing the recent policy initiatives in higher education.

This chapter explores the dynamics of Union-state relations and higher education in India. It discusses the implications of such an imbalance on higher educational outcomes and why the recent policy efforts to overhaul the Union-state financial relations in higher education, through National Higher Education Mission (Rashtriya Uchchatar Shiksha Abhiyan, RUSA), is inadequate, if not a complete failure. The plan of the chapter is as follows. The first section discusses the complex federal type higher education system in India. The second section illustrates the dynamics of Indian federalism and higher education by emphasizing two important features: (1) how the regulation in higher education has emerged to be a Union-heavy regulatory structure and (2) notwithstanding the Union-heavy regulatory structure, how the responsibility of governing majority of the HEIs fall on the state governments. The fourth section then goes on to discuss the horizontal imbalances, particularly, highlighting the disparities in the fiscal capacity of different states and their limitations in financing of higher education. As a possible consequence, the dominance of the private sector in provisioning and financing of state governed HEIs is discussed in the fifth section. The sixth section presents a critical appraisal of the policy initiative of RUSA in addressing the inadequate transfer of funds from the Union to the states as well as to eradicate disparities in educational outcomes across states. The chapter ends with a conclusion.

2. Union-State Relations and Funding Responsibilities

Espousing the spirit of federalism, the Constitution of India (1950) distributes governmental powers and functions among different levels[1] of polity. It allocates subjects to the Union and the states under the Union List and the State List, respectively, with overlapping functions contained in a separate Concurrent List (Indian Constitution, Seventh Schedule). Further, the Constitution also makes provisions regarding taxation and borrowing powers of the Union and the states so that they generate resources to fulfil their respective functions (Indian Constitution, Article 268–81). In reality, however, a one-to-one correspondence between the governmental functions on the one hand and the availability of power (to regulate and govern) and access to financial resources (through taxation and borrowing) on the other hand is impossible in any federal polity (Bhasin 2017). The Indian polity, in particular, is characterized by both vertical (Union-states) as well as horizontal (among states) imbalances in governmental

---

[1] Although the Constitution of India mentions about the distribution of powers and functions among Union, State and the local governments, this chapter focuses on Union-state relations only.

functions as well as availability of power and access to financial resources (Bhasin 2017).

The vertical imbalance can be illustrated by the prevalent Union-heavy fiscal federalism in the country. When compared to the states, not only does the Union garner a relatively significant proportion of tax revenue from major sources but also its borrowing (internal and external) powers are, relatively, flexible (Bhasin 2017). Despite the constitutional provisions for transferring of funds from the Union to the states through several modalities, it is argued that the states receive only a miniscule amount of financial assistance from the Union (Chakraborty and Gupta 2016). The Constitution provides for the Union-to-states transfer of funds via devolution of taxes on the basis of a transfer formula of the finance commission; the Union assistance to the state and loans disbursement by the erstwhile Planning Commission before and the NITI Aayog (National Institution for Transforming India) at present; as well as discretionary Union-to-state transfers for centrally sponsored schemes (Indian Constitution, Article 268–81). Notwithstanding this provisioning, there is an inadequacy of financial resources available to the states from the Union to perform the series of functions assigned to them. The vertical imbalances are further complicated by the horizontal imbalances.

The horizontal imbalances can be illustrated by the disparities among the states, both in terms of their socioeconomic development and their fiscal capacities. Furthermore, 'the political and economic influence or the importance of the states affect the transfers they receive from the Union, in ways that are not necessarily captured in transfer formulae' (Rao and Singh 2001: 2). The negative effect of vertical and horizontal imbalances is accentuated across the sectors where the functions and responsibility of provisioning and governing fall, invariably, more on one level of government than on the other. Higher education is one such sector in India. A significant portion of the HEIs, including the private HEIs (PHEIs), exist under the governance of the state governments; yet, the roles and responsibilities of maintaining standards and quality in higher education fall on the Union. The situation is further accentuated with interstate disparities in fiscal capacities and space. It is the context of vertical (Union-states) as well as horizontal (among states) imbalances of powers and functions as well as imbalances in access to financial resources, that characterizes the dynamics of Indian federal polity and higher education.

The Indian higher education landscape has experienced massive increase in the number of HEIs since independence (see Chapter 1, Introduction). Exercising the constitutional power vested in the Union, Union level institutions – Institutions of National Importance (INIs), Central Universities (CUs) and the like – and some autonomous institutions were established, which were under the purview of the Ministry of Education (MoE, erstwhile Ministry of Human Resource Development, MHRD) and other ministries[2] of the Union government. Apart from the INIs and the CUs, the Union government was also bestowed with powers under Section 3 of the University Grants Commission (UGC) Act to notify an institution as deemed-to-be university (DU) on the advice of the UGC. This allowed the declaration of institutions established under the purview of the states to come under the purview of the Union.

Under the purview of the States, the state universities are established. Apart from this, the, universities also affiliate constituent colleges which are maintained by the universities themselves. Some of these colleges have acquired the status of 'autonomous college' under the UGC scheme of autonomous colleges.[3] Apart from state universities and affiliated institutions, there are few HEIs established under the state legislature act. For example, Sanjay Gandhi Postgraduate Institute of Medical Sciences (SGPGIMS) is a medical institute under State Legislature Act of Uttar Pradesh. Similarly, Nizam's Institute of Medical Sciences (NIMS) is an institute under State Legislature Act in the city of Hyderabad, in the state of Telangana.

One of the features of the Indian higher education landscape is the recent rise in the establishment of state private universities (SPUs). The total number of SPUs has gone up from 42 in 2009 to 304 in 2018–19 (MoE 2019). Apart from these HEIs, there are several, so-called stand-alone institutions which come under the purview of regulatory bodies like the All India Council for Technical Education (AICTE); these HEIs have the authority to award diplomas. All in all, the Indian higher education system emerges to be a complex federal-type higher education system (Froumin and Leshukov 2018). That is, the higher education system comprises several levels of governance and thereby have HEIs under different governmental levels.

---

[2] Some HEIs are under the administrative control of Ministry of Shipping, Ministry of External Affairs, Ministry of Agriculture, Ministry of Sports, Ministry of Textiles and Ministry of Chemicals & Fertilizers. For instance, National Institute of Fashion Technology (NIFT) is under the Ministry of Textiles; seven National Institutes of Pharmaceutical Education and Research (NIPERs) under the Department of Pharmaceuticals, Ministry of Chemicals and Fertilizers; Rajiv Gandhi National Institute of Youth Development, Sriperumbudur, under the Ministry of Youth Affairs & Sports; Rajiv Gandhi Institute of Petroleum Technology, Raibareli, under the Ministry of Petroleum & Natural Gas; and Indian Institute of Engineering Science & Technology, Shibpur, West Bengal, formerly under the state government of West Bengal.
[3] https://www.ugc.ac.in/pdfnews/5353052_Scheme-of-autonomous-colleges.pdf

3. Dynamics of Indian Federalism and Higher Education in India

Although the Constitution of India distributes powers and functions between the Union and the states, over time, the political and economic factors and legal discourse have gained importance, which has shaped the dynamics of Indian federalism. In the post-independence era, the framers of the Constitution of India felt the importance of ensuring national integration and promoting the idea of unity in diversity; this led to the formation of a Union-heavy, federal structure (Austin 1999). With the establishment of the extra-constitutional body, namely, the planning commission, with the prime minister as its chairman, the Union government ensured its control over expenditure of the state governments (Tilak 1989). This was made possible by making it mandatory for the states to get their socioeconomic development plans – and, consequently, expenditure requirements – approved by the Planning Commission. The Union-heavy federal structure was further supported by the stable political reign of a single national party not only at the Union but also at all state levels. However, this began to change since the late 1960s with the emergence of regional parties on the political landscape of the country. This era, therefore, marked the beginning of conflict negotiation between the Union and the states over power and resources (Rao and Singh 2001).

After 1991, the Union adopted a 'sound financed paradigm' by aiming to keep fiscal deficit within limits by discouraging fiscal profligacy (Chakraborty and Gupta 2016). States were then directed to control their state fiscal deficits with an acceleration in the curtailment of flow of funds from the Union to the states, shrinking the fiscal capacities of the state governments. In the limited fiscal space, the post-reforms era is, therefore, characterized by competition among the states for not only central resources but also resources from the private sector (Chakraborty and Gupta 2016). Quite recently, with the scrapping of the planning commission and the establishment of the NITI Aayog, there has been an emphasis on economic efficiency through decentralization to promote cooperative *and* competitive federalism (GoI 2020d).[4] The evolving dynamics of Union-state relations exerts a particular influence over the higher education sector.

---

[4] Another important policy reform is the introduction of the Goods and Services Tax (GST) which aims to transform India into a common market, in line with the common market of the European Union (CGST Act) (GoI 2017a). The GST will subsume all indirect taxes levied by the Union and the states by creating a single tax. States get a share from the centre's collection of GST. It is argued that this arrangement has denied the states to exercise autonomy over a significant amount of tax collection by the states on their own.

4. Union-Heavy Regulatory Structure in Higher Education

Exercising the power vested with the Union under the Entry 66 of the Union List, the UGC was set up in 1956 with the larger objective of promotion and coordination of university education and for the determination and maintenance of standards of teaching, examination and research universities. It is noteworthy that UGC is an exclusive statutory body meant for the Union to discharge its power under Entry 66. The need for coordinated educational experience was felt in the pre-independence era (Tilak 1989). The establishment of the Central Advisory Board of Education (CABE) in 1920 and its revival in 1935 can be attributed to this cause. Similarly, on the recommendation of the Lytton Committee, an all India university body called the Inter-University Board was established in 1924 (Austin 1999). However, a university grants body in the line of the British University Grants Committee was recommended by the Sargent Commission in 1943 (Tilak 1989). While in 1945, the UGC was appointed, it was in 1952 that the government of India resolved to establish the UGC. The UGC Act was passed in 1956. Since then, the UGC, the MoE, the government of India and its various ministries have established a number of councils and regulatory bodies to achieve its aforementioned larger objectives.

In the case of *Yashpal Sharma and Others v. the State of Chhattisgarh*, Professor Yashpal, as a petitioner, contested that all colleges instituted by the Chhattisgarh state under the Private Universities Act of 2002 ignored guidelines and regulations of the UGC resulting in the establishment of universities of pathetic quality. The state of Chhattisgarh argued that the act was well within the legislative competence as per Entry 32 of List II of the Seventh Schedule dealing with incorporation of universities. The court agreed with the petitioner and declared the act unconstitutional. The court discussed the meaning of 'universities' and significance of 'a degree' to argue that the state lacked legislative competence to do justice to the conception of university and what a degree stands for. Kapur and Khosla (2017) pointed out that the actual reasons could have been possibly that the impugned act suffered from excessive delegation (Kapur and Khosla 2017: 228–9), and the state hence acted against the objective of centre's act, that is, to maintain quality standards. The reconciliation between Entry 32 of List II and Entry 66 of List I (dealing with the coordination of standards) was achieved by arguing that the Parliament would lay down standards of education while a state may be allowed to establish a university (Kapur and Khosla 2017). Kapur and Khosla (2017) argued that the Supreme Court could have asked the state to be careful while enacting legislation. The court was actually dealing with private universities and to what extent the UGC would have control over the private universities remains debatable.

The higher education regulatory regime has emerged as a conundrum with overlapping mandates across regulatory bodies adopting a top-down approach to the formulation and implementation of policies and schemes. The problem gets aggravated by the unavailability of efficient state level bodies to coordinate between the Union and the states and the ineffectiveness of the existing body like the state higher education council (SHEC)[5].

5. Union-State Financial Relations and Higher Education

Funding Responsibilities

The governance and financing of higher education in India is the joint responsibility of both the Union and the states as higher education is in the Concurrent List of the Indian Constitution. However, as a matter of fact, in the year 2018–19, close to 17.5 per cent of the universities are centrally funded and nearly 53 per cent universities are funded by various state governments (MoE 2019). The remaining 29.5 per cent of the universities fall under the governance of the state governments, funded by the private sector. Around 77.76 per cent of the colleges are funded by the private sector (including private colleges receiving aid from the state governments mostly). The remaining 22.24 per cent of the colleges are funded by the public sector, again, mostly by the state governments (MoE 2019). When it comes to the enrolment, out of the total enrolment in the public sector-funded HEIs, only 6 per cent are enrolled in the centrally funded HEIs, and the remaining 94 per cent are in the state-funded institutions (MoE 2019). However, it is the Union that has been assigned the important task of coordinating and maintaining standards in higher education with overriding powers over the states.[6] Further, education policy is conceptualized and formulated at the level of the Union.

---

[5] SHECs were recommended by an act of National Policy on Education (NPE), 1986, primarily for state-level planning and coordination of higher education.

[6] This was made evident in the outcome of *Yashpal Sharma and Others v. the State of Chhattisgarh*, when the Supreme Court of India declared a number of private institutions established in the state without the approval of the UGC in the state of Chhattisgarh as null and void, and ultra vires were ordered to be closed down.

Coming to the apex funds granting agency in higher education, namely, the UGC, it can fund only those colleges which are eligible under Sections 12(B) and 12(f) of the UGC Act of 1956 (UGC Act 1956). Broadly, eligibility is measured by having proper infrastructure in place. This excluded 33 per cent of universities and 51 per cent of the colleges in 2012–13 from funding (MoE 2013). This effectively meant that the colleges which were in poor shape could not avail themselves of UGC funding to pull themselves up. This led to further worsening of the disparities in the quality of infrastructure that exist in the colleges. Moreover, majority of the UGC grants goes to CUs while a significant number of the state-level HEIs remain in dire need of funds. If we look at the UGC grants (both revenue and capital expenditure) in the year 2018–19, only 5.76 per cent goes to the state universities and colleges (GoI 2019a: 33).

Yet, when it comes to financing of higher education, in 2013–14, out of total public expenditure on higher education (general and technical), only 39.78 per cent was borne by the Union and 60.22 per cent was borne by the states. Over the last few years, the share of state government expenditure on higher education has gone up. In 2016–17, the share of state expenditure on higher education was 64.40 per cent, and it increased to 65.43 per cent in 2017–18 (Figure 5.1).

This is not a surprising fact as a significant portion of the higher education in India, both in terms of number of HEIs and enrolment, falls under the governance of state governments. Thereby, a lion's share of public expenditure on higher education is bound to be borne by the state governments.

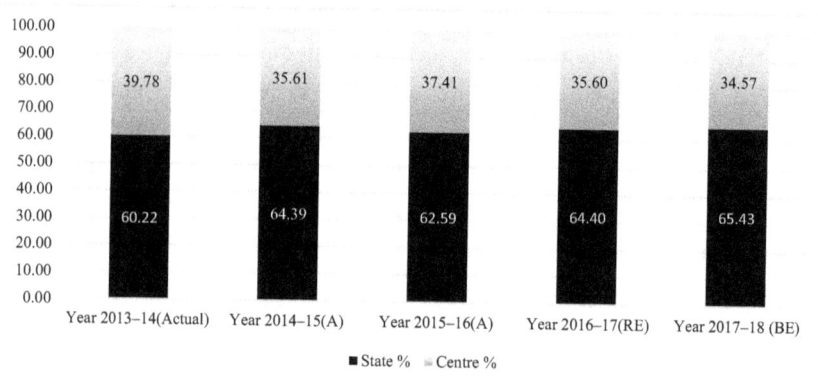

Figure 5.1 Share of union and states/union territories' expenditure in the total expenditure on higher education (general and technical education, revenue account) between 2013–14 and 2017–18.

Source: Authors, based on an analysis of Budget, MoE, GoI, various years.

Interstate Disparities in Fiscal Capacities

While it is clear that states bear a significant portion of public expenditure on higher education in India vis-à-vis the Union, it is noteworthy that not all the states are on equal footing when it comes to their fiscal capacity and space.

On the basis of the existing information, we calculated average indicators for fiscal capacities of the states and educational indicators for the year 2017–18 (Table 5.1). For fiscal capacities of the states, we looked at net state domestic product (NSDP) per capita, the revenue deficit to gross state domestic product ratio (RD/GSDP) and the gross fiscal deficit to the gross state domestic product ratios (GFD/GSDP). To get the actual figures of these indicators, we relied on the data from the *State Finances: A Study of Budget 2019-20* from the Reserve Bank of India (RBI 2019).

For state-wise expenditure on higher education, we looked at the *Analysis of Budgeted Expenditure on Education 2018-19* from the MoE (2018). It is noteworthy that all the expenditure on higher higher education is incurred by the Department of Higher Education in the respective states. For educational indicators, we calculated the average gross enrolment ratio (GER) and average number of PHEIs. For educational indicators, we relied on *All India Survey of Higher Education, 2018-19* from the MoE. We calculated the average fiscal as well as educational indicators across three categories of states: high-income states; low-income states; and northeast (NE) states and the hilly states. The NE states and the hilly states are treated separately because of their terrain and remoteness. It is to be stated that we did not calculate these values for union territories (UTs) to avoid anomalies. The findings of these calculations are presented in the Tables 5.1 and 5.2. Table 5.1 represents state-wise comparison of GER and PHEIs in 2017–18 and Table 5.2 represents state-wise comparison of deficit indicators and budget allocation for higher education.

The average GER of high-income states is 31.2 in 2017–18 whereas the average GER of low-income states is only 21.2. The NE states and hilly states have an average GER of 26.9. Certainly, low incomes states have low average GER values than the high-income states. One also observes the prevalence of PHEIs in the high-income states vis-à-vis the NE states and the hilly states. The rich states have an average of 2085 PHEIs whereas the low-income states have an average of 877 PHEIs.[7] The NE states and the hilly states have only fifty-six PHEIs. Clearly,

---

[7] A meaningful comparison would require some indicators for the sizes of states' higher education sector or state population.

Table 5.1 State-Wise Comparison of Net State Domestic Product Per Capita, Gross Enrolment Ratio and Private Higher Education Institutions, 2017–18

States	NSDP per capita 2017–18	GER 2017–18	Private higher education institutions			
			Private university	Private college	Private aided	Total PHEIs
High-income states						
Goa	321289	28.0	0	10	23	33
Haryana	159892	28.7	21	641	115	777
Uttar Pradesh	147204	25.9	34	5160	650	5844
Karnataka	143827	27.8	25	2431	445	2901
Gujarat	142068	20.1	33	1380	500	1913
Maharashtra	140724	31.1	18	2463	978	3459
Kerala	138368	36.2	1	842	203	1046
Tamil Nadu	133029	48.6	28	1883	250	2161
Telangana	132293	35.7	0	1571	114	1685
Punjab	110802	30.3	16	643	180	839
Andhra Pradesh	103214	30.9	5	2105	165	2275
Average	**152066**	**31.2**				**2085**
Low-income states						
Rajasthan	74441	21.7	51	2027	189	2267
Odisha	72760	22.0	5	281	421	707
Chhattisgarh	66122	18.4	8	322	70	400
West Bengal	64007	18.7	10	603	249	862
Madhya Pradesh	54264	21.2	22	1236	210	1468
Jharkhand	52277	18.0	9	129	26	164
Bihar	26699	13.0	1	186	86	273
Average	**58653**	**19.0**				**877**
Northeast states and hilly states						
Sikkim	232483	37.4	5	5	1	11
Mizoram	106537	22.9	1	2	0	3
Arunachal Pradesh	90727	29.7	6	11	1	18
Tripura	76358	21.2	1	6	2	9
Nagaland	68456	17.8	3	10	35	48
Meghalaya	61789	24.7	6	14	15	35
Assam	57835	18.2	5	60	13	78
Manipur	51211	31.8	0	28	13	41
Himachal Pradesh	130644	37.9	17	131	20	168
Jammu & Kashmir	62984	27.7	0	129	22	151
Uttarakhand	42798	36.3	17	192	62	271
Average	**93902**	**27.0**				**56**

Source: Authors, derived from *All India Survey on Higher Education* (MoE 2018) and Central Statistical Organisation.

Table 5.2 State-Wise Comparison of Deficit Indicators and Budget Allocation for Higher Education, 2017–18 (Budget Estimate)

States	Revenue deficit/ gross state domestic product (2017–18)	Gross fiscal deficit/ gross state domestic product (2017–18)	Total capital expenditure on education/ Total expenditure on education (revenue +capital) (2017–18 budgetary estimate (BE)	Total capital expenditure on university and higher education and technical education/ Total capital expenditure (2017–18 BE)	Total revenue expenditure on university and higher education and technical education/ Total revenue expenditure (2017–18 BE)
High-income states					
Goa	−0.7	2.30	7.70	54.37	24.22
Haryana	1.7	3.10	3.97	69.31	14.92
Uttar Pradesh	−0.9	2.00	1.89	44.18	5.34
Karnataka	−0.3	2.30	5.10	22.92	17.25
Gujarat	−0.4	1.60	4.81	24.06	13.57
Maharashtra	−0.1	1.00	0.31	51.99	77.88
Kerala	2.4	3.80	1.47	45.48	23.66
Tamil Nadu	1.5	2.70	1.89	90.26	10.74
Telangana	−0.5	3.50	1.52	52.20	22.29
Punjab	2.0	2.60	3.22	20.93	7.06
Andhra Pradesh	2.0	4.00	2.34	69.82	15.26
Average	0.6	2.63	3.11	49.59	21.11
Low-income states					
Rajasthan	2.20	3.00	1.45	27.05	6.13
Odisha	−3.10	2.10	2.84	74.33	16.97
Chhattisgarh	−1.20	2.40	7.49	30.29	8.26
West Bengal	1.00	2.90	2.53	10.49	21.02
Madhya Pradesh	−0.60	3.10	5.14	49.40	12.00
Jharkhand	−0.70	4.30	4.71	88.12	21.05
Bihar	−3.10	3.00	7.22	87.88	27.74
Average	−0.79	2.97	4.48	52.51	16.17
Northeast states and hilly states					
Sikkim	−4.50	2.00	3.33	51.34	5.90
Mizoram	−9.60	1.80	2.04	0.00	16.51
Arunachal Pradesh	−13.00	1.40	7.96	73.84	25.78
Tripura	0.60	4.50	1.09	24.95	7.15

States	Revenue deficit/ gross state domestic product (2017–18)	Gross fiscal deficit/ gross state domestic product (2017–18)	Total capital expenditure on education/ Total expenditure on education (revenue +capital) (2017–18 budgetary estimate (BE)	Total capital expenditure on university and higher education and technical education/ Total capital expenditure (2017–18 BE)	Total revenue expenditure on university and higher education and technical education/ Total revenue expenditure (2017–18 BE)
Nagaland	2.00	2.60	3.22	20.93	7.06
Meghalaya	−2.80	0.50	1.20	64.57	15.67
Assam	0.50	3.20	1.33	44.12	16.17
Manipur	−4.50	1.40	2.84	11.20	30.18
Himachal Pradesh	−0.20	2.80	3.85	64.53	9.53
Jammu & Kashmir	−5.50	2.00	11.13	41.17	18.08
Uttarakhand	0.90	3.70	1.41	50.87	8.32
Average	−3.70	2.22	3.80	39.67	15.20

Source: Authors, using data from RBI (2019) and MoE (2018).

private sector in higher education is dominant in the high-income and non-NE states and non-hilly states.

When it comes to the fiscal capacities of the states, the average GFD/GSDP of the high-income states is 2.6 whereas the average GFD/GSDP for low-income states is 3.1. Given the geographical location of NE states and the hilly states, the average GFD/GSDP is 2.2. The high average GFD/GSDP for low-income states vis-à-vis the high-income states is possibly because of low revenue base compared to the developmental needs in the low-income states. However, the average GFD/GSDP is the lowest for the NE states and the hilly states because these states are treated differently in terms of central grants. The average RD/GSDP values which is indicative of the extent of the government borrowing being used for revenue or committed expenditure in the concerned fiscal year is the lowest for the NE states and the hilly states. In fact, the average RD/GSDP is -3.7, which indicates a surplus on the budget of these states. The average RD/GSDP is higher for high-income states (0.6) than for low-income states (-0.8), which are in surplus.

Coming to the state-wise expenditure on higher education, it is clear that, on an average, the revenue expenditure on higher education (university as well as technical education) as a percentage of total revenue expenditure on higher education of high-income states (21.1) is more than that of the low-income states (16.2) as well as NE states and the hilly states (15.2). However, when it comes to the average capital expenditure on higher education as a percentage of total capital expenditure on education, low-income states (52.5) spend slightly more than the high-income states (49.6). Yet, average capital expenditure as percentage of total expenditure on higher education remains low across all states. Average capital expenditure as percentage of total expenditure on higher education is 3.1 in high-income states, 4.5 in low-income states and 3.8 in NE states and hilly states. This indicates limited resources are available for expansion of the facilities in higher education.

Because of the decision to expand the higher education by setting up new institutions to meet the rising demands in the low-income states, the extent of capital expenditure is slightly lower than that of the high-income states. Interestingly, average capital expenditure on technical education as a percentage of total capital expenditure is highest in the low-income states (37.5), followed by the NE states and the hilly states (27.1), and it is the lowest in the high-income states (24.7).

With the implementation of the new economic policy and emphasis on curbing the fiscal deficit of both the Union and the states, the states have found it difficult to spend adequately on higher education. The growth in the state expenditure on higher education has been slow (MoE 2018). The inability of the states to spend more is further evident if one looks at the composition of the expenditure. The states spend mostly on operational- and maintenance-related items to the extent of nearly 80 per cent and spend only 10–15 per cent on capital expenses which contribute to the expansion (MoE 2018). Owing to the lack of capital expenditure on higher education, the state-level HEIs have focused on augmenting and generating resources through privatization and commercialization (Prakash 2007). The states have focused more on giving affiliations to the new colleges, raising fees and opening of self-financing colleges, which led to the rising cost of education coupled with a deterioration in the quality (Prakash 2007). This was compounded by the issue of separation of teaching and research in higher education in India. University administration came under tremendous pressure to administer the ever-increasing number of affiliated colleges. This led to the complete loss of autonomy of the colleges to design curriculum as well as experiment and innovate with teaching-learning methods and research. Dynamism of the sector was badly missing and therefore quality suffered. The orientation was more towards granting degrees in most of the state level HEIs. It is noteworthy that a large number of HEIs under the governance of the state governments are ultimately financed by the private sector. Wide differences in the fiscal situation in the states compounding the problem of disparities in budgetary allocations by the state government paved the way for a de facto privatization.

6. Empowering the States?

Regulatory Interventions: States Approving Private Higher Education Institutions

Approximately 75 per cent HEIs in India are either completely or partially financed and/or managed by the private sector. It is noteworthy that while PHEIs exist all over the country, they are particularly dominant in the richly endowed states/UTs (here defined in terms of states and UTs with high GSDP per capita). It is noteworthy that while the internal governance of PHEIs is under the aegis of the institutional leadership and governance body, the external governance of the institution is carried out by the state/UT governmental bodies. Hence, it can be argued that while state HEIs enrol a significant number of students and have a larger proportion of HEIs, it is the PHEIs that are a characterizing feature of state-level higher education.

As private sector comes to dominate the state higher educational landscape, a noteworthy feature of PHEI at the state level is the rise of SPUs in India. An SPU is established by the concerned state legislature; however, it should abide by the standards set by the regulatory bodies at the Union level. The predominance of PHEIs have grave implications for quality as well as equity in higher education (Tilak 2018).

So far, the two-fold inherent imbalances in the Union-state relations pertaining to the rules and regulations as well as functions and financing of higher education in India have been discussed. First, it has been established that there exists a vertical imbalance between Union and the states/UTs leading to a power struggle between them over power and resources. Second, horizontal imbalances which exist among the states lead to a competitive tussle for mobilizing resources for investment not only from the Union but also from the private sector. The predominance of PHEIs have implications on quality as well as equity in higher education. The government of India recently adopted a policy initiative – RUSA – to address these imbalances in Union-state relations in higher education. The next section discusses the nature of the initiative, its ontological assumptions and the need to address the real challenges of quality and equity in higher education which are arising because of the asymmetrical power positioning of the Union vis-à-vis the states and of the richer states vis-à-vis the poorer states.

Channelling Funds through the National Higher Education Mission

In order to address the imbalances emerging from inefficient allocation of central funds to the state-level institutions and to tackle the interstate disparities, the MoE adopted the National Higher Education Mission, also known as RUSA, in 2014. It is a higher education scheme sponsored by the central sector which is funded by both the MoE and the state governments. It aims at providing strategic funding to eligible state HEIs through the state governments and state-level autonomous bodies, namely the SHECs. The central funding is in the ratio of 65:35 for general category states and 90:10 for special category states. The funding would be norm based and outcome dependent.

The RUSA committed to spend a total sum of INR 32,460 crore on higher education in two phases in the period from 2012–13 to 2017–18 (phase I) and then from 2018–19 to 2019–20 (phase II). The Union committed to spend 72 per cent of the total funds and the rest 28 per cent was expected to be spent by the various state governments. As on 2020–1, a total of INR 7449.4 crore[8] (3690.98 million USD PPP) was allocated by the Union government. This is to say that only 32 per cent of the total funds committed by the Union is actually allocated for higher education during the period of the scheme. To make matters worse, only a fraction of the funds allocated to the HEIs are actually disbursed. Clearly, the technocratic-managerialist solution based on performance, efficiency and accountability did not help in improving the Union-state financial relations in higher education. But why? The issue is that the 'sound financial paradigm' is based on a conceptualization that efficiency of resources utilization is an overarching guiding force of any governmental allocation and disbursement of funds in higher education. Thereby, fiscal compression and curtailing fiscal deficit become matters of primary concern rather than investigating, acknowledging and addressing the real fiscal and developmental constraints faced by the Union and the state governments. To develop a ten-year perspective plan, annual plan and budgets are to be prepared for implementation in a phased manner. While

---

[8] One crore equals 10 million.

the centre-state ratio in funding is 90:10 for NE, Himachal Pradesh, Jammu and Kashmir, Sikkim and Uttarakhand, for the rest the ratio is at 65:35. Institutional plans are to be incorporated in the SHEC's plan and a consolidated plan is be prepared which would include public- and the private-funded HEIs. This would help overcome the inadequacy of budgetary allocations by the states.

The small disbursement under the RUSA scheme is often attributed to the unwillingness of the states to readily understand, adopt and respond to the Union's vision. The shift from block grants to strategic funding under the RUSA would entail a technocratic-managerial fiscal federalism. Under the RUSA, after receiving approval from the Parliamentary Approval Board (PAB), state universities are provided direct funding from the Union through the SHECs (non-existent in many states, even now). The states are asked to develop their state higher education plan by assessing their past performance, evaluating their current status and estimating projections of their future targets based on a given set of parameters, which includes enrolment, gender parity, accreditation and student-teacher ratio. On need-cum-performance basis, the PAB sanctions funds relying on the basis of a given fund equalization formula (MHRD 2013).

We hypothesize that, despite due emphasis placed on fiscal needs, RUSA funding might be regressive. In other words, richer states may get more funding vis-à-vis the poorer states. It was our assumption that the presence of SHECs must have enabled the eight states to get more funds as compared to the states with no SHECs. On the contrary, the states without SHECs have received more (assuming that the sanctioned amount has actually been disbursed as states could keep aside their shares) (Table 5.3). A deeper investigation is needed as to why SHECs do not count or have no impact. Which are the states that have SHECs? How healthy are these states? In our analysis, we have excluded Delhi and UTs as well as seven out of eight NE states. However, we have included Assam, as this NE state is large, both geographically and in terms of income. The reason for excluding other NE states from our analysis is because they fall under special category states owing to their hilly terrain and location; another reason was to ensure representativeness of the all categories (high-income, low-income as well as NE states and hilly states).

As mentioned earlier, the high-income states have high GER and a larger presence of private institutions (measured in terms of population). Fiscal health is better for high per capita income (PCI) states, but low PCI states spend more on university education.

We wanted to see whether the high-income states gain more in terms of RUSA grants. We had adopted two measures of sanctions: (1) grants sanctioned as a

Table 5.3 A Comparison between States with and without State Higher Education Councils

Indicators	States with SHEC	States w/o SHEC
Per capita income (2014–15)	109687	99572
Total RUSA funds sanction as a percentage of total government expenditure on higher education[a]	0.0016	0.0028
Total RUSA funds sanction per capita eligible student	4.76	12.07
Primary deficit/gross state domestic product (GSDP)	3.050	3.000
Gross Enrolment Ratio (GER) (2014–15), Male	28.600	24.177
GER (2014–15), Female	26.800	23.369
GER (2014–15), Total	27.725	23.831
Expenditure on higher education (university/scholarship) (as a percentage of GSDP)	0.330	0.493
Expenditure on technical education (as a percentage of GSDP)	0.104	0.084
Expenditure on higher education (total) (as a percentage of GSDP)	0.434	0.577
Number of PHEIs per 1 lakh of eligible population	2047	1296

[a] RUSA funds allocated till the 10th Project Approval Meeting of RUSA in 2016.

Note: The states with SHECs are Andhra Pradesh, Gujarat, Karnataka, Kerala, Maharashtra, Tamil Nadu, Uttar Pradesh and West Bengal. 1 lakh = 0.1 million.

Source: Authors, based on *Handbook of Statistics for the Indian Economy*, MHRD (2014–15), Analysis of Budget Expenditure 2018–19, and MoE, GoI and RUSA websites; GoI 2019a.

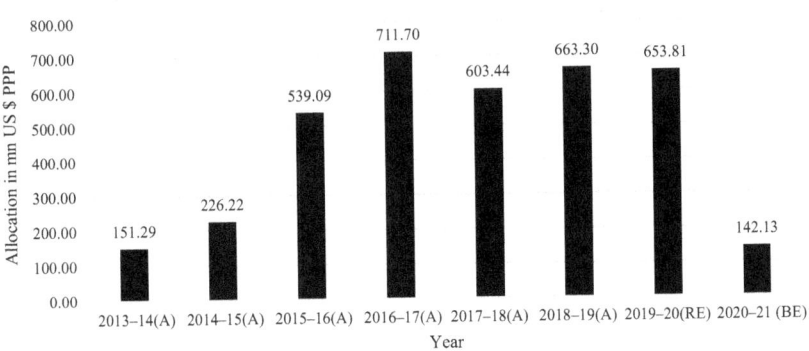

Figure 5.2 Central government allocation on National Higher Education Mission (RUSA) (in million USD Purchasing Power Parity).
Source: Authors, based on Union Budget of India, various years.

Table 5.4 A Comparison of High and Low Per Capita Income States and National Higher Education Mission (RUSA) Funds Allocation

Indicators	High PCI states	Low PCI states
Average per capita income (2014–15)	141085	61999
Total RUSA funds sanctioned as a percentage of total government expenditure on higher education	0.0022	0.0025
Total RUSA funds sanctioned per capita eligible student	10.82	7.60
Primary deficit/GSDP	2.67	3.40
GER (2014–15), Male	30.05	21.26
GER (2014–15), Female	30.14	18.67
GER (2014–15), Total	30.16	19.98
Expenditure on higher education (university/scholarship) (as a percentage of GSDP)	0.31	0.57
Expenditure on technical education (as a percentage of GSDP)	0.11	0.07
Expenditure on higher education (total) (as a percentage of GSDP)	0.42	0.64
Number of PHEIs per 1 lakh of eligible population	2094	1019

Source: Authors, based on *Handbook of Statistics for the Indian Economy*, MHRD (2014–15), analysis of budget expenditure 2018–19, and MoE, GoI and RUSA websites; GoI (2019a).

percentage of state government expenditure on higher education, and (2) RUSA sanction grants per student in the age cohort of eighteen to twenty-three years. High PCI states get more RUSA grants compared to the low PCI states on a per capita basis and not in terms of government expenditure on higher education as a whole (Table 5.4). Thus, RUSA emerged to be inadequate if not a complete failure. The issues that follow, in particular, can be flagged.

Setting up State Higher Education Councils

The Constitution of India gives exclusive powers to the Union to make laws for coordination and determination of standards in institutions for higher education or research and scientific and technical institutions. Thus, although education comes under the Concurrent List, it is the Union that determines the standard of HEIs. The Union has established the UGC as a statutory body for coordination and implementation of university education. Therefore, states cannot set up universities without UGC's approval. This was made evident in the case *Yashpal Sharma and Others v. the State of Chhattisgarh*, when the Supreme Court of India declared a number of private institutions opened in the state of Chhattisgarh as ultra vires and were ordered to be shut down. It seems, in the absence of any state level regulatory body, the state governments tend to use their power to make laws on education which are in accordance with their vested interests.

Most of the educational reforms and policies, especially, concerning the quality of higher education is ushered in a top-down fashion. The Department of Higher Education at the state level, therefore, faces a binding constraint set by the Union. It acts as the intermediary between the regulatory bodies at the Union including the MoE and the state-level HEIs. It is busy with complying with the rules rather than implementing reforms in a meaningful manner. SHECs have not been established in every state and have proven to be advisory bodies with little or no influence.

Concerns Regarding the Functioning of the State Higher Education Councils

At one level, the expansion of the higher education sector should have been well coordinated with strict enforcement of standards to ensure quality between the Union and the states. But the underlying disparities in the fiscal situation of the Union and the states during the last two decades, rapid privatization in some states and the differences in the underlying socioeconomic conditions across the states have led to an uncoordinated and virtually unregulated expansion. This has resulted in a serious compromise with respect to quality and confusion which exemplifies how much ground work and negotiation is still required in a federal state to arrive at some consensus and to ensure uniformity in educational standards as well as conformity and congruity between the states and the Union – by balancing the interests of the states having varying needs with the Union's legitimate and justified concerns on the standard of higher education quality.

This confusing state of affairs regarding regulation and funding with respect to the individual roles of the centre and the states is partly structural and is partly an outcome of faulty design. Absence of any clear demarcation in the role of SHECs vis-à-vis the states as well as the Union when it comes to regulation, planning, accreditation, academic matters and funding for expansion has sent misleading and confusing signals to the governments and the academia. Although the idea to give more powers to the states would help them deal with the local level challenges, at the same time, this very autonomy would result in varying standards and practices – an outcome which is also not desirable at one level. Keeping that in mind, a clear understanding of the respective jurisdictions of the Union and the states is the need of the hour.

However, the Union has expressed its desire to ensure coordination in planning, regulation and funding of the higher education system between the Union and the states. This is evident from the Union's decision to set up the SHECs based on the recommendation of the National Policy of Education in 1986, in view of the Constitutional Amendment in 1976 which included education in the Concurrent List of the Indian Constitution. This became necessary as states are required to have a much larger share – in terms of both the number of institutes and enrolment – when compared to that of the Union. The Programme of Action (PoA) plan based on the modification of the National Policy on Education (NPE) in 1992 pointed out that the SHECs were supposed to develop plans and programmes for the expansion and revitalization of the HEIs, decide on the courses and curriculum as well as respond to the local needs. These plans are supposed to be consolidated by the UGC and to be implemented under their supervision. Based on the NPE guidelines, it was decided that the SHECs will be constituted as statutory bodies that are far removed from the arms of the state governments so as to avoid interference. Unfortunately, so far only eight or nine states have set up SHECs, which is not a good sign. Also, it can be noted that only the developed states have set up these councils, which is a matter for worry as SHECs are no less important for the low-income states.

The National Higher Education Mission seeks to reiterate the role of SHECs to rejuvenate the dialogue between the Union and the states, but its performance so far has been far from satisfactory. RUSA makes it mandatory for the states to constitute SHECs to channelize funds from the Union to the states. States are visualized as the partners, and there should evolve a transparent mechanism to devolve funds. However, several issues emerged (Anandakrishnan 2016):

1. There was a lack of clarity regarding the flow of funds and confusion regarding the positional hierarchy between SHECs and the state governments and with respect to other funding agencies and decision-making bodies.
2. The SHECs are supposed to be independent bodies as per the guideline. But in practice the state governments may not want it to be so. It is indeed very difficult for the state governments to retain power, exercise discretion in appointments of faculty and the vice chancellor, and take decisions on various other academic matters.

3. The SHECs are not adequately empowered to execute their decisions due to want of expertise and resources.
4. The SHECs had limited freedom in taking decision in academic matters.
5. The distinction between regulation and decision-making power has often led to confusion about the jobs SHECs are supposed to be carrying out.

7. Conclusion

Governance of the higher education sector as a whole and at the institutional level faces challenges in a federal system because of the differences in the vertical and horizontal imbalances, as pointed in this chapter, in addition to other issues specific to the higher education sector. While it is most desirable that the governance and financing of higher education in India is the joint responsibility of both the Union and the states as higher education is on the Concurrent List of the Indian Constitution, the associated challenges affect the functioning and the delivery of the system. Although one of the characterizing features of Indian federalism in the context of higher education sector is that it is regulated by the Union, functional responsibilities, including financing of a large part of higher education, ultimately fall on the state governments.

By invoking secondary data, the chapter highlighted how the state governments vis-à-vis the Union defrayed a greater share of public expenditure on higher education. It was observed that the states spend mostly on operational- and maintenance-related items to the extent of nearly 80 per cent and only 10–15 per cent on capital expenses towards expansion (MoE 2015). There were several disparities in fiscal capacities as well as the educational outcome indicators such as the GER among the states/UTs. However, this does not mean that the richer states (with high GSDP per capita), invariably, spent more on higher education than the poorer states (with low GSDP per capita). When it comes to the outcome indicators in higher education such as GER, the richer states emerged to perform better than the poorer states. This is despite the relatively low state government expenditure on higher education. The apparent paradox can be explained by studying the intensity of private sector participation in higher education in the richer states/UTs vis-à-vis the poorer states/UTs. By capitalizing on the purchasing power capacity of the households in the richer states, the PHEIs dominate the higher education landscape of the richer states by substituting and augmenting state government expenditure. The predominance of PHEIs have implications on quality as well as equity in higher education (Tilak

2018). While the Union is patting its back on ushering in new age reforms in higher education in conformation to the rise of performativity ideals in higher education policymaking, it has paid scant attention to understand, organically, the ground level challenges and opportunities faced by majority of the state-level institutions (Srivastava and Koshal 2018). Resource-crunched state-level institutions are even incapable of complying with the National Assessment and Accreditation Council (NAAC) procedure and are beyond the coverage of the National Institutional Ranking Framework (NIRF).[9] The situation becomes worse when funding is attached to these performance indicators.

The RUSA, one of the recent policy moves of the Union government to rectify the vertical (Union-states) as well as horizontal (among states) imbalances in Union state financial relations in higher education, is inadequate. This is to say that only 32 per cent of the total funds committed by the Union is actually allocated for higher education since the scheme's inception. To make matters worse, only a fraction of the funds allocated to the HEIs are actually disbursed. Clearly, the technocratic-managerialist solution based on performance, efficiency and accountability did not help in improving the Union-state financial relations in higher education.

---

[9] As NIRF considers only top 100 institutions across various categories.

6

Changing Contours of Regulation in Indian Higher Education

Saumen Chattopadhyay and Emon Nandi

1. Introduction

The efficacy and mode of regulatory interventions have remained the most debatable area in Indian higher education policymaking. It was only to be expected that regulation would be unwieldy and unmanageable in a federal country with twenty-nine states and eight union territories with growing private participation and poor university governance. In view of this, the nature and the extent of government intervention poses a daunting challenge for the government as India gears up to address development needs of the country in the context of changing landscape of global higher education. The demand for institutional and teacher autonomy and averseness of the private sector towards regulatory interventions in the context of the government's concern to achieve inclusive expansion and excellence has rendered regulation an extremely important area for critical reflection.

This chapter makes an attempt to critically look at the complexities involved in higher education and how the future is shaping up in the context of some significant policies being implemented by the government. We begin with a brief account of the existing regulatory framework in the context of Indian higher education. This is followed by an attempt to identify the major dilemmas and conflicts as policymakers seek to negotiate with critical trade-offs between public and the private, centre and the states and general and professional education. We then take up the discussion of the recent policy measures mooted by some of the important policy initiatives on reforming the regulatory structure of Indian higher education sector. We end with a discussion on the possible implications for the overall higher education sector in India arising out of the proposed regulations on the basis of their purpose, form and impacts.

2. Rationale for Regulation in Higher Education

Regulations have aimed to intervene in primarily two different spheres to achieve the very objectives of higher education, inclusive expansion and quality education and no less importantly to curb and prevent malpractices the education process remains vulnerable to. One is in the realm of the university functioning or what may be called conduct regulation and two, in the higher education sector as a whole primarily to construct a regulated market, albeit a quasi-market (Jongbloed 2004). The purpose of the former intervention refers to the realization of technical efficiency while the latter refers to the attainment of allocation efficiency. The rationale for technical efficiency arises in absence of a well-defined technology or educational production function to convert the human capital embodied in the teachers and the students to university output. This is an imperative because the teachers and the students are essentially self-optimizing agents, as the neoliberals and the mainstream economists claim when they are ideally expected to be intrinsically motivated in their academic pursuits. This self-interestedness may lead to a lack of synchronization between the objectives of teachers and the students and their propensity to indulge in subversive practices involved in teaching-learning and research which is prominently present in the Indian context (Chattopadhyay 2012; Chandra 2017). This forms the basis of new public management (NPM) which seeks to install an audit culture based on accounting of university activities for the purpose of performance assessment.

Market construction is advocated to attain allocative efficiency because regulatory intervention is expected to eliminate market segmentation and allow for the exercise of sovereignty by the students and the institutions to foster competition. For the purpose of achieving excellence, higher education market cannot operate like a typical consumption good market (Marginson 2016). However, a market for education undermines concern for those who are at the margins of the society and those who are meritorious (Chattopadhyay 2009) unless adequate safeguard measures are adopted. Market operates based on selection-based competition (Glennerster 1991), which leads to the convergence of the best of the teachers and students among the best of the universities. This in effect rigidifies the hierarchical order in the higher education sector as evident in university ranking tables.

3. The Regulatory Interventions: Tracing Back, Taking Stock

At present, the two main agencies responsible for regulating this huge sector are the University Grants Commission (UGC) and the All India Council for Technical Education (AICTE) along with other professional councils and the National Assessment and Accreditation Council (NAAC).

The UGC has been discharging two major functions: to provide funds to the higher education institutions (HEIs) and to coordinate, determine and maintain the standards of university education in India. The UGC was established in 1945 with the task of overseeing the work of the three Central Universities (CUs) of Aligarh, Banaras and Delhi on the basis of the recommendations made in the Report of the Central Advisory Board of Education (CABE). In 1948, the University Education Commission under the Chairmanship of Dr S. Radhakrishnan recommended for the reconstitution of the UGC on the basis of the UK model. In 1956, it was formally established as a statutory body of the government of India through an act of Parliament.

The AICTE was initially established in 1945 as a national-level apex advisory body to conduct a survey on the facilities available for technical education and to promote development in the country in a coordinated and integrated manner. Eventually, based on the suggestions made by the National Policy of Education (1986), the AICTE emerged as a statutory authority for planning, formulation and maintenance of norms and standards in technical education with the entrusted tasks of assuring quality through accreditation; providing funding in priority areas; monitoring and evaluating programmes; maintaining parity of certification and awards; and managing the technical education sector in the country.

Apart from these, there are various councils for regulating specific fields of professional education in India. These are as follows: Distance Education Council, Indian Council of Agriculture Research, Bar Council of India, National Council for Teacher Education, Rehabilitation Council of India, Medical Council of India, Pharmacy Council of India, India Nursing Council, Dental Council of India, Central Council of Homeopathy, Central Council of Indian Medicine, Veterinary Council, Council of Architecture. Also, some of the ministries have the power to regulate the specific HEIs.

Among the major quality assurance agencies in India, the NAAC, an autonomous body under the UGC is the most important one. It was established in 1994 following the recommendations of the National Policy of Education (1986) and the Programme of Action (PoA) plan (1992). According to the NAAC, the major role of an HEI is to promote the values inherent in education. These core values as specified for Indian higher education system are as follows: (1) contributing to national development, (2) fostering global competence among students, (3) inculcating a value system among the students, (4) promoting use of technology and (5) quest for excellence.

The National Board of Accreditation (NBA) under the AICTE was established in 1994 to offer accreditation to the programmes in technical institutions which are approved of by the AICTE. Under the provisions of the AICTE Act of 1987, all diploma, degree and postgraduate programmes coming under certain disciplines (engineering and technology, management, architecture, pharmacy, hotel management and catering technology, town and country planning, applied arts and crafts) are covered under accreditation by the NBA.

The regulatory architecture proposed by the National Knowledge Commission (NKC) (GoI 2009) and the Yash Pal Committee (YPC) National Commission of Higher Education and Research (NCHER) had common elements despite differences in their approaches (Ayyar 2016). Both sought to cover the entire higher education sector being oblivious of the fact that the professional bodies had played an important role in maintaining quality and regulating entry of education providers. The Medical Council of India is one such example. However, both NKC and the YPC-NCHER recommended divestment of regulatory functions of the professional councils. The bill introduced by the centre showed a clear tendency towards centralization. The important question is whether a super regulatory body in a federal structure would eventually succeed in making meaningful and efficacious regulatory interventions which require consensus among the states and their active participation. The NKC wanted a single window clearance to facilitate entry whereas the YPC-NCHER wanted the UGC to deal with the entire higher education sector.

Education remained under the sole control of the government with the UGC acting as a regulatory agency. In the beginning, it was much easier for the government to regulate a sector with only a handful of universities run by the government or registered philanthropic trusts often aided by the government. Input-based funding systems were in place, and HEIs used to receive funds depending on the scale, capacity and pre-approved requirements. The HEIs had to abide by the government rules on recruitment policies, course curriculum, fee structure and selection of students. However, at the institutional level, management and governance were left to the discretion of the vice chancellors or the principals.

In the wake of serious concerns regarding the lack of motivation and poor governance in various public HEIs along with the problem of rampant commercialization in private HEIs, the traditional input-based funding of the HEIs by the government has been criticized by many scholars. Agarwal (2006, 2009) argued for a change in the existing funding mechanism and introducing competitive grants to incentivize teachers to perform. He also stressed on the role of ranking and accreditation to make the system more competitive. Kaul (2006) also felt that role of private sector was gaining increasing importance in today's world, and there was no justification for controlling these unaided institutions by imposing the state regulations on them.

With mounting pressure from global forces to open up, eventually the government has shifted its role from a service provider to a regulator and then to a facilitator in the higher education market. Two major challenges emerged for the regulator-cum-facilitator-state. One, to tackle the problem of subversion of norms in low-quality HEIs and to maintain a minimum standard; and two, to promote excellence in the good quality HEIs irrespective of the type of management, public or private. Structural regulations (such as entry, exit, approval) were tightened, while conduct regulations[1] (such as Performance-Based Appraisal System; PBAS) were also introduced.

4. Challenges before the Existing Regulatory System

Regulation of the higher education system is inherently beset with conflicts and trade-offs in view of the underlying diversity of the Indian higher education system in terms of their mandates and emerging challenges. Any regulatory intervention comes at a price as in the process of achieving the stated objective, there lurks in the background a possible compromise with another objective. The regulatory system in Indian higher education is often criticized as corrupt and ineffective in the wake of serious concerns about its inability to check rampant commercialization and deterioration of quality of education. Varghese (2015) argued that the most crucial challenge related to the regulatory reforms

---

[1] These two spheres of interventions find resemblance in Jongbloed (2004). It is divided into three different types: the structure of the market, regulating the process and the administrative regulations.

is centred around the issues of the adequacy and the implementation of the existing regulations in the Indian higher education sector. Varghese and Malik (2016) pointed out that the most crucial question is to decide if more regulations are further needed, or a better implementation of the existing regulations would be a preferable solution. The huge size of the sector; overlapping regulatory spaces between several regulatory agencies; the strained relationship between the centre and the states; increasing growth of private institutions in terms of number and enrolments; balancing between accountability and autonomy; as well as managing local, national and global concerns have complicated the situation. Some of these points are discussed below.

Regulation in a Federal Country

Though education is under the Concurrent List of the Indian Constitution, it is the central government which mainly controls the standard and quality of the regulatory bodies. Tilak (2017) has pointed out that the sharing of responsibility between the Union and the states has always been subject to the 'political power struggles' between the union and the state governments. Almost three-fourths of universities and 90 per cent of undergraduate colleges are in the states, but no proper mechanism of involving the states in policy formulation is visibly clear (Thorat 2016). Tilak (2017) argued that the Union government has assumed the key role of determining policies while the state governments are responsible only for implementing these policies.

Also, governance of higher education in states is under tremendous pressure from local politicians. As a consequence, the states have mainly concentrated on expanding the system without caring much for quality (Carnoy and Dossani 2013). Kulandaiswamy (2005) argued that with this affiliating system and the huge number of undergraduate colleges lacking in adequate infrastructure and qualified faculty members, any measure to make the system more effective would be unsuccessful unless the very structure of this regulatory system is reconstituted. Hatekar (2009) analysed the situation of state universities which are trapped in the vicious cycle of resource crunch, shortage of faculty, bureaucracy and political interference, outdated pedagogic methods and lack of flexibility in allocating resources. The affiliating system has also been inefficient, as pointed out in the National Education Policy 2020 (NEP 2020) (Anandakrishnan 2007; GoI 2020c). Kumar (2013) is extremely critical of the affiliating system for creating a rift between teaching and research, which has in turn created a major structural problem for the Indian higher education system.

Regulating Private Institutions

The conflict between the state and central regulatory authorities has gained a new dimension with the establishment of private universities. But with the proliferation of private universities and private unaided institutions, determining the desirable degree of applicability of the regulations on the private HEIs has become a serious challenge for the regulatory agencies.[2] With the increasing dominance of private unaided institutions, the role of UGC and AICTE in regulating the higher education sector became extremely limited (Tilak 2017). The extent and applicability of the control exercised by these union regulatory authorities on the private institutions has been questioned from time to time. Though these private institutions are supposed to follow the norms and guidelines issued by the UGC and AICTE, ensuring full compliance to these is a herculean task for these central regulatory authorities. Gupta (2016) pointed out that in the absence of stringent regulation on private institutions, the judiciary had to play a crucial role.[3] The fact that private universities and the colleges are mainly under the jurisdiction of state authorities makes the situation more complex, and this ultimately led to a good number of court cases regarding overlapping of the space for regulation between the centre and the states.[4] Kapur and Khosla (2017) argued that the Supreme Court had become a 'critical institutional actor' and their judgements played a crucial role in shaping the policies in the field of higher education in India.

The initiation of the new economic policy in the early 1990s began to change the way higher education sector was being funded and regulated. It took almost a decade eventually for the private sector to occupy an increasing space in the Indian education sector. It was justified on the grounds of expanding the sector and meeting the huge demand for professional courses. Even then, profiteering in education was not morally and legally accepted. Private players entered through the non-profit trusts mainly in professional courses.[5] They were encouraged so

---

[2] At present there are 197 private universities, 90 deemed-to-be private universities and the private self-financing colleges which comprise 61 per cent of all colleges in India (2014–15). In 2014–15, the proportion of enrolment in unaided private colleges was 43 per cent, in aided private colleges, it was 23 per cent, and in the government colleges, it was 34 per cent.

[3] See Appendix Table 6A.1 for some of the interesting court cases.

[4] Kapur and Khosla (2017) found a steady rise in the number of the court cases on higher education: from 29 in 1970–9 to 206 in 2000–9 (an average of 20.6 cases per year). Also, the number of cases filed by the private HEIs and the state government has increased over these years. In 2000–9, 18.8 per cent of the cases were filed by the private sector and 41.2 per cent by the state government. In 2000–9, 34.4 per cent of the cases were filed on the issue of faculty and administrative staff; 17.8 per cent on admission and 16 per cent on recognition, establishment, and affiliation.

[5] Profit making in education is not legally permitted in India.

as to meet the rising demand for higher education, help increase the GER as well as prepare a pool of skilled labour force fit for the global market. These institutions were also directly regulated by the government regulatory agencies. But, with the proliferation of private colleges in professional courses, the existing regulatory structure failed miserably to ensure even a minimum standard. Rampant corruption, subversion of norms and violation of rules resulted in a murky situation with poor quality of education becoming the centre of the debate. The government introduced the Private Universities (Establishment and Regulation) Bill in response to the rising number of proposals for self-financing universities. The bill was never passed but the elements of the bill were incorporated in the state legislations (Establishments and Standards of in Private Universities Regulations 2003).

In 2000, the changes in the rules allowed even a new HEI to acquire the status of a deemed university. This was a very attractive proposition for deemed universities, and soon their numbers began to flourish. The Supreme Court in the case *Bharathidasan University* v. *All India Council of Technical Education and Others* (2001) ruled that universities were not required to seek the permission of the AICTE to set up a technical institute or to introduce a technical course. A deemed university could cater to the entire country. In absence of the Private Universities Bill mooted by the UGC, the state of Chhattisgarh allowed universities to be established which turned out to be teaching shops with abysmal quality of infrastructure. The ruling of the Supreme Court case *Yashpal Sharma and Others* v. *the State of Chhattisgarh* (2005) led the UGC to issue regulations in 2003 which resulted in a metamorphosis of the UGC as it evolved to be a powerful organization (Ayyar 2015).

Overlapping powers between central and state departments and confusion among different regulatory agencies worsened the situation. In many cases, courts had to step in. The judgements of High Courts and Supreme Courts became the guiding factors for regulating Indian higher education. There was a steady rise in cases related to higher education from just twenty-nine cases in the period of 1970–9 to 206 during 2000–9, a seven-fold increase during the three decades (Kapur and Khosla 2017: 209). This rapid rise could be attributable to a variety of factors including the significant growth of higher education, governance challenges in the sector and a general tendency of seeking judicial remedies reflecting deficiencies in legislative and executive organs of the state. However, there has been a tapering of the growth and in fact a stabilization in the number of cases appearing before the Supreme Court. To deal with the regulatory morass and poorly governed universities, the courts became the last resorts; however, the courts are poor remedies and make matters worse (Kapur and Khosla 2017).

High Degree of Centralization and Corruption

Kapur and Mehta (2004) have criticized the existing system for being extensively centralized and politicized and for not providing any incentives to the teachers to perform better. They emphasized the need to have competitive measures for evaluating teachers' performances and linking it to their promotion and tenure. Chattopadhyay (2012) has pointed out how in various ways educational processes in terms of teaching-learning, evaluation and in conduct of research are routinely subverted resulting in poor university governance and delivery of quality of teaching and research. Kapur and Mehta (2017: 11) argued that 'the core of the governance problem lies in the nature of the highly centralized state regulation' that seeks to micromanage the HEIs'. Regulations also failed to cope up with the sheer size of the system which has grown hundred-fold while the regulatory bodies remain 'poorly staffed' (Kapur and Mehta 2017: 19). Kapur and Mehta (2017) also observed that the quality of politicians who have become governors and who are the statutory heads of the state universities has also fallen. The president of India, the visitor of the centrally funded universities, has to look after over a hundred HEIs (Kapur and Mehta 2017: 17). Kapur and Mehta (2017) argued that the involvement of Ministry of Human Resources Development (MHRD), bureaucrats and ministers in Indian higher education have hindered the effective functioning of the sector in various ways.

Anandakrishnan (2007) expressed his concerns that autonomy is eroded through the appointments of vice chancellors and the governing boards, and no reform can yield results unless the political and bureaucratic controls are eliminated. Bhushan (2016) has cited the regulation and control responsible for increasing the 'bureaucracy' and undermining the 'autonomy' of the Indian higher education sector. The reforms which are often imposed from top without any consensus or public reasoning, according to him, would inevitably fail to yield desirable results. He also argued the rules and regulations formed by the UGC for recruitment and promotion of the faculty have failed to attract the best minds. The role of the AICTE was severely criticized by Ayyar (2015) who argued that the substandard technical education was an inevitable fallout of the corrupt practices of the council. Excessive monopolistic power in the hands of the AICTE led to rampant corruption and the regulations became just an 'empty ritual'.⁶ Consequences include creating obstacles for private sector to cater to the demands, adverse selection of educational entrepreneurs, concentration of private HEIs in professional fields, 'significant market failures in acquiring physical assets' as well as limited room for creativity and innovation.

As Varghese (2015) noted, eventually the performance-based funding system was implemented instead of the input-based criteria for disbursement of funds. This is also evident from the Rashtriya Uchchatar Shiksha Abhiyan (RUSA) or National Higher Education Mission which suggested the implementation of performance-based funding in higher education (GoI 2013). The introduction of Choice Based Credit System (CBCS) can also be viewed as giving freedom to the students to choose courses, and it is a pre-requisite for fostering competition.

Inefficacious University Grants Commission's Regulations

There have been several changes since the time the UGC regulations were introduced in 2010 to regulate and monitor the career progression of the teachers employed in the government-funded HEIs and recruitments of the new faculty along with the processes associated with the conduct of research undertaken by the students pursuing MPhil/PhD degrees. One major purpose of establishing regulations has been to improve the standard of the quality of research carried out by the faculty and the students – that is to ensure that the teachers allocate their time judiciously and across a range of activities to address the university mandate. However compliance with the regulations by the faculty led to their academic freedom being compromised on various counts, including teacher autonomy at the individual level in pursuit of teaching, conduct of research guidance, and research and its dissemination, at the disciplinary levels and at the university level, but because of the structural differences in the university activities and university missions (Das and Chattopadhyay 2014), it was felt to be a necessity in view of the substandard performance of a majority of the public-funded universities. Dandekar (1991) criticized the entire system as it protects the interests of only the teachers. He argues for introducing a system which would incentivize those teachers who perform better as competition among the teachers is essential. The UGC regulations are rightly argued to be binding with detailed prescriptions. Consequently, universities are unable to

---

⁶ In 2009, the chairman and secretary of AICTE were suspended. In 2008–9 several members of the senior staff faced police FIRs filed against them, and seven AICTE employees were convicted and were put in jail.

attract and retain talent to culture of research, which did not take root with no scholarship either (Kapur and Mehta 2017: 13).

The Draft National Education Policy (DNEP) (2019) (GoI 2019b) identified the inefficacy of the UGC regulations as one major reason for the failure of the Indian university system to deliver quality output. Further, the DNEP observed that micromanagement at the levels of teaching and research suffocate the autonomy of the teachers and stifle their creativity and innovativeness. However, the introduction of the regulations failed to usher in any significant improvement in the quality (GoI 2019b) because of the deficiency in the various provisions of the regulations and indulgence in unethical practices against the backdrop of poor infrastructure and low level of motivation among the faculty and the students.

The points assigned to various academic activities like teaching, research guidance, publications, and attending seminars and conferences are essentially indicators of how these various activities are valued by the policymakers. Since the points can be scored by choosing a combination of publications or research works, the rise in the number of publications show that the teachers have mostly resorted to the route which is associated with questionable quality rather than high quality (Appendix Table 6A.1; GoI 2018b, Table 2: 105; GoI 2018a). Jayaram (2006) has also made a scathing remark about the poor governance of the Indian universities where faculty promotions are mainly based on seniority. The DNEP echoes the same concern about seniority-based promotion despite the UGC regulations. The proliferation of substandard journals is symptomatic of abuse of regulations, the DNEP argues. Unethical practices in the process of teaching and research are hard to define. One can accumulate the required points as the journals/books have their ISSN and ISBN numbers but the publications remain devoid of quality. An increase in quantity as indicated in the accumulation of number of points need not mean production of quality.

5. Changing Contours: Evidence from Recent Policy

The neoliberal approach in managing higher education systems has ushered in some crucial changes at the institutional, national and the global level (Chattopadhyay 2020). To tackle the twin challenges of maintaining minimum standard and promoting excellence, the policymakers took recourse of the neoliberal approaches of constructing a market and fostering competition among the HEIs while regulating the poorly performing HEIs. We discuss these below.

Graded Autonomy

In 2018 (GoI 2018a), the UGC proposed graded autonomy[7] for universities which would inform the degree of regulation and therefore the extent of autonomy the different categories of universities would have. The universities would be categorized at three levels based on their scores awarded by NAAC or any other reputed external quality assurance agency and/or ranks in popular global university rankings such as Times Higher Education or QS. Universities in Category I would enjoy freedom to start a new course/programme/school/centre or off-campus activities without the approval of the UGC or related authority. They can collaborate with private partners and foreign educational institutions featuring in top 500 list of global rankings, recruit foreign faculty and admit foreign students (up to 20 per cent), install incentive structures for faculty members as well as offering of open and distance learning courses subject to minimum requirements without approval of the UGC. These institutions would be exempted from any supervisory inspections by the regulatory authorities. For Category II and Category III institutions, the degree of autonomy enjoyed in all these aspects is reduced in accordance with their status.

The graded autonomy is based on the understanding that those institutes who are capable of managing autonomy should be made free of regulation and also therefore bureaucratic hassles or red-tapism in order to achieve excellence. On the other hand, those who have failed to deliver must remain under the strict regulation of the authorities to ensure a minimum standard (Chattopadhyay 2020). The rationale for awarding autonomy is therefore based on performances.

A Category I university is allowed to start a new course/programme/department/school/centre in disciplines that form a part of its existing academic framework without the approval of the UGC as long as the university does not require any additional funding from the government. These Category I universities are allowed to open off-campus centres within its geographical jurisdiction, without the approval of the UGC, provided they garner both recurring and non-recurring revenue to sustain their activities and expect no financial assistance from the UGC or the government. These universities may also start skill courses, consistent with the National Skills Qualification Framework, open research parks, incubation centres, university-society linkage centres in self-financing mode, either on its own or in partnership with private

---

[7] UGC [categorization of universities (only) for grant of graded autonomy] regulations, 2018.

partners, without the approval of the UGC and without asking for any funds from the government.

Universities, subject to the rules, regulations and guidelines, are given the freedom to hire including foreign faculty (up to a limit of 20 per cent of total staff) and admit foreign students without the approval of the UGC.

These universities may offer incentives to the faculty as long as the additional expenses arising out of the implementation of the incentivized pay structure are defrayed out of their own revenue sources. Such an incentive structure, though not necessarily universal, must be strictly merit based with clearly defined, transparent and objective criteria.

To promote excellence and to encourage the HEIs to perform better, the UGC issued notifications for private and public institutes aspiring to be Institutions of Eminence (IoEs) in 2017.[8] With the view of improving the quality of education and enabling Indian HEIs to become world class, these policies also aim to reform the regulatory structure by pushing it towards self-regulation.

Universities are also allowed to offer courses in the open and distance learning mode, without the approval of the commission, provided it satisfies all the conditions laid down under UGC (Open and Distance Learning) Regulations, 2017 (GoI 2017c) and amendments therein from time to time.

National Education Policy 2020

Based on the argument that micromanagement of the faculty's conduct by the UGC regulations has failed to produce quality research and dampened enthusiasm, the NEP recommends that regulations should be 'light but tight' indicating the importance of strict compliance with only a few regulations rather than pervasive non-compliance with the entire gamut of regulations almost in every sphere of university operations (GoI 2020c). The concept of autonomy which is a hallmark of a university system has to be upheld but in a controlled manner. It is recommended that autonomy is essential for fostering innovation and creativity. The HEIs should have autonomy in all three spheres: academic, administrative and financial. The overall regulatory structure is set to be reconfigured with four independent verticals within one umbrella institution, the Higher Education Commission of India (HECI). HECI is the single point regulator which will ensure independence and effectiveness of other four verticals (see Figure 6.1). The first vertical of the HECI is

---

[8] UGC (Institutions of Eminence Deemed to Be Universities) Regulations, 2017, for private institutions and guidelines; UGC (Declaration of Government Educational Institutions as Institutions of Eminence) Guidelines, 2017, for public institutions (GoI 2017b) (as on 7 September 2017).

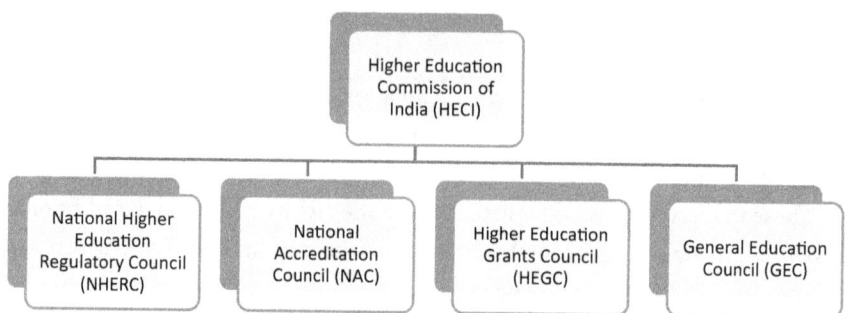

Figure 6.1 The proposed regulatory structure in National Education Policy 2020.
Source: Based on NEP 2020 (GoI 2020c).

the National Higher Education Regulatory Council (NHERC) which would oversee the entire higher education sector with the exception of medical and legal education. The NHERC will focus on financial probity and audit, governance, transparency as well as educational outcomes. It will act as a facilitator in expanding the scope of the higher education market by ensuring HEIs provide necessary information to the stakeholders, adopt a method of cost-recovery and the new managerial practices, and deliver output within a competitive setup and survive in the system. Another important role of NHERC would be addressing customers' (i.e. students') grievances.

The second vertical of HECI is the National Accreditation Council (NAC) envisaged as a 'meta-accrediting body' which will coordinate between several accrediting institutions. Through accreditation, the HEIs would seek to attain certain benchmarks and eventually progress towards achieving the highest level of accreditation. Once achieved, the HEIs would be granted autonomy and the power to self-regulate. The NEP has suggested binary accreditation which would intensify competition in the proposed construction of the higher education market (Chattopadhyay 2020).

The third vertical of HECI, the Higher Education Grants Council (HEGC), will look after financing of the HEIs. Based on the institutional developmental plans (IDP) submitted by the HEIs to articulate their future plan of academic activities and progress, funds would be disbursed to the HEIs. Also, it would look into the means and ways of supporting students from financially weak backgrounds. The future goals of the institutions have to be identified and mentioned in the IDP. After the approval of the board of governors, the IDP would be submitted to the funding authority which will allocate and disburse funds after a thorough review of the document. Though on paper the institutions have the liberty to set their own goals, in practice they will be forced to align their priorities to conform with the national level ranking and quality assurance indicators and for some, the global ranking parameters. The collective and democratic process of preparing the IDP by all the teachers could be difficult to attain in reality (Chattopadhyay 2020). A fast-track system for promotion for the faculty with excellent performance would be put in place to incentivize the career progression scheme. This is a major departure from the existing regulatory system which seeks to ensure minimum standard.

The fourth vertical, the General Education Council (GEC), is entrusted with the most contentious task of framing the expected learning outcomes or 'graduate attributes' for the higher education programmes. Apart from developing a National Higher Education Qualification Framework (NHEQF) and aligning it with National Skills Qualification Framework (NSQF), the GEC will also outline the set of skills required from the university graduates. The system of framing a set of common graduate attributes would indirectly force the HEIs to offer similar kinds of programmes through similar processes across the nation. Identifying the common attributes may be easier for the skill development programmes, but it would be extremely difficult in a diverse higher education system. In a way, it is a move towards homogenization of the HEIs in India.

Also, the National Research Foundation (NRF) is supposed to allocate research funding based on merit. The performance-based competitive funding is expected to make the HEIs more concerned about their performance which in turn would have serious implications for the internal governance of the institutions. It is expected that the HEIs would monitor each and every activity of its staff and students to reduce the cost inefficiencies and incentivize them for being more productive and to peform better. Promotions, salaries and the job tenures of staff members would be related to their performances, and failing to perform would lead to the termination of contracts. The NEP notes that this is a clear step towards this 'funding-based governance system' (Chattopadhyay 2020).

The government has also been actively promoting the use of e-platforms like massive open online courses (MOOCs). During the pandemic, the UGC issued notifications to popularize the courses the students are now allowed to opt for 40 per cent of the credits per semester through various e-platforms like Study Web of Active Young Aspiring Minds (SWAYAM) (GoI 2020f).

6. Policy Implications

Efficiency Does not Mean Quality

The purpose of any regulatory intervention is to ensure best possible utilization of resources – human resources in particular – to deliver the best possible quality.

However, differences in quality are intrinsic because of the variation in the quality of human capital embodied – the teachers and the students across the universities. Compliance is a necessary condition but not a sufficient one for achieving excellence because compliance, which is often a merely ritualistic process, does not guarantee the best possible efforts. For quality, two major conditions are to be fulfilled: dedication and robust foundational situation to ensure that the teachers and the students are provided with a congenial and supportive system. This requires adequate financial support, autonomy and trust on the academic community. The graded autonomy system proposed by the UGC is supposed to impose minimal regulations for Category I while subjecting Category II to limited regulation with some autonomy and Category III to full regulation.

Teacher Autonomy, Institutional Autonomy and Financial Autonomy

The NEP has strongly argued for teacher autonomy and institutional autonomy. We will examine how are these two related and whether the teachers and the institutions are supposed to have autonomy for both their dynamism and creativity. There is a need to recognize the relationship between teacher autonomy and institutional autonomy. Institutional autonomy does not guarantee teacher autonomy as the institutional mandates in a highly competitive situation would expect the teachers to deliver in accordance with the objectives prioritized by the institutions. A major part of the regulatory structure is to develop relationships among the university, the state and the market in the presence of the quality assurance agencies and the ranking agencies. The shifting of accountability has therefore led to an erosion of the teacher autonomy, despite the fact that, at the ground level, the NEP talks about bestowing teachers with autonomy in both teaching and research.

Clark's Triangle of Coordination

The approach to reform as proposed by the NEP is a variant of the neoliberal approach because the NEP suggests an increase in public funding and curbing commercial practices while indicating the setting up of a regulated quasi-market for higher education. The channels of regulations highlight the importance of the two kinds of efficiencies – allocational and technical – which are identifiable in the 'triangle of coordination' proposed by Clark (1983), in which the three vertices – academic oligarchy, the state and the market – constitute the major institutions of the higher education system as a whole (Figure 6.2).

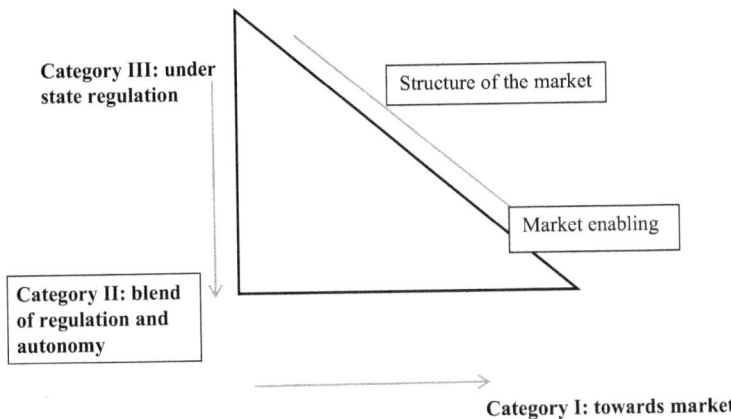

Figure 6.2 Academic freedom and Burton Clark's triangle.
Source: Clark (1983)

Though the attempt of the government is to correct the market failure, it looks forward to gain from the attributes of the market; to bestow sovereignty to the students as the consumers and the HEIs; and foster competition to get the best of the participants, the individuals and the institutions. The NEP provides for student sovereignty by giving them the choice to exit their studies with the option or rejoining at a later time; it also allows students to opt for courses offered in the e-platform as well as those offered by the foreign universities. The NEP recommends setting up of the ABC (Academic Bank of Credits). This will enable the students to deposit credits successfully earned. After earning the requisite number of credits, they become eligible to claim their certificates. This student sovereignty will infuse competition in the higher education sector (Chattopadhyay 2020). Therefore, the steps needed to construct the market for higher education would be directed towards the university and towards the students and the teachers to respond to the market and setting up of institutions to foster the construction of the market. The scheme of graded autonomy or rather graded regulation is shown in Figure 6.2.

7. Conclusion

The implementation of the scheme of graded autonomy, according the status of IoEs to a select set of universities and the possible entry of the foreign universities, will contribute to the further accentuation of the hierarchical order in the Indian higher education sector. This will dilute the public good character of higher education. Category II and III institutions will follow affirmative policies while selection-based competition will be encouraged among the Category I institutions and the IoEs. This will reinforce the 'positional good' character of higher education as equalization of access and diversity among the student community gets restricted to Category II and III HEIs. This highlights the conflict between achieving excellence and equity.

But the possible clash between academic autonomy and financial autonomy will hamper the realization of quality for the Category I institutions with the exception of the IoEs as they are assured of additional funding during the next ten years.

Without dedication, high moral standard and recognition for scholarship, the efficacy of regulation to improve quality will remain limited. The widespread malpractices in almost every sphere of higher education activity in various manifestations are deep rooted. Accountability to peer group has not worked for India with the formation of exclusionary networks that have had damaging consequences on the delivery of quality, whether it is in terms of examiners' list, deciding on the panel of experts for faculty recruitment or peer-review process. The leadership, barring a few exceptional cases, has failed in their duties because they were not made accountable to the academic community, nor did they strive for excellence. Rather they became trapped in issues inimical to academic excellence which emanated both from within the university as well as from outside.

Appendix

Table 6A.1 Methodology for University and College Teachers for Calculating Academic/Research Score

S.N.	Academic/research activity/faculty of sciences	Engineering/agriculture/ medical/veterinary sciences	Faculty of languages/humanities/arts/social sciences/ library/education/physical/education/commerce/ management & other related disciplines
1	**Research papers in peer-reviewed or UGC-listed journals**	08 per paper	10 per paper
2	**Publications (other than Research papers)**		
	(a) Books authored which are published by:		
	International publishers	12	12
	National publishers	10	10
	Chapter in edited book	05	05
	Editor of book by international publisher	10	10
	Editor of book by national publisher	08	08
	(b) Translation works in Indian and Foreign language by qualified faculties		
	Chapter or research paper	03	03
	Book	08	08
3	**Creation of ICT-mediated teaching learning pedagogy and content and development of new and innovative courses and curricula**		
	(a) Development of innovative pedagogy	05	05
	(b) Design of new curricula and courses	02 per curricula/course	02 per curricula/course
	(c) MOOCs		
	Development of complete MOOCs in 4 quadrants (4 credit course) (in case of MOOCs of lesser credits 05 marks/credit)	20	20

S.N.	Academic/research activity/faculty of sciences	Engineering/agriculture/medical/veterinary sciences	Faculty of languages/humanities/arts/social sciences/library/education/physical/education/commerce/management & other related disciplines
	MOOCs (developed in 4 quadrant) per module/lecture	05	05
	Content writer/subject matter expert for each module of MOOCs (at least 1 quadrant)	02	02
	Course coordinator for MOOCs (4 credit course) (in case of MOOCs of lesser credits 02 marks/credit)	08	08
	(d) E-Content		
	Development of e-Content in 4 quadrants for a complete course/e-book	12	12
	E-content (developed in 4 quadrants) per module	05	05
	Contribution to development of e-content module in complete course/paper/e-book (at least one quadrant)	02	02
	Editor of e-content for complete course/paper/e-book	10	10
4	**(a) Research guidance**		
	PhD	10 per degree awarded	10 per degree awarded
		05 per thesis submitted	05 per thesis submitted
	MPhil/PG dissertation	02 per degree awarded	02 per degree awarded
	(b) Research projects completed		
	More than 10 lakhs	10	10
	Less than 10 lakhs	05	05

(c) Research projects ongoing		
More than 10 lakhs		05
Less than 10 lakhs		02
(d) Consultancy		03
(a) Patents		
International		10
National		07

5. **(b) *Policy document** (Submitted to an international body/organization like UNO/UNESCO/World Bank/International Monetary Fund etc. or central government or state government)

International	10
National	07
State	05

(c) Awards/Fellowship	
International	07
National	05

6. ***Invited lectures/resource person/paper presentation in seminars/conferences/full paper in conference proceedings** (Paper presented in seminars/conferences and also published as full paper in conference proceedings will be counted only once)

International (abroad)	**07**
International (within country)	**05**
National	**03**
State/University	**02**

(Assessment must be based on evidence produced by the teacher such as: copy of publications, project sanction letter, utilization and completion certificates issued by the university and acknowledgements for patent filing and approval letters, students' PhD award letter etc.)

The research score for research papers would be augmented as follows:

Peer-reviewed or UGC-listed journals (impact factor to be determined as per Thomson Reuters list):

(i) Paper in refereed journals without impact factor 5 Points

(ii) Paper with impact factor less than 1 10 Points

S.N.	Academic/research activity/faculty of sciences	Engineering/agriculture/ medical/veterinary sciences	Faculty of languages/humanities/arts/social sciences/ library/education/physical/education/commerce/ management & other related disciplines
	(iii) Paper with impact factor between 1 and 2	15 Points	
	(iv) Paper with impact factor between 2 and 5	20 Points	
	(v) Paper with impact factor between 5 and 10	25 Points	
	(vi) Paper with impact factor >10	30 Points	
	(a) Two authors: 70% of total value of publication for each author.		
	(b) More than two authors: 70% of total value of publication for the first/principal/corresponding author and 30% of total value of publication for each of the joint authors.		
	Joint projects: Principal investigator and co-investigator would get 50% each.		

*For the purpose of calculating research score of the teacher, the combined research score from the categories of 5(b) (Policy document) and 6 (Invited lectures/resource person/paper presentation) shall have an upper capping of 30% of the total research score of the teacher concerned.

Note:

Paper presented if part of edited book or proceeding, then it can be claimed only once.

For joint supervision of research students, the formula shall be 70% of the total score for supervisor and co-supervisor. Supervisor and co-supervisor both shall get 7 marks each.

The research score shall be from the minimum of three categories out of six categories.

Source: Author, using material from GoI (2018c: 106–7).

7

Internationalization of Indian Higher Education: Issues and Challenges

Saumen Chattopadhyay

1. Introduction

India's connection with the rest of the world in the realm of knowledge production and its dissemination can be traced to the country's ancient past. Taxila, which was established in 700 BC and Nalanda, in c.700 AD, were truly international universities. Nalanda University had 10,000 students and 2000 teachers. Foreign participation was high with students coming from China, Indonesia, Korea, Japan, Turkey and Persia (Varghese 2020b). After independence, the international influence on Indian higher education continued as some of the universities were modelled on Euro-American systems. Over time the renewed connection took a different form as the number of Indian students as well as skilled personnel and IT professionals going abroad for further studies and for work, respectively, began to swell. In a way, India's connection with the rest of the world in terms of mobility of human capital embodied, finished or semi-finished in the form migrating students reflect, in fact, the state of India's higher education and economic development, broadly speaking. Production of knowledge and knowledge produced are intrinsically integral to the global knowledge economy. The issue is how does internationalization help Indian higher education in achieving excellence and growth in an inclusive manner. There is a need to identify the risks and challenges associated with the growing tendencies towards internationalization.

There is a clear and sound policy thrust on fostering internationalization of Indian higher education in the recent years. Arguably, this is also being recognized as one way of achieving quality and global recognition as, after all, India has the second largest higher education sector in the world in terms of enrolment. Some of the recent policy initiatives by the government like the scheme of graded autonomy and setting up of Institutions of Eminence (IoEs) in addition to a few other policy initiatives by the University Grants Commission (UGC) and government of India are indicative of global aspiration which entails internationalization of various processes of teaching-learning and research. This is in sync with the global trend as evident from the weightage given to the internationalization in the form of foreign students and teachers by the world ranking agencies. India is also keen to extend soft power to promote internationalization based on bilateral relationships between India and other countries (Varghese 2020b). However, embracing globalization in higher education in the sense of promoting trade has received mixed responses. While collaborative nature of research across the borders and teacher-student exchange contribute to the making of higher education as a global public good, participation in the global market comes at a cost as all the universities are not in a position to negotiate with the imperatives at all three levels: local, national and global.

This chapter seeks to take stock of the major trends in various aspects of internationalization of Indian higher education and examine the policy initiatives which purports to promote internationalization in view of India's attempt to strike a delicate balance between national and global compulsions. We begin this chapter with an attempt to situate India's position in the global knowledge economy. We then take up issues related to programme mobility, student mobility, institutional mobility and movement of skilled persons from India. This is followed by an appraisal of the recent policy initiatives and programmes being run by international bodies to encourage academic exchange across the borders. This chapter ends with a discussion of the possible implications of internationalization for the Indian higher education.

2. Setting the Context: Four Modes of the General Agreement on Trade in Services (GATS)

Globalization is discussed as mobility under four modes: Mode 1: Cross-border supply of education which facilitates programme mobility; Mode 2: Consumption of education abroad or student mobility as students go abroad to pursue higher studies; Mode 3: Commercial presence or institution mobility (examples include opening up of local branches, or, satellite campuses and partnerships with local institutions); Mode 4: Movement of natural persons. We adopt this classification to discuss various aspects of internationalization of higher education.

The main deliverables of higher education institutions (HEIs) in the form of teaching-learning and knowledge generated in research are amenable to transformations in their articulations in the context of information and communication technology (ICT) driven globalization. Teaching as a service requires (1) contemporaneous presence of the service provider and the consumer, the teacher and the student and (2) physical proximity of the two (Nayyar 2007). Digital technology has made it possible for us to join a virtual community from anywhere in the world. Since teaching can be recorded and saved as a digital product, simultaneous presence is no longer necessary for the transaction. This is ushering in radical transformations in the university space by redefining time and space associated with a university. This new development which gained considerable momentum in the post-COVID era has added a new dimension to the conventional notion of mobility because of the need to separate virtual mobility from physical mobility. Further, with the rapid rise in the use of technology in teaching-learning particularly in the post-COVID era, the distinction between 'internationalization at home' and 'internationalization abroad' has gained relevance. Therefore, each of the aspects can potentially have these two different aspects of internationalization, at home and abroad. New ways of connecting with the rest of world are gaining traction in the wake of this technological advancement (Wadhwa 2019).

Internationalization at Home and Abroad

Internationalization at home comprises designing of global curriculum and students in India attending classes in the virtual space of a foreign university either operating in India or abroad. With the sudden disruption of travel during the lockdown, students who were intending to migrate to pursue higher studies abroad were instead attending classes conducted by their universities located abroad from their home. Internationalization abroad would entail conventional mobility of students and teachers/scholars, and Indian HEIs opening up off-shore campuses or international branch campuses (IBCs). All this has made transnational education which involves cross-border education more acceptable and more popular. Doing collaborative research across the border need not necessarily require cross-border movement of scholars.

For programme mobility and institutional mobility, there could be both internationalization at home as well as the conventional internationalization

Table 7.1 Top Six Countries by Research Output (All Publications Type), 2018–19

	2018	2019	Rate of growth (%)
China	607281	687492	13.2
United States	699743	683702	-2.3
UK	217806	213605	-1.9
India	178470	187432	5.0
Germany	182904	182092	-0.4
Japan	135831	133054	-2.0

Source: Author, derived from International Facts and Figures 2020 (Universities UK International), Original data source: SciVal as of April 2020.

abroad under Mode 1 and Mode 3 of GATS. Setting up off-shore campuses or IBCs is an example of internationalization abroad.

3. India in the Global Knowledge Economy

While internationalization is natural to the process of knowledge production and its dissemination, internationalization is a policy being actively pursued to feature in the global knowledge space. Before we discuss various aspects of internationalization, we begin with India's position in the global knowledge production (Table 7.1).

Though it may not feature in the world ranking of the universities, India occupies fourth position in terms of total number publications after China, United States and UK in that order (International Facts and Figures 2020). If we consider a different estimate, India recorded 11.1 per cent growth during 2006–16 in terms of science publications (Marginson 2020b). India surpassing Germany to occupy the fourth position has raised eyebrows, and it is legitimately so (Bothwell 2020). Proliferation of fake journals was noted by the Draft National Education Policy (DNEP) 2019 (GoI 2019c) and maximization of publications to score points by the teachers as required by the UGC regulations for becoming eligible for career promotion and recruitments are the possible reasons.[1] The other measure would be to look at the proportion of internationally co-authored publications which

---

[1] It is also important to note that India is the third largest higher education sector in the world with 1.4 million teachers. So in terms of per capita productivity, India would be lower down the ladder. This is also evident as in terms of citation index – India occupies twelfth position (Ramaswamy 2020). See Chapter 6 on regulation for the possible reason.

Table 7.2 Proportion of Internationally Co-authored Publications

	2010	2019	Growth during the period (%)
France	44.6	58.0	30.0
Australia	40.2	57.5	43.6
UK	39.8	57.2	43.7
Canada	41.5	54.6	31.6
Germany	42.4	51.7	21.9
United States	25.8	37.0	43.4
China	14.4	23.4	62.5
India	16.7	18.1	8.4

Source: Author, derived from International Facts and Figures 2020 (Universities UK International), Original data source: SciVal as of April 2020.

is presumably, an indication of quality research. The share of internationally co-authored publications in India's total publication at around 18 per cent is rather low compared to that of other countries (Table 7.2). India ranks tenth in the list of ten largest research systems in the world (Marginson 2020b), which is defined as the percentage of all science papers that were internationally co-authored.

The other side of the questionable quality of this large volume of research publications is the concentration of high quality research in a few good universities within the large number of HEIs in India. On the international scale, the growth rate is highest for China where not only has there been a phenomenal expansion of the higher education sector, there has been a great increase in the number of world ranking universities during the decade 2010–19. The share in the co-authored publications is the highest for France followed by Australia, UK, Canada and Germany. The United States has a lower share possibly because the country has the largest concentration of reputed scholars in the world.

Indian Universities in the Global Rankings

It would also be of interest to see how Indian universities are ranked in the world ranking for 2020–1 by the three ranking agencies: the Academic Ranking of World Universities (ARWU), the Times Higher Education (THE) World University Rankings, and the QS World University Rankings, all of which are recognized by the Indian policymakers and are set as targets for the best of the HEIs (Table 7.3).

Indian universities did not feature in the top 200 in 2020 in the global league of world ranking universities published by the two major world university ranking agencies, the ARWU and the THE. Because of high importance given to present

Table 7.3 World Ranking of Indian Universities (Select) and their National Ranking in National Institutional Ranking Framework, 2020

	Universities	ARWU ranks	Universities	THE ranks	Universities	QS ranks
1	IISc Bengaluru	501–600 (2)	IISc Bengaluru	301–350 (2)	IIT Bombay	152 (4)
2	IIT Madras	601–700 (1)	IIT Ropar	301–350 (39)	IISc Bengaluru	184 (2)
3	University of Calcutta	601–700 (11)	IIT Indore	351–400 (23)	IIT Delhi	182 (3)
4	University of Delhi	601–700 (18)	IIT Bombay	401–500 (4)	IIT Madras	271 (1)
5	IIT Delhi	701–800 (3)	IIT Delhi	401–500 (3)	IIT Kharagpur	281 (5)
6	IIT Kharagpur	701–800 (5)	IIT Kharagpur	401–500 (5)	IIT Kanpur	291 (6)
7	JNU	701–800 (8)	Institute of Chemical Technology	501–600 (34)	IIT Roorkee	383 (9)
8	AMU	801–900 (31)	IIT Guwahati	501–600 (7)	University of Delhi	474 (18)
9	VIT	801–900 (28)	IIT Roorkee	501–600 (9)	University of Hyderabad	651–700 (15)

Note: In the parentheses, the overall ranking in the NIRF for 2020 are indicated corresponding to their world ranking.

Source: Compiled by author based on public website data. For ARWU, http://www.shanghairanking.com/World-University-Rankings-2020/India.html; for Times Higher Education (THE) World University Rankings, https://www.timeshighereducation.com/world-university-rankings/2020/world-ranking#!/page/0/length/25/locations/IN/sort_by/rank/sort_order/asc/cols/stats; for QS World University Rankings, https://www.topuniversities.com/university-rankings/world-university-rankings/2020; for NIRF, https://www.nirfindia.org/2020/OverallRanking.html.

and past research and that too importance being given to the Nobel Laureates and winners of field medals, the ranking of Indian HEIs start after 500th rank with Indian Institute of Science (IISc) Bengaluru and Indian Institute of Technology (IIT) Madras in 501–600 band. The University of Calcutta and University of Delhi rank in the range of 601–700 above the ranking of the two IITs, Delhi and Kharagpur in ARWU. The IISc ranks in the range of 301–350 in the THE World University Rankings which is followed by IIT Ropar and IIT Indore much ahead of the old and reputed IIT Delhi and IIT Bombay with National Institutional Ranking Framework (NIRF) ranking 3 and 4 respectively. In the QS World Ranking 2020, the top Indian HEI IIT Bombay ranked 152 followed by the IISc Bengaluru at 184. In terms of overall ranking in the NIRF, these institutions, IIT Bombay and the IISc ranked fourth and second respectively while IIT Madras ranked first followed by IIT Delhi at the second position. In QS World University Rankings, which are less research centric, the Indian universities do relatively better.

4. Globalization under Four Modes

Mobility of Students

Though Kothari Commission (1964–6) referred to the emigration of students to study abroad as 'brain drain', it did not get much recognition either in the commission's report or in the policy documents such as in the science and technology policy (Khadria 2016). Khadria argues that, by early 1990s, the narrative of 'brain drain' which was in the discussion during 1960s–70s was replaced by the new concept of 'brain bank' abroad during 1980s–90s. In the twenty-first century, the emigration of IT professionals and return of some of them was being considered as 'brain gain' in the context of the debate on internationalization of human capital. The success of the IT professionals abroad brought to the fore the issue of migration of skilled workers in the policy discourse. In an investigative report initiated by the daily the *Indian Express* (27 December 2020) to track where are the school board toppers settled, it was found that more than half of the toppers between the age group of twenty-one and forty-two years are in foreign countries, with three out of every four settled in the United States. Four out of ten are working in the IT sector in the Silicon Valley followed by medicine and finance.

Outward student mobility from India witnessed a rise by 4.5 times during 2000–17 as the outward mobility rose from 66,700 to 305,000 in 2017 (Varghese 2020b). Australia, Canada and New Zealand have become popular countries

Table 7.4 Outward and Inward Mobility for India

	India	China	South Africa	Brazil
Students abroad	375,055	993,367	9130	67,183
Percentage of total mobile students	6.7	17.8	0.2	1.2
Outward mobility ratio	1.1	2.2	0.8	0.8
Students hosted				
Total number of mobile students hosted	47424	201,177	42267	21181
Percentage of mobile students	0.9	3.6	0.8	0.4
Inbound mobility ratio	0.1	0.4	3.6	0.2

Source: Author, using data from http://uis.unesco.org/en/uis-student-flow (accessed 26 November 2020).

mainly because they offer bright job prospects. Indian students have been observed to be 'highly price sensitive' and 'value maximizers' (Varghese 2020b).

The outward mobility of students has experienced a steady rise until the pandemic applied a brake in the process. The total stock of international students which was 5.1 million in 2016 is expected to rise to 8 million by 2025. As on December 2020, a total of 375,055 Indian students were pursuing higher studies abroad as compared to only 47,424 foreign students who were studying in India.[2] Indian students constitute 6.7 per cent of total number of mobile students world over. This is, however, only 1.1 per cent of total number Indian students in higher education because of the large size of the student population (around 34 million). In contrast, India as the host country accounts for only 1 per cent of total number of international students. Given the small size of the foreign students studying in India, this is merely 0.1 per cent of total Indian students enrolled in HEIs in India. The ratio of inbound to outbound mobility is therefore 1:10 (Table 7.4).

India has emerged to be the second largest country in sending students abroad for higher studies. China sent almost close to 1 million students abroad which is nearly 18 per cent of total students who went abroad for higher studies. South Africa and Brazil – countries chosen purely for the sake of comparison – send much fewer students. Inward and outward mobility of students are indicative of the global recognition of the host countries among other factors such as costs of studying and language or medium of instruction. English as a medium of instruction in the majority of Indian HEIs has facilitated the outward mobility

[2] These figures are reported by the *All India Survey on Higher Education* (AISHE) (GoI 2020h) which also figure in the UNESCO list.

of students. As per the latest AISHE 2019-20 (GoI 2021d) there were 49,348 foreign students studying in India with top ten countries constituting 63.9 per cent of the foreign students.

Out of those Indian students who are studying abroad, the share of students going to the United States has seen a decline from 78.5 per cent in 1995 to 44.4 per cent in 2018 (Varghese 2020a) and 36.0 per cent in 2020 (Appendix Table 7A.1). This is followed by 19.55 per cent in Australia, 9.25 per cent in Canada, 5.23 per cent in the UK and 4.13 per cent in Germany. Adding UAE and New Zealand to this list, the top seven destination countries would account for nearly 80 per cent of the Indian students pursuing higher studies abroad. In comparison, Nepal sends 26.8 per cent students of the total inward students, followed by 9.82 per cent from Afghanistan, 4.38 per cent from Bangladesh and 3.81 per cent from Bhutan. The sending countries for India are therefore widely diverse in comparison to the host countries of the outward students as twenty-six countries account for 80 per cent of the inward students (GoI 2020a).

Foreign students prefer Indian private institutions possibly because of better infrastructure and easy admission policies. Manipal University and Pune as a city have emerged to be the popular destinations for foreign students (see All India Survey for Higher Education 2018–19, in GoI 2020a). It is often difficult for foreign students to get admission in the best of the universities if their command over English language and training obtained in their home countries are found to be inadequate. Indian public universities are under no compulsion to advertise and promote university brands abroad as fees charged to foreign students constitute an insignificant share of total university income. For all the HEIs, the permissible number is merely 10 per cent of the total number of students enrolled; some HEIs are allowed to take foreign students up to 15 per cent. In practice, the actual number of foreign students admitted is way below these limits – in fact, it is just 0.13 per cent (Varghese 2020b).

Foreign students who come to India prefer to pursue undergraduate (UG) followed by postgraduate (PG) degrees which make for nearly 90 per cent of the inward students (Table 7.5). The percentage of female students is around 46 per cent. If we adopt Marginson's classification of internationalization (Marginson 2020b), India with barely around 1570 foreign students pursuing research degrees would be far down the list of countries with low degree of internationalization which is defined as the proportion of research degree students and doctoral students being less than 15 per cent in 2016.

The 1:10 inward to outward mobility ratio in fact confirms India's rather weak position in the global knowledge economy. As indicated, the reputation

Table 7.5 Gender-Wise and Course-Wise Distribution of Foreign Students

	Male	Female	Total	Percentage
PhD	1201	369	1570	3.31
MPhil	56	10	66	0.14
PG	5352	2309	7661	16.15
UG	23376	11454	34830	73.44
PG diploma	37	36	73	0.15
Diploma	1793	322	2115	4.46
Certificate	235	258	493	1.04
Integrated	348	271	619	1.31
Total	**32398**	**15029**	**47427**	**100.00**

Source: Author, derived from *All India Survey of Higher Education*, 2018–19, T-16 (GoI 2020a).

of Indian universities in the world academia is low barring a select set of universities. Rising middle-class incomes, lure of settling abroad and intense competition to get admission in the best of the Indian HEIs are the major drivers for outward student mobility. Engineering and management institutions like IITs and Indian Institutes of Management (IIMs) are of world repute but securing admission to these institutes is extremely difficult. Based on the interviews conducted by the *Indian Express*, Indian toppers lauded the better research and job opportunities and overall a better and congenial ecosystem abroad. 'Higher education is the primary reason why toppers left the country' as 70 per cent of those who were interviewed migrated to study abroad, but only around 12 per cent of total 86 per cent took up jobs abroad (*The Indian Express* 2020).

It has been a major debate as to how the outward mobility of Indian students has contributed to the health of the Indian universities. Brain drain involves loss of precious human capital in two ways as averred by Khadria (2016): (1) loss of skills embodied and (2) loss of investment made on student education. The Indian market is yet to be in a position to absorb graduates, even in the case of doctoral students from science disciplines. Loss of investment is not merely the money spent on education; the actual loss also includes the total amount of income these individuals would have generated had they stayed back during their life time. This brain drain needs to be weighed by the three benefits India appropriates (Khadria 2016), namely, remittances, transfer of technology and return migration of human capital. Migration of the skilled workers and students are positive indicators of a holistic and appropriate assessment of the Indian higher education sector.

Mobility of Programmes

Promotion of massive open online courses (MOOCs) has a huge potential to contribute to the expansion and internationalization of higher education attracting students from all over the world. Study Web of Active Young Aspiring Minds (SWAYAM) is being actively popularized by the government and making it an integral part of the existing courses being offered by the universities. The National Education Policy (NEP) (GoI 2020c) also recommended that credits acquired in foreign universities will be permitted to be counted for students pursuing degrees in India. Internationalization of programmes and thereby improvement in the content of the curriculum can enhance the quality of education provided. Sovereignty being bestowed on the students would infuse competitiveness in the higher education sector, which may pose challenges for the HEIs with questionable performances (Chattopadhyay 2020).

Mobility of Institutions: International Branch Campuses

In December 2020, five private HEIs set up twelve IBCs (Table 7.6). In 2016, the number of IBCs was seven (Wadhwa 2019) and this number was growing in the early phase of 2000 when there were around seventeen such campuses (Chanda 2016). The preferred destinations are UAE and Singapore. Among the developed countries, Australia is the only host country for Indian institutions.

Table 7.6 International Branch Campuses: Home Country India

	Name of the institution	Host country
1	Amity University, Dubai	UAE
2	Amity Institute of Higher Education, Mauritius	Mauritius
3	Amity University, Tashkent Campus	Uzbekistan
4	Amity University, Singapore	Singapore
5	Birla Institute of Technology and Science, Dubai	UAE
6	Institute of Management Technology, Dubai	UAE
7	Manipal College of Medical Sciences, Manipal	Nepal
8	Manipal University, Colombo	Sri Lanka
9	Manipal University, Dubai	UAE
10	S. P. Jain School of Global Management, Dubai	UAE
11	S. P. Jain School of Global Management, Sydney	Australia
12	S. P. Jain School of Global Management, Singapore	Singapore

The reasons for establishing IBCs by the private HEIs are to augment the revenue base, to wriggle out of stifling regulations and to maximize on the intake of foreign students. The choice of the countries shows that one intention may be to tap the large Indian expatriate population settled in the Middle East and in the countries such as Singapore and Mauritius. The IoEs (GoI 2021b) have now been allowed to open up IBCs (GoI 2021) with the same norms and standards prescribed by the UGC or concerned statutory councils for establishing similar institutions in India. India is one of the thirty-seven countries with 306 IBCs across the world (Cross-Border Education Research Team 2020). Other modes of cross-border movement would actually complement commercial presence; a part of it can be through online modes.

Inward Mobility of Investment and Institutions: Foreign Direct Investment and Foreign Universities

Foreign education providers began their operations in 1991-2 with the setting up of the study and examination centres (Bhushan 2009). Their second mode of operations which involved twinning and teacher-student exchange began in 1995-6. The third mode involved programmatic collaborations through the growth of joint degrees around that time. In the fourth mode, foreign providers started offering complete foreign degrees in India marking deeper involvement between the Indian institutions and the foreign partners (Bhushan 2009). Education provided by the foreign institutions are flexible with easy exit options, focus on life-long education and impart job-oriented training. The advantage of such an association with foreign universities provided the impetus for the internationalization of curriculum which needed a massive improvement.

India's presence in the commercial sector in the sphere of global higher education is rather small (Chanda 2016). In April 2000, foreign direct investment (FDI) inflows in the education sector was only 1 per cent of total FDI inflows for the April 2000 to July 2014 period (Chanda 2016). This low investment is attributable to the regulatory barriers to the entry and operations of foreign institutions in India. The NEP (GoI 2020c) has suggested suitable legislative changes to allow the top 100 world ranking universities to operate in India. As per the clauses of the Foreign Educational Institutions Regulation of Entry and Operations (Maintenance of Quality and Prevention of Commercialisation) Bill 2010, foreign universities could enter the Indian higher education market and offer degrees and diplomas upon fulfilment of several conditions. It was stipulated that those foreign universities intending to operate in India should have INR 500 million, which was later reduced to INR 250 million, in the form of corpus fund which would be forfeited if conditions are found to have been violated. Out of the total income or surplus generated by the foreign providers, 75 per cent was required to be reinvested. They were also required to be registered under the Section 25 or as non-profit companies under the Companies Act. The universities were required to be from the list of 400 universities ranked by the three ranking agencies. The approval by the UGC was a prerequisite for their entry and operation. This bill did not get the necessary approval which reflects lack of consensus among the stakeholders. Though the norms and the conditions were relaxed later, foreign universities did not show much interest. To bypass this strict regulatory compliance requirements, foreign institutions preferred to enter into tie-ups and twinning arrangements.

In 2011, there were 161 foreign educational institutions operating in India. In addition, there joint degree programmes were developed with foreign universities in professional courses such as IT, management and engineering. In 2012, over 400 foreign institutions were engaged in franchise or liaising activities (Bhushan 2009). Most of these were operating without any formal approval from the concerned regulatory authority (Chanda 2016). In 2012, there was an attempt to encourage joint academic programmes between the Indian and foreign universities under the UGC Promotion and Maintenance of Standards of Academic Collaborations between Indian and Foreign Educational Institutional Regulations 2012 to collaborate with Indian universities subject, of course, to the approval granted by the UGC (Chanda 2016). The picture remains hazy to date because of the lack of clarity and regulatory jurisdictions until a new legislation comes into effect.

Chattopadhyay (2010) argued against the entry of the foreign education providers because it had the potential to accentuate the selection-based market mechanism which would further differentiate the higher education market which would push the Indian universities to the receiving end. With rising fees, not only access would suffer, but replication of quality by these foreign universities would be a difficult proposition in their branch campuses located in India. With the rapid advancement of digital technology and acceptance of internationalization at home, the possible quality difference would get narrower but campus experiences in the host countries would remain coveted by the students intending to study abroad.

Until a legislation is put in place to facilitate the operation of the foreign providers in India, the inflow from FDI will remain limited and will be mainly through such partnerships.

5. Recent Policy Initiatives for Fostering Internationalization

In its strategic framework, the Twelfth Five Year Plan (GoI 2013) recognized the importance of promoting internationalization to achieve excellence. To promote internationalization, the policymakers have introduced necessary changes in the regulations and schemes. The most prominent of these are the steps to build-up world class universities (WCUs) – what are referred to as IoEs – and the scheme of graded autonomy (GoI 2017b, 2018a).

Building WCUs requires policy support from the government. As pointed out by Salmi (2008), there are two broad strategies which are pursued by the governments for the purpose of enabling universities to feature in the list of world ranking universities. One is 'rewarding quality', and the other is 'picking winners'. The first strategy is to rely on the ranking and accreditation score to generate competition with the purpose of creating differentiation among the universities followed by dedication of resources to the top few who have performed as per the standard set by the policymakers. The second strategy involves the government infusing resources to a select group of universities which have the potential to become world class. The selection may involve competitive bidding. An example of the first strategy is the policy of graded autonomy (GoI 2018a), according to which the Category I institutions are bestowed with financial autonomy rather than additional financial support.[3] The policy to accord the status of IoE (GoI 2017b) is one of initiatives towards implementing the second strategy.

Making Policy for Institutions of Eminence

In 2017, GoI announced the scheme of according the status of IoEs to a select set of ten public and ten private universities based on their potential and strategies to achieve world class standards.

To develop strategically concentrating resources in a select set of universities has now become a global phenomenon. Salmi (2009) suggests three important factors which gives us an overview of the challenges faced by the countries in setting up WCU along with suggestions to overcome these challenges. Basically there are three sets of complementary factors which are

---

[3] The universities are categorized mainly as follows Category I: National Assessment and Accreditation Council (NAAC) score of 3.5 and above or in the top 500 of world ranking universities as per the QS and the THE; Category II: NAAC score between 3.01 and 3.49; Category III: Neither I nor II as above. Featuring in the NIRF as a criterion for classification has been discontinued with as per the revised policy (GoI 2018a).

essential to set the stage for launching the project of building the WCUs: (1) concentration of the good quality human capital, embodied in students and teachers, in the top-ranking universities; (2) liberal funding of resources to achieve world class excellence in teaching and research; and (3) a nimble and accommodative governance structure supportive of designing which would bestow academic freedom to teachers and students to minimize bureaucratic interference. All these three are recognized in the policy of according the status of IoEs (GoI 2017b).

While fixing the target, the selected IoEs are assured of autonomy in the process and selection of inputs, the students and the teachers. The selection of students should be merit based and if needed, the meritorious will be financially supported. The IoEs have freedom to hire foreign faculty and build-up an incentive structure as long as the additional resources required are generated by the university. They are assured of administrative, financial and academic freedom. Other than this, a significant proportion of international students and cutting-edge research with high social impact in addition to 1:10 faculty to student ratio are mandated – all these resonate with the ranking parameters of THE World University Rankings and the World University Rankings as discussed above.

These factors are critical for the IoEs to feature in the top 500 of any of the world renowned ranking frameworks (such as the THE or QS or Shanghai Jiao Tong University) (GoI 2017b: 17). Over time, the IoEs are expected to rank in the top 100 world ranking universities. The policy of IoEs reflects the fact that quality publications are important, where quality is conceptualized in line with the parameters used by the world ranking agencies.

The IoE notification states thus:

> The Institution of Eminence Deemed to be University should be known for promoting a culture where faculty are encouraged to publish regularly in peer-reviewed journals and engage academically with the issues of concern to the society. It should have a record of research publications at the mean rate of at least one per faculty member each year in reputed peer reviewed international journals based on publication made by top 100 global Universities in these journals. For this purpose ... 'Any paper published in international publications which are included in Scopus, Web of Science or similar international agencies can be counted.' (GoI 2017: 4.12.12)

The institutional autonomy bestowed on the IoEs appears to be in conflict with the financial autonomy granted to them as exercise of institutional autonomy in the true sense of the term entails liberal public funding. Altbach (2018) favours creation of an entirely new set of institutions to become WCUs as it is doubtful whether the existing constraints can be successfully overcome by the existing IoEs.

Graded Autonomy

If academic autonomy is crucial to the attainment of excellence, there is a need to restrict the purview of regulations. This is based on the understanding that regulation seeks to help realize the potential of the universities by seeking compliance. This constitutes the rationale for categorizing universities based on their performances and subject them to different degrees of regulations. This is articulated in the scheme of graded autonomy announced by the government in 2018 (GoI 2018b). The freedom to internationalize in various dimensions of university functioning, governance and selection of inputs are given to Category I universities.

We find almost a similar set of freedoms as given to the IoEs are also extended to the Category I universities. They can hire up to 20 per cent of the total sanctioned faculty strength from abroad – faculty that are teaching in the top 500 universities ranked by the THE World University Rankings or the QS World University Rankings – without approval of the government. Universities are also allowed to take in foreign students on merit – up to 20 per cent of the approved quota allotted to domestic students can be admitted. Universities can also design an incentive structure to attract talented faculty which has to be financed out of the university's own sources of revenue.

Universities are also encouraged to engage in academic collaborations with top-ranked foreign educational institutions (universities in the top 500 of THE World University Rankings or QS World University Rankings, or in the top 200 of discipline specific ranking as per the UGC (Promotion and Maintenance of Standards of Academic Collaboration between Indian and Foreign Educational Institutions) Regulations, 2016).

Such policy initiatives provide the impetus for the top performing institutions to embrace a greater degree of internationalization in order to meet their aspirations of becoming world ranking universities. There is hence an unmistakable need for fixing the criteria – in line with the parameters used by the THE World University Rankings and QS World University Rankings for universities – which universities can meet that will in turn to enable them to be placed among the select set of WCUs.

National Education Policy 2020

The NEP (GoI 2020c) seeks to promote internationalization in research and in teaching-learning to improve quality of publications in continuation with the existing policy initiatives. The NEP recommends that India should be promoted as a global study destination with each host university in India to open an international student office. To this effect, as mentioned earlier, the IoEs are now allowed to start new off-campus centres with maximum of three campuses in five years and not more than one in any given academic year with same teacher-student ratio of 1:20, which is to be improved to 1:10 after five years.

Schemes and Programmes to Make India Count

The finance minister in her Union Budget Speech for 2020–1 stated that India should be a preferred destination for higher education. Hence, under its 'Study in India' programme, Ind-SAT (Scholastic Aptitude Test) is proposed to be held in Asian and African countries. It shall be used for benchmarking foreign candidates who will receive scholarships for studying in Indian higher education centres GoI 2020b: 11). The Study in India was launched with 2500 scholarships. In 2018, this programme attracted 6000 students from thirty countries. By 2024, the number of scholarships is to be raised to 50,000. The 'PM Scholars Return to India' has been launched to bring back Indian scholars working abroad. The MOOCs platform SWAYAM is also being promoted to attract foreign students; the e-content is available as open access resources.[4] Global Initiative for Academic Networks (GIAN) was launched in 2017–18 as an initiative which 'aimed at tapping the talent pool of scientists and entrepreneurs, internationally to encourage their engagement with the institutes of Higher Education in India so as to augment the country's existing academic resources, accelerate the pace of quality reform, and elevate India's scientific and technological capacity to global excellence'.[5] Around 1800 schemes for fifty-six countries offered courses during 2017–18 to 2018–19 (Varghese 2020b).

There is another scheme available for foreign nationals which provides scholarships in line with the Junior Research Fellowship (JRF) meant for the Indian students for which a master's degree is a prerequisite. Research

---

[4] The e-PG Pathshala had received several international visitors: around 6990 from the United States, 1030 from China and 611 from the Russian Federation (e-PG Pathshala. https://epgp.inflibnet.ac.in/#, accessed on 28 January 2021).

[5] https://www.indiascienceandtechnology.gov.in/programme-schemes/human-resource-and-development/gian-global-initiative-academic-networks (accessed on 29 June 2021).

associateship are also available for the foreign nationals, this provides scholarship equivalent to the Indian eligible students which is INR 25,000 per month in addition to other benefits. The General Cultural Scholarship Scheme (GCSC) implemented through the Indian Council of Cultural Research (ICCR) is meant for students hailing from Latin America, Africa and Asia.

The Scheme for Promotion of Academic and Research Collaboration (SPARC) was launched in 2018 to promote research collaboration between reputed institutes abroad and the Indian institutes. Institutional grants have been given to sixty-six selected proposals under the MHRD-SPARC Study in India (2500 scholarships to 60,000 students from thirty countries in 2018).

UK-India Education and Research Initiative

The UK-India Education and Research Initiative (UKIERI) is a bilateral pilot programme between the UK and India. It has been primarily conceived to promote short-term outward UG student mobility from the UK to India which could not only contribute to the foreign students' understanding of India's cultural diversity but also provide international experiences which will help them appreciate India's role in knowledge creation at the global level, which can in turn enhance employment opportunities for the UK graduates. This programme seeks to extend support to the UK universities interested in collaborating with Indian partners. Concomitantly it supports internationalization of Indian HEIs under the GoI's 'Study in India' programme. The objective is to seed deeper institutional partnership and research collaboration. There are 105 higher education partnerships and seven skills partnership programmes involving over 100 institutes – which are among the top-ranking HEIs in the NIRF with high national accreditation scores – from India. Around 500 senior educators from the engineering field have got opportunities under the UKIERI-AICTE technical leadership programme. The budget is in excess of GBP 1 million while the upper limit is pegged at GBP 60,000.

Fulbright-Nehru Fellowship

The Fulbright-Nehru Fellowship seeks to provide funds for the scholars, teachers and students who want to teach and conduct research in the United States. This also includes professional development programmes for university administrators to develop leadership capabilities. Students can pursue a master's degree or attend a US university as a visiting researcher. Recognizing India's vibrant democracy, rich history and enchanting diversity as new vistas for research, the US-India Educational Foundation (USIEF) has set up initiatives for students wanting to study and to conduct research in India. The USIEF is also connected with Study in India programme. Since its inception in 1950, it has administered over 20,000 grants for Indian and US citizens.

According to the Institute of International Education's 2020 Open Doors report, over 3300 US students studied in India during the 2018–19 academic years. Since 2000–1, this figure has more than quadrupled (USIEF 2020).

In addition, individual home universities provide financial aid packages to help students fund their studies abroad (e.g. the Benjamin A. Gilman International Scholarship Program, the David L. Boren Undergraduate and Graduate Scholarships and the Critical Language Scholarships).

6. Conclusion

The pertinent question is as the extent of internationalization grows, what would be the long-term implications for the Indian higher education. Specifically speaking, what happens to access to higher education system and quality of higher education in terms of teaching-learning and research. Different aspects of internationalization with varying implications can be read as signs of development of the Indian higher education system – these are unambiguously beneficial as well as contradictory. This is related to the question of how, and to what extent, internationalization can contribute to the pursuit of quality and foster 'publicness' of higher education at the national level as well as at the global level as a global public good. Marginson and van der Wende (2007) point out that internationalization – which depends on its extent and content, cooperation and competition, and the relationship between national and global elements – is ambiguous with both zero-sum aspects and positive sum aspects. Internationalization of higher education involves two tendencies which run commensurately (Teichler 2015): on the one hand, internationalization encourages the selection-based mechanism and accentuates the hierarchical ordering as the globally mobile students and the teachers tend to converge among the top-ranking world reputed universities, and on the other through forging international collaborations, it results in the collaborating departments and universities across the borders become more diverse, which contributes to enrichment of teaching-learning processes and conduct of research.

The global market in higher education is more competitive now than it was ever in the past. This competitiveness is attributable to the growing dominance of global ranking of universities which strengthens the selection-based efficiency involving the students and the faculty. Global integration enlarges the market and expands the range of opportunities but it comes with challenges.

The higher education system is intrinsically heterogeneous devoid of a level-playing field among the HEIs. By opening up to the global market, opportunities to get integrated will expand and with it, the costs too. Not all HEIs will get access to a mobile pool of students and faculty. And not all HEIs will survive the competition because the top ones will occupy a larger share resulting in a bipolar market. Despite concentration of quality human capital among the top-ranking universities, the overall quality is likely to improve due to benchmarking of quality in a system which is an uncertain and contextual blend of cooperation and competitiveness. The increasing usage of ICT will enable the top-ranked HEIs to expand and overcome the constraints posed by the scarce availability of quality inputs, students and teachers. The emergence of ICT and online classes may also garner more participation and improve quality of content; however, quality in the broad sense which includes socialization and self-formation would suffer relegation. As the extent of internationalization is likely to remain restricted to the top HEIs (public and private), these very institutions get 'disembedded' from the national context as pointed out by Marginson and van der Wende (2007).

India, so far, has failed to reap the benefits of internationalization in a big way. Bhushan (2009) refers to the duality of higher education, whether it is a social service or a tradable service, in the context of India agreeing to be a party to the General Agreement on Trade in Services (GATS). In a developing country context like India, this renders policymaking, which involves embracing the global space through measures to promote internationalization, rather delicate and in fact challenging.

The entry of foreign universities will add to the competitiveness of the national higher education market. Expansion may improve quality, but increased differentiation would dilute and defy the purpose of inclusive expansion. Inviting foreign universities may not be a remedy for quality, or it could be only to a certain extent. This does not, of course, militate against the rationale for internationalization. This only means that the government should build up a robust and sturdy higher education system to cater to the national needs in the best possible manner as internationalization continues to grow.

As noted, outward mobility of students is ten times higher than inward mobility. India is basically an exporter of human capital and an importer of knowledge. A good number of Indian scholars are working abroad. We have also seen that despite a large share in world of publications, collaborations are not so prominent compared to other countries. This goes on to validate our observations that, given the total volume of publications, quality remains a major issue. India is therefore yet to emerge as a strong contender or competitor in the world of knowledge.

As we emerge out of the pandemic, it remains uncertain how the future of internationalization will unfold as the process of internationalization undergoes structural changes, some of which will prove to be irreversible with the likelihood of internationalization at home gaining wider acceptance.

India must build up a sound and a competitive higher education system to reap the benefits of internationalization even if it will be more 'at home' in the near future.

Appendix

Table 7A.1 Inward and Outward Student Mobility, India, 2018

Outward mobility: Indian students to other countries				Inward mobility: Students from other countries			
United States	135940	36.25	36.25	Nepal	12747	26.88	26.88
Australia	73316	19.55	55.79	Afghanistan	4657	9.82	36.70
Canada	34806	9.28	65.07	Bangladesh	2075	4.38	41.07
UK	19599	5.23	70.30	Bhutan	1809	3.81	44.89
Germany	15473	4.13	74.42	Nigeria	1614	3.40	48.29
UAE	13370	3.56	77.99	United States	1517	3.20	51.49
New Zealand	11604	3.09	81.08	Yemen	1498	3.16	54.65
Ukraine	10698	2.85	83.94	Sri Lanka	1252	2.64	57.29
Kyrgyzstan	8662	2.31	86.25	Iran	1127	2.38	59.67
Georgia	5832	1.55	87.80	Malaysia	1087	2.29	61.96
Cyprus	4038	1.08	88.88	UAE	1050	2.21	64.17
Italy	3880	1.03	89.91	Tanzania	968	2.04	66.21
Kazakhstan	3719	0.99	90.90	Ethiopia	870	1.83	68.05
France	3252	0.87	91.77	Somalia	670	1.41	69.46
Malaysia	2810	0.75	92.52	Canada	527	1.11	70.57
Ireland	2606	0.69	93.21	Iraq	498	1.05	71.62
Poland	2497	0.67	93.88	Kenya	489	1.03	72.65
Netherlands	2438	0.65	94.53	Saudi Arabia	470	0.99	73.64
Sweden	2086	0.56	95.09	Zimbabwe	467	0.98	74.63

Outward mobility: Indian students to other countries				Inward mobility: Students from other countries			
Latvia	1233	0.33	95.42	Syrian Arab Republic	453	0.96	75.58
Armenia	1218	0.32	95.74	Thailand	398	0.84	76.42
Saudi Arabia	1154	0.31	96.05	Congo	379	0.80	77.22
Japan	962	0.26	96.30	Oman	361	0.76	77.98
Indonesia	947	0.25	96.56	Qatar	356	0.75	78.73
Korea Republic	886	0.24	96.79	Kuwait	338	0.71	79.45
Switzerland	792	0.21	97.00	Bahrain	284	0.60	80.05
Finland	761	0.20	97.21	Ghana	252	0.53	80.58
Mauritius	758	0.20	97.41	Turkmenistan	249	0.53	81.10
China, Hong Kong	719	0.19	97.60	Mauritius	240	0.51	81.61
Czechia	685	0.18	97.78	Uganda	240	0.51	82.11
Qatar	659	0.18	97.96	Vietnam	240	0.51	82.62
Lithuania	637	0.17	98.13	Rwanda	233	0.49	83.11
Spain	626	0.17	98.30	Mozambique	231	0.49	83.60
Oman	600	0.16	98.46	Malawi	206	0.43	84.03
Tajikistan	573	0.15	98.61	Côte d'Ivoire	201	0.42	84.46
Bahrain	572	0.15	98.76	Indonesia	190	0.40	84.86
Hungary	506	0.13	98.90	Korea, Republic	173	0.36	85.22
South Africa	408	0.11	99.00	South Africa	164	0.35	85.57
Denmark	400	0.11	99.11	Mali	159	0.34	85.90
Austria	387	0.10	99.21	UK	151	0.32	86.22
Norway	354	0.09	99.31	Maldives	149	0.31	86.54
Other countries	2592	0.69	100.00	Other countries	6385	13.46	100.00
Total	375055	100.00		Total	47424	100.00	

Source: Author using data from http://uis.unesco.org/en/uis-student-flow (accessed 26 November 2020). For the most recent data, see GoI 2021d.

8

Engineering Education in India

Jandhyala B. G. Tilak and Pradeep Kumar Choudhury

1. Introduction

Similar to global trends, higher education has experienced remarkable growth during the post-independence period, and more impressively during the last three to four decades, in such a way that it has become the second largest educational system in the world after China, pushing the United States to the third place. Growing aspirations of young Indians, particularly in the critical phase of 'demographic dividend' the country is passing through on the one hand and India's resolve to create a knowledge society on the other, have contributed to the tendencies towards massification of higher education. However, within higher education, technical education, and more specifically engineering education, has been recognised for a long period as an important factor for technological advancement and socioeconomic development of the nation. Engineering, science and technology have transformed the world we live in, contributing to significantly longer life expectancy and enhanced quality of life for large numbers of the world's population (UNESCO 2010). The contributions of engineering education in India that started largely with building roads and bridges are currently addressing several new and emerging challenges like providing more equitable access to information for our populations, environmental protection and natural resource management, artificial intelligence, natural and man-made disaster mitigation and so on.

During the last three decades, engineering education in India has experienced an extraordinary high rate of growth, and it has gone through, like the rest of higher education, several pertinent transitions, experiencing several internal and external shocks, the major ones being rapid growth of private sector, declining public investment, shortage of faculty, and declining quality. It is also associated with limited research output, rising student fees and overall costs of education, raising questions of affordability and inequalities in access, growing unemployment, falling wages of engineering graduates and the like. Some of these problems are attributable to the unplanned and unbridled growth of the engineering education, a very rapid growth of private sector, and weak and ineffective governance mechanisms. The path of rapid growth has been affected by economic slowdowns, which brought a recession in the global economy. Globally, engineering education is experiencing an increasing pressure on graduate employability, particularly in the context of the changing environment in the labour market. The complexities found in the global engineering labour market have changed the discourse on engineering education. Understanding engineering education nowadays is becoming quite complex in India, particularly with the emergence of different kinds of players with different interests, and a very large number of private unaided institutions.

This chapter is an attempt to identify and explore the major issues and new challenges faced by engineering education in the contemporary times. Using secondary data available form Ministry of Human Resource Development (MHRD), All India Council for Technical Education (AICTE) and the University Grants Commission (UGC), and household level data collected by the National Sample Survey Office (NSSO), the chapter analyses three major dimensions: the trends and patterns in the growth of engineering education in India considering the expansion in terms of number of institutions and enrolment; the inequalities in growth in engineering education both at the regional and state level, concentrating on regional imbalances in the growth of engineering education, besides inequalities in access by caste and gender; and the quality concerns of engineering education.

2. Growth of Engineering Education in India: Trends and Patterns

The economic reform policies introduced in the early 1990s in India gave impetus to the growth of the service sector and within the service sector to the growth of the information and technology (IT) industry. As a result, starting from 1990s, demand for technical education in India rose significantly, and pursuing engineering education became a significant attraction to students as India became the leading provider of IT and engineering, outsourcing services to the world, and employment opportunities in this field started growing exponentially (UNESCO 2010; Dubey et al. 2019). Economic liberalization and growth of service sector (relating to IT services) led to high demand for engineering graduates both within the country (Dubey et al. 2019) and abroad. As a result, many new engineering institutions, particularly private engineering/technological universities and colleges in the self-financing mode, were established in India.

An important outcome of the rapid growth is that engineering education that was considered as an exclusive space for Indian elites until the 1990s took a new turn by catering to the growing ambitions of middle-class families. The elite nature of engineering education to a great extent slowly vanished. Today engineering education in India attracts new waves of low- and middle-income students to meet their aspirations for getting trained in technical fields. An engineering degree has been a preferred option for most of senior secondary school graduates, and not just the academically bright and economically well-off students. With the expectation of higher returns in Indian and global labour markets from engineering studies, and also high returns in the marriage market in the form of dowries (Mishra 2011), demand for engineering education has reached more segments of society. Engineering education is seen as linked to social mobility, for some families even as essential to reaching a higher level of socioeconomic status. Thus, more 'new middle-class' parents have come to aspire to send their children to engineering institutions (Fernandez 2006).

The net result has been that overall enrolments in engineering education have improved dramatically. Enrolments in engineering and technology have increased from 96,000 in 1975–6 to 4.1 million in 2018–19. In 2018–19, enrolments in engineering and technology constituted 10.9 per cent of the total enrolments in higher education. The corresponding figure was a little below 4 per cent in 1975–6, as shown in Table 8.1.

The number of degree level engineering institutions (excluding polytechnics) increased from a meagre 109 (in 1975–6) to 3124 in 2018–19, that is, it multiplied 28.6 times in the last forty-five years. Likewise, student enrolment in engineering studies has risen from 96,000 in 1975–6 to 4,076,000 in 2018–19 (multiplication by 42.4 times). The rate of growth of both institutions and enrolments in engineering education was higher than the rate of growth of overall higher education. However, recent years have seen a marginal decline in the number of engineering institutions. For instance, the number of degree level engineering institutions has come down by 247 between 2012–13 and 2018–19, falling from 3371 in 2012–13 to 3124 in 2018–19. Similarly, the share of engineering education in enrolments in higher education reached the highest proportion of 15.5 per cent in 2012–13 and declined afterwards.

Table 8.1 Growth of Engineering Institutions and Enrolment in India

Year	Institutions			Enrolment		
	Higher education	Engineering education	Share of engineering in higher education (%)	Higher education ('000)	Engineering education ('000)	Share of engineering in higher education (%)
1975–6	4,124	109	2.64	2,426.11	96.06	3.96
1980–1	4,396	149	3.38	2,752.44	128.94	4.68
1985–6	5,427	242	4.46	3,605.02	176.54	4.90
1990–1	6,323	277	4.38	4,924.87	216.84	4.40
1995–6	8,188	355	4.34	6,574.00	315.72	4.80
2000–1	11,568	678	5.86	8,399.44	529.47	6.30
2005–6	20,769	1,562	7.52	12,043.05	795.12	6.60
2008–9	25,951	2,237	8.62	15,768.42	1,313.70	8.33
2012–13	37,204	3,371	9.06	21,501.15	3,333.16	15.50
2015–16	42,188	3,364	7.97	34,584.78	4,885.13	14.13
2018–19	42,846	3,124	7.29	37,399.39	4,076.28	10.90
Growth rate[a]	5.59	8.11	-	6.57	9.10	-

[a] Compound rate of growth per annum (%).
Source: Authors, using data from *UGC Annual Report* (various years).

While higher education as a whole grew at a rate of 6.6 per cent per annum, enrolments in engineering education increased at a rate of 9.1 per cent during this period of nearly two and a half decades. Growth in enrolments has probably been faster than anywhere else in the world, and India is now regarded as having the second largest number of engineering students in the world. Around 25 per cent of the world's engineers are in India (Madheswari and Mageswari 2020: 215).

However, at the same time, the nature of growth of engineering education has its own effects. Growing demand for technical education coupled with the inability of the state to invest further in technical education led to the liberalization of technical education (Mani and Arun 2012), and the private sector seized the opportunity and almost invaded the engineering education sector (Choudhury 2016). Starting with the late 1980s, the private sector slowly started participating in engineering education, and in time it expanded to a large scale. Private engineering colleges and 'institutions deemed-to-be-universities', known briefly as deemed universities, under self-financing mode have been established in large numbers in a very short period, and today the Indian engineering education system is characterised by the preponderance of private (self-financing) colleges and deemed universities.

The private sector, which accounted for just 15 per cent of the enrolments in 1960, accounted for 86 per cent of admissions by 2019 and for a similar proportion of all engineering institutions in India (Kapur and Mehta 2004; AICTE 2019). The growth of the private institutions is, however, not even across all the states in India. In states like Andhra Pradesh, Kerala, Karnataka, Tamil Nadu, Telangana and Maharashtra, the growth of private institutions has been so high that in 2019 more than 90 per cent of total engineering institutions were private engineering colleges (Table 8.2).

Interestingly, a majority of the economically better-off states (with per capita net state domestic product (NSDP) higher than the national average) have a higher share of private engineering institutions than their counterparts, that is, states with low per capita NSDP, with very few exceptions. At the macro-level, a direct relationship seems to exist between economic growth and private participation in engineering education and also between the total number of engineering institutions (per 1 million population) and NSDP per capita, as the logarithmic trend lines in Figure 8.1 make it clear. The simple coefficient of correlation between NSDP per capita and the private institutions is 0.47.

Apart from the level of economic development, is there any other factor that explains the growth of private sector? First, we note that other variables like population of the age-group (eighteen to twenty-three), which is the main pool

Table 8.2 Private Engineering Institutions in India (As % of All Engineering Institutions), 2018–19

	%	All (number)		%	All (number)		%	All (number)
Telangana	94.6	239	Haryana	86.2	130	Jharkhand	60	20
Andhra Pradesh	94.5	305	Chhattisgarh	84.8	46	Bihar	47.4	38
Madhya Pradesh	91.9	186	Gujarat	84.1	126	Delhi	47.1	17
Maharashtra	91.7	363	Rajasthan	83.8	117	Jammu & Kashmir	45.5	11
Punjab	89.7	97	Puducherry	82.4	17	Assam	42.1	19
Tamil Nadu	89.5	533	West Bengal	79.6	93			
Odisha	89.4	94	Himachal Pradesh	76.5	17			
Uttar Pradesh	88.9	253	Uttarakhand	72.4	29			
Karnataka	87.6	193	Kerala	71.3	160	All India	86.8	3124

Source: Authors, derived from *All India Survey of Higher Education, 2018–19.*

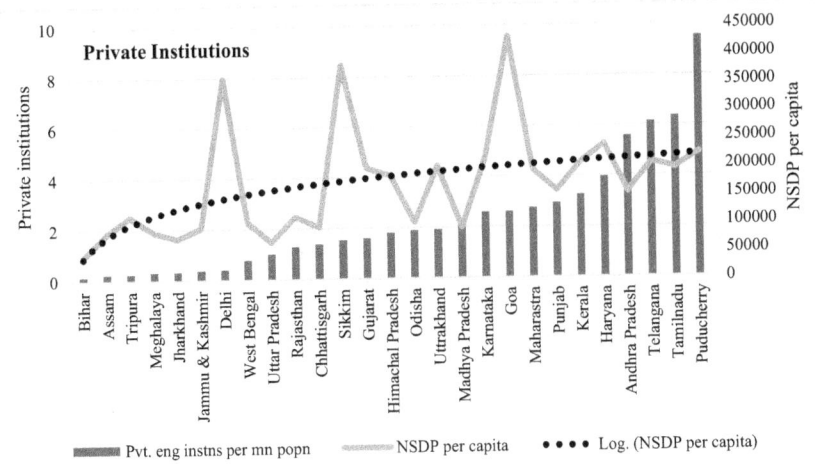

Figure 8.1 Economic growth and number of engineering institutions (per 1 million population), 2018–19.

from which demand for higher education emerges, or government expenditure on engineering education, inadequacy of which will encourage the private sector to take advantage of the situation and open private institutions, are not found to be statistically significant factors in explaining the variations between several states in the growth of all engineering institutions. State income per capita is the most important factor that positively influences the growth of the number of institutions, in addition to industrial production (gross value added as percentage of gross state domestic product (GSDP)) which also influences positively the growth in the number of institutions (in 2012–13). But in another equation for 2018–19, we included rate of graduate unemployment,[1] which is also found to be having a positive effect on the number of institutions. That is, higher the overall graduate unemployment, the higher would be the demand for engineering education. After all, employment prospects for engineering (and other professional) graduates are generally believed to be brighter than those for graduates of general higher education. With the inclusion of unemployment in the equation, industrial production has turned out to be not statistically significant. Second, we get similar results for the equation that is estimated to explain interstate variations in private institutions (Table 8.3).

After all, as the public sector institutions are relatively small in number in every state, it is not surprising that the results are similar. However, in case of private

---

[1] Graduate unemployment refers to all graduates, as we do not have data separately for engineering graduates by states. Also, this was not available for 2012–13.

Table 8.3 Factors Influencing Growth of Engineering Institutions (Dependent Variable: Natural Log of Institutions per One Million Population)

	All Institutions		Private Institutions	
	2012–13	2018–19	2012–13	2018–19
Ln NSDP	1.2349***	0.9946***	1.1238***	1.0993***
	(0.431)	(0.309)	(0.451)	(0.303)
Ln Population (age-group 18–23)	−2.1668	−0.3686	−4.551*	−1.4316
	−2.108	(0.880)	(2.90)	(2.424)
Ln Gross value added from industry as % of GSDP	0.4235**	0.0222	0.656***	0.4745**
	(0.209)	(0.029)	(0.241)	(0.178)
Ln Public expenditure on education as % of GSDP	−0.1783	−0.0032	−0.332*	−0.1209
	(0.159)	(0.101)	(0.173)	(0.122)
Ln Graduate unemployment rate		0.8031**		−0.6751
		(0.416)		(0.537)
Intercept	−9.6964	−12.9716	−4.089	−12.6079
	(5.772)	(3.591)	(7.236)	(7.315)
Number of observations	25	26	23	26
F-value	8.01	5.12	6.97	5.12
R-square	0.531	0.553	0.525	0.552

*** $p<0.01$, ** $p<0.05$, * $p<0.10$.

Note: Figures in () are robust standard errors.

Source: Authors.

institutions, industrial production turned out to be important both in 2012–13 and in 2018–19. Further public expenditure is negatively related to growth in private institutions in 2012–13; the coefficient is statistically significant at 90 per cent level of confidence. As one expects, as the government expenditure on engineering education declines, private sector takes advantage and opens more and more institutions.

The alarming growth of the private sector has been in response to the growing aspirations of low and middle classes coupled with the opening up of the Indian economy. As the government engineering institutions are not sufficient to meet the increasing demand, private actors played a dominant role, as establishment of these institutions became easy with a flexible permissions system of state governments and an equally straightforward approval mechanism of the AICTE (the apex body for technical education in India). Several private registered trusts and societies, including mainly those with commercial interests, have contributed to this phenomenal growth of engineering education in the country.

The proliferation and wholesale privatization of engineering education in India has led to many more problems (Dubey et al. 2019); important ones include inequality in the access to engineering education and decline in the quality of engineering education. The two are related and are briefly discussed in the following sections of the chapter.

3. Inequalities in Engineering Education

Tilak (2015) has shown that inequalities in higher education by gender have narrowed in India over the years to minimum levels; inequalities by caste have also improved at an impressive rate, though the situation is far from satisfactory; and regional disparities were reduced, but the improvement is very modest. More importantly, Tilak (2015) also found that inequalities between the rich and the poor have been very high, and the gap has widened over the years. We shall examine whether in case of engineering education the situation is similar or different.

Regional Disparities: Interregional and Interstate

The regional imbalance continues to be a major issue despite expansion of higher education in India in recent years, despite the fact that it was seriously taken up as a major issue in the National Policy on Education (1986), when it stated that 'steps will be taken to facilitate interregional mobility by providing equal access to every Indian of requisite merit, regardless, of his origins as [far as] the higher and technical education is concerned' (GoI 1986: 6). Around two-thirds of India's engineering institutions at the undergraduate level are located in the states of Tamil Nadu, Karnataka, Andhra Pradesh and Maharashtra in spite of these states accounting for less than one-third of the total population of the country. The southern region alone has almost half the number of total engineering institutions, whereas there are very few in eastern region (Table 8.4). As per the latest statistics available from AICTE, there are around 1447 degree level engineering institutions (46.6 per cent of the total institutions in India) in 2018–19 in the southern region, which consist of five states and one union territory, namely Andhra Pradesh, Karnataka, Kerala, Puducherry, Tamil Nadu and Telangana, whereas there are only 226 institutions in the four major states of eastern region which includes Assam, Jharkhand, Odisha and West Bengal (7.2 per cent of the total institutions in India). Interestingly, ten states and two union territories in the eastern and northern regions (Bihar, Jharkhand, Odisha, West

Table 8.4 Regional Concentration of Engineering Institutions and Intake in India, by Management, 2012–13 and 2018–19

Regions	Institutions			Enrolment		
	Government	Private	Total	Government	Private	Total
2012–13						
Southern	35.3	47.6	46.6	38.81	50.59	49.36
Northern	10.5	11.3	11.2	8.66	9.74	9.62
Eastern	14.0	5.6	6.2	9.46	5.40	5.95
Western	8.0	11.4	11.1	7.75	12.19	11.74
Central	15.4	11.1	11.5	19.60	12.35	13.04
Northwest	16.8	13.0	13.3	15.72	9.73	10.30
All India	100.0	100.0	100.0	100.00	100.00	100.00
	(286)	(3085)	(3371)	(94.5)	(871.7)	(967.8)
2018–19						
Southern	38.26	47.55	46.32	49.14	57.55	55.78
Northern	13.56	9.74	10.24	10.02	7.36	7.92
Eastern	13.56	6.57	7.23	9.59	5.39	6.27
Western	7.51	12.43	11.78	6.91	13.49	12.10
Central	10.17	11.66	11.46	11.57	9.74	10.13
North West	16.95	11.91	12.58	12.77	6.48	7.80
All India	100.00	100.00	100.00	100.00	100.00	100.00
	(413)	(2711)	(3124)	(151.0)	(566.6)	(717.6)

Note: Figures on enrolment in ( ) for 'All India' are in thousands.
Source: Authors, original data from AICTE database.

Bengal, Haryana, Himachal Pradesh, Jammu & Kashmir, Punjab, Uttarakhand, Uttar Pradesh, Delhi and Chandigarh), accounting for 45.3 per cent of India's population, have only about 17.4 per cent of the total engineering institutions, with an intake capacity of 15 per cent.

The region-wise student intake for student admissions and actual enrolments also reveals more or less a similar pattern. Six southern states account for 49.3 per cent of the total intake (and 55.8 per cent of enrolment) in degree level engineering institutions in 2018–19, while the eastern region accounts for only about 6.5 per cent of the total intake (and 6.3 per cent of enrolments) in India. Ten out of the twenty-eight states (Tamil Nadu, Andhra Pradesh, Maharashtra, Uttar Pradesh, Telangana, Karnataka, Madhya Pradesh, Gujarat, Kerala and Haryana) and eight union territories together account for 80 per cent of the total student places for admission in the country (AICTE 2019). Statistics clearly suggest the glaring regional imbalance that exists in the field of engineering education in

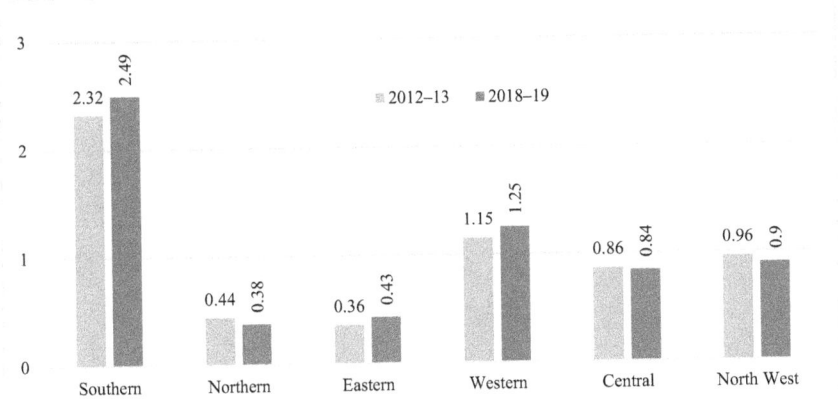

Figure 8.2 Ratio of regional concentration of engineering institutions.
Source: Authors, based on *All India Survey of Higher Education*, 2012–13 and 2018–19.

India, leading to oversupply in some regions and states and shortages in others (Rao 2003; Roach 2007). A careful look at the growth of institutions reveals that the regional imbalance is not only due to the establishment of a large number of private colleges in southern region and a lack of them in other regions, but also due to imbalanced public supply of government engineering colleges.

In fact, if we look at the geographic concentration of engineering institutions, we note a very high degree of regional imbalance. The extent of interregional disparity is clearly highlighted in our analysis of the concentration ratio, which is estimated here as a ratio of the share of institutions in a region in the national total to the share of region's population in the national population(Figure 8.2). If the value of the ratio equals 1, it means that the distribution of institutions is proportionate to the distribution of population; if the ratio is above 1, it shows over concentration, and if it is below 1, the state is underserved in relation to population. We also note that the regional concentration has intensified between 2012–13 and 2018–19, with the ratio increasing in case of southern and western regions. Though there is a small increase in case of eastern region, the number is insignificant, while the disadvantages of the northern region and northwestern region increased.

Similar analysis by states provides further details on interstate inequalities (Table 8.5). For instance, Tamil Nadu, Telangana and Andhra Pradesh have the highest numbers of engineering institutions per 1 lakh population. Corresponding numbers are: seventy per 1 lakh population in Tamil Nadu, sixty in Telangana, and fifty-eight in Andhra Pradesh. On the other end, we have states like Bihar and Jharkhand with just three and five, respectively, per 1 lakh population! Assam

Table 8.5 State-Wise Engineering Institutions per 1 Million Population in India, 2018–19

State and UTs	Institutions per 1 million Population		Concentration ratio	
	2012–13	2018–19	2012–13	2018–19
Andhra Pradesh	7.15	5.87	2.58	2.55
Assam	0.44	0.56	0.16	0.23
Bihar	0.21	0.32	0.09	0.15
Chandigarh	2.80	3.43	0.82	0.93
Chhattisgarh	1.93	1.62	0.69	0.66
Delhi	1.05	0.87	0.35	0.33
Goa	3.40	3.27	1.31	1.25
Gujarat	1.79	1.88	0.64	0.79
Haryana	6.17	4.60	2.08	1.86
Himachal Pradesh	3.03	2.34	1.13	1.08
Jammu & Kashmir	0.65	0.84	0.24	0.39
Jharkhand	0.42	0.54	0.16	0.24
Karnataka	3.11	2.96	1.09	1.27
Kerala	4.55	4.58	2.03	2.46
Madhya Pradesh	3.06	2.29	1.09	0.94
Maharashtra	3.25	3.00	1.14	1.25
Odisha	2.31	2.10	0.87	0.93
Puducherry	10.95	11.56	4.31	4.64
Punjab	3.68	3.27	1.27	1.41
Rajasthan	1.97	1.53	0.68	0.59
Tamil Nadu	7.06	7.07	2.80	3.48
Telangana	9.66	6.47	3.41	2.76
Uttar Pradesh	1.58	1.14	0.56	0.46
Uttarakhand	3.42	2.63	1.18	1.10
West Bengal	0.90	0.97	0.32	0.39
All India	2.75	2.37	1.00	1.00
Coef. of Variation	0.847	0.874		

Source: Authors, data assembled from AICTE database; Census of India.

and Jammu & Kashmir similarly have lower numbers. The interstate inequality has increased marginally, as the coefficient of variation increases from 0.84 to 0.87. The concentration ratios given in Table 8.5 show the extent of interstate inequalities in the growth of engineering education. They also confirm that, even after adjusting for population, states such as Telangana, Tamil Nadu, Kerala, Haryana and Andhra Pradesh dominate the scene of engineering institutions in the country. The interstate inequality is also mainly due to the predominant role of the private sector, which, ignoring concerns for regional balanced development, has concentrated on states where there is apparently high demand.

The concentration ratio ranges between 0.86 in Bihar and 4.31 in Puducherry in 2012–13. In 2018–19, these two states were still placed at the two extreme ends of the ratio in terms of concentration. There is a very high concentration in Puducherry, Telangana and Tamil Nadu with a ratio above 3. Tamil Nadu which was the third in concentration ratio among the major states in 2012–13 rose to second position in 2018–19. There are as many as twelve states with over-concentration and about the same number with under-provision. Between 2012–13 and 2018–19, one does not find any significant change in concentration, implying that no special effective measures were taken to improve regional balanced development or clearly to deconcentrate the spatial growth of engineering institutions in the country.

Inequality by Gender

Over the decades, there has been a phenomenal growth in the enrolment of female students in higher education in India, and their share in total enrolment has reached 48.6 per cent in 2018–19, suggesting achievement of near gender parity (Table 8.6). In 2018–19, of the total enrolment of 37.4 million students in higher education in India, 18.2 million were women (MHRD 2019). The gross enrolment ratio (GER) in higher education among girls is the same as in case of males (26.4 per cent among females, and 26.3 per cent among males). But the picture is not the same with respect to all branches of higher education. In arts/social sciences, basic science and medicine, the representation of females is higher than males, while in commerce/management and engineering/technology female enrolment is less than that of males. For instance, out of the total student population among males in higher education, 18.7 per cent are pursuing engineering studies, while only 8 per cent of females do the same.

In the case of engineering education, women constitute nearly 30 per cent of the enrolments in 2018–19. This marks a big increase from a meagre 2.2 per cent in 1975–6 with an annual average growth rate of 15.9 per cent (Table 8.6). This rate of growth in women's enrolment in engineering education in the last four decades is higher than the growth in their enrolment in overall higher education which is 8.3 per cent. However, women's enrolments in engineering are still not at par with that of males. Often, it is argued that engineering and technical education is a masculine domain and hence out of reach for women. Those who support this line of argument reproduce certain untenable social

Table 8.6 Enrolment of Women in Higher and Engineering Education in India

Year	Higher education		Engineering education	
	Total (in lakhs)	% Share	Total (in lakhs)	% Share
1975–6	6.0	24.5	0.021	2.2
1980–1	7.5	27.2	0.050	3.0
1985–6	10.7	29.6	0.122	6.9
1990–1	14.4	29.2	0.171	7.9
1995–6	21.9	33.3	0.264	8.4
2000–1	30.1	35.9	1.09	20.6
2005–6	44.7	37.1	1.86	23.4
2010–11	70.5	41.5	8.01	28.0
2015–16	134.7	47.3	13.60	27.8
2016–17	141.6	48.1	13.65	28.5
2017–18	174.4	47.6	12.34	29.0
2018–19	181.9	48.6	11.93	29.3
Growth rate[a]	8.27	–	15.94	–

Note:
[a] Compound rate of growth per annum.

Source: Authors, derived from *Selected Educational Statistics* (various years), *UGC Annual Report* (various years), and *All India Survey of Higher Education* (various years).

myths, such as the idea that women are emotional, technology is strictly logical and they do not go together. There is also view that men are good at mathematics and machines, while women have no clue about these (Rao 2007: 187). But all this does not seem to be true. Nevertheless, quite a few studies have found that technical and professional education is, by and large, dominated by males more than is general education, in which females constitute a larger proportion (Salim 2008; Ghuman et al. 2009). Despite this, the improvement in the participation of women in engineering education during the last four decades highlights the gradual rise women's interest in this discipline of study.

Inequality by Caste

Wide variations in the access to higher education between different social groups exist in India. In 2018–19, the GER in higher education is 23 per cent for scheduled castes (SCs), and 17.2 per cent for scheduled tribes (STs), as compared to the ratio of 26.3 per cent for all at the all-India level (MHRD 2019). Furthermore, it is generally felt that engineering and technical education in India has been highly selective in terms of providing access to the disadvantaged sections of the society such as SCs and STs (Rao 2006), as it is relatively more

Table 8.7 Enrolments of Scheduled Castes and Scheduled Tribes in Engineering Education in India

Year	Scheduled Castes			Scheduled Tribes		
	Male	Female	Total	Male	Female	Total
1985–6	3.61	0.22	3.83	0.99	0.04	1.03
1990–1	5.70	0.67	6.36	1.12	0.08	1.19
1995–6	3.91	0.46	4.37	1.61	0.18	1.79
2000–1	5.23	1.67	6.90	2.26	0.33	2.59
2005–6	15.06	5.38	20.44	5.31	1.88	7.19
2010–11	5.64	2.33	7.97	1.91	0.64	2.57
2015–16	7.26	2.85	10.11	1.89	0.62	2.51
2018–19	7.65	1.96	11.04	2.07	0.74	2.81

Source: Authors, using data in *Selected Educational Statistics* (various years), UGC Annual Report (various years), *All India Survey of Higher Education* (various years).

expensive than other branches and it also requires strong academic background at school level.

The percentage of enrolment of SCs in engineering education is 11 per cent in 2018–19 as compared to a mere 3.8 per cent in 1985–6, registering an increase by three times. Similarly, the enrolment of STs in engineering education has increased from 1 per cent in the total enrolment to 2.8 per cent in a period over thirty years (Table 8.7). Ghuman et al. (2009), using the data collected from a primary survey of 2085 students in rural Punjab, found that as high as three-fourths of the total number of students from rural areas studying in different professional education programmes belonged to forward castes. It shows that while students from rural areas go to professional education in large numbers, the socially backward groups lag far behind others in terms of access to professional education. Furthermore, the access to engineering education among females belonging to different disadvantaged social groups appeared to be worse. Being a woman belonging to scheduled groups means double disadvantage. Currently only 7.7 per cent of SC females and 0.7 per cent of ST females are accessing engineering education in India. As Varma and Kapur (2010) found, a large number of students belonging to upper and middle castes/classes get admitted into Indian Institutes of Technology (IITs) in India. It was also pointed out that once admitted, students belonging to upper and middle castes/classes are likely to have much more positive experience and higher success rate than those belonging to lower castes and classes. Therefore, as widely criticised, education at the IITs has been for the privileged sections of Indian society. However, the situation is gradually, though slowly changing.

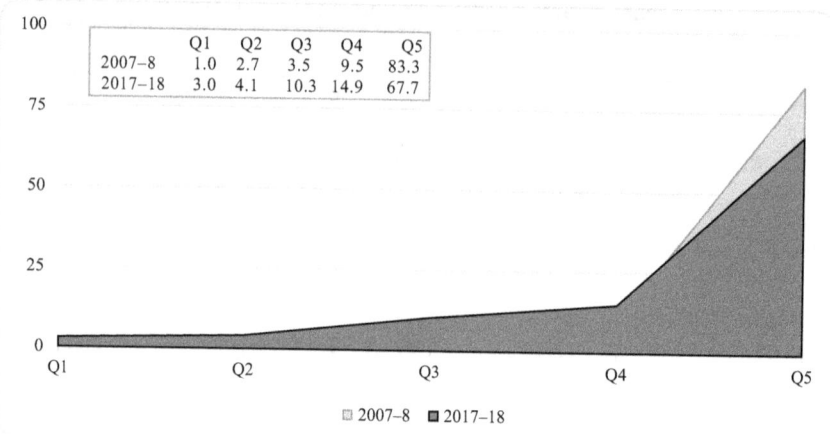

Figure 8.3 Distribution of enrolments in engineering education, by household quintiles, India (%).
Source: Authors, based on NSSO data.

Unequal Participation by Economic Classes

NSSO provides data on enrolment of students at various levels of education by average per capita monthly consumption expenditure of households. Considering household consumption expenditure as reflective of its income levels, we can analyse enrolment pattern in engineering education by economic levels of households. Figure 8.3 shows the extent of inequalities in enrolments in engineering education. About 80 per cent of the students belong to the top-income quintile and about 7 per cent is accounted by the bottom 60 per cent of the population in 2007–8. The situation marginally improved by 2017–18: the share of the top quintile coming down to 68 per cent; the bottom two quintiles accounting for 7.1 per cent, and the third quintile accounting for another 10.3 per cent.

Still a high degree of inequality persists. After all, engineering education is expensive, and the public support in the form of schemes of reimbursement of fee, fee-waivers, loans and so on are not effective enough to mitigate the inequalities.

Disciplinary Imbalance

We have already seen that the growth of higher education in India has been uneven, creating a more imbalanced system of higher education in terms of different branches of study. Within the broad stream of engineering also, we notice a high degree of imbalance between several sub-streams, as growth of student enrolments in engineering education varied significantly by different

Table 8.8 Enrolment in Engineering (First Degree) Programmes, by Sub-stream (%)

	2010–11	2018–19	Change
Computer engineering	22.25	22.85	0.60
Mechanical engineering	16.64	20.32	3.68
Electronics engineering	25.34	16.39	-8.95
Civil engineering	8.65	13.93	5.28
Electrical engineering	13.46	10.23	-3.23
Other engineering & technology	–	5.96	–
Information technology	11.45	4.88	-6.57
Architecture	–	2.11	–
Chemical engineering	1.36	1.33	-0.02
Agriculture engineering	0.215	0.552	0.34
Aeronautical engineering	–	0.441	–
Food technology	–	0.349	–
Metallurgical engineering	0.313	0.249	-0.06
Mining engineering	0.093	0.198	0.10
Marine engineering	0.189	0.109	-0.07
Dairy technology	0.066	0.078	0.02
Planning	–	0.024	–
Engineering & technology total	100.0	100.0	
Total in million	1.11	3.85	17.1

Source: Authors, derived from MHRD (2011a, 2019).

sub-disciplines. The engineering stream has seventeen sub-streams, such as electronics engineering, computer engineering, mechanical engineering, electrical engineering and so on. The top five sub-streams in terms of enrolments in 2018–19 are computer engineering with 8.8 lakh students, mechanical engineering with 7.8 lakh students, electronics engineering with 6.3 lakh students, civil engineering with 5.4 lakh students and electrical engineering with 3.9 lakh students enrolled. In information technology/computer application stream, there were 7.5 lakh students enrolled. These five disciplines account for more than 80 per cent of the total enrolments in engineering education. Distribution of enrolments across seventeen sub-streams of engineering in 2010–11 and 2018–19 is given in Table 8.8.

With economic liberalization and globalization, the Indian software services industry got a big boost, which resulted in the demand for engineers trained in electronics and IT-related disciplines such as computer science and engineering, and electronics and communications. These streams are more popular branches among students. The number of students opting to study traditionally popular branches such as electrical, civil and mechanical engineering has gone down considerably. The boom in the IT sector led to the opening up of several electronics and IT-related fields of study in newly established engineering institutions in India. Engineering institutions established after the 1990 largely concentrate only on offering electronics and IT-related streams (Banerjee and Muley 2008). As a result, India produces larger numbers of engineers in computer science and IT than in any other discipline. This was clearly linked with the labour market expectations of the engineering graduates as degrees in electronics and IT-related degree programmes helped them secure jobs relatively easily and quickly as compared to degrees in traditional subjects like civil and mechanical engineering. However, by 2010–11, the situation seems to have reached the peak, and the IT boom seems to have ended, as after 2010, we notice a declining trend in the demand for these popular branches of engineering education, necessitating closure of institutions and reduction in further growth of private engineering institutions. However, many of these institutions were opened – and this was done after receiving the required permission to offer these programmes, but – not necessarily on the basis of any reliable planning exercises by the state or by the private institutions. The resultant unplanned and unregulated growth has led to excess supply thereby compelling the introduction of tougher measures in recent years.

4. Quality of Engineering Education

We have noted that engineering education has expanded rapidly during the last few decades. However, the expansion has taken place at the expense of compromising on the quality of education, as reflected in low rates of employability of the graduates, high rates of graduate unemployment, low wages and the like. While quality has several dimensions, we briefly review some of the factors leading to poor quality. The three issues we discuss include teacher shortage, production of PhDs and quality of faculty, and excess supply of engineering graduates.

Teacher Shortage

Quality of education critically depends upon the teacher. After all, the teacher is considered the pivot of the education system. The entire higher education system in India is suffering from acute shortage of faculty and is functioning with very limited faculty – far below the minimum requirements. This problem compounded over the years, as is has been building up for the past two to three decades. Even the IITs suffer from severe shortage of faculty. The problem is grave in NITs and other national institutes as well as in state institutes of engineering and technology.

Production of Research Degrees and the Quality of Faculty

Faculty shortage is due to several factors. The first reason is a limited supply of qualified graduates. A research degree (PhD) is an essential qualification for a teaching position in higher education. The number of PhDs in a field like engineering and technology is very limited; very few bachelor's degree holders go to master's level studies and even fewer to research programmes. Graduates are reluctant to go into teaching profession because of poor academic environment, on the one hand, and better opportunities in job market even for bachelor's degree holders, on the other. So there is a big supply constraint. Added to this is the inability of the institutions to recruit faculty due to bureaucratic and legal hurdles. Another reason is the reluctance of many institutions, particularly private ones, to hire faculty, as it results in incurring higher levels of expenditures on salary accounts. These institutions try to manage with a smaller number of teachers, who are less qualified and are recruited through questionable hiring practices. All this has increased the student-faculty ratio from 9.9 in 2017–18 to 11.39 in 2018–19 (AICTE 2019).

The number of PhD degrees awarded in the discipline of engineering and technology in 2018–19 in India was 7160 (AICTE 2019). This shows an increase of about 46 per cent from the previous academic year (2017–18). Yet the number of PhDs awarded as a proportion of total undergraduate out-turn in India is less than 1 per cent (0.86 per cent), though it has gone up substantially in the recent years. This figure was merely 0.39 per cent in 2011–12 (Table 8.9). The recent sudden increase in the number of PhDs produced may be due to special efforts initiated by the government, but more importantly due to the gloomy labour market conditions for the engineering graduates completing undergraduate level studies. As a result of the latter, instead of remaining idle, these graduates may be opting for higher studies with the expectation of better jobs, a phenomenon which is generally described in the literature as the 'baby-sitting' role of higher education.

Not only the number but also the quality of teachers is important. Only a small number of faculty members in engineering institutions hold PhD degrees, and in many self-financing colleges, bachelor's degree holders occupy teaching

Table 8.9 Growth in the Number of PhDs Awarded in Engineering/Technology and as a Proportion of Total Undergraduate Out-turn in India

Year	Number of PhDs awarded	PhDs relative to undergraduate out-turn (%)
2011–12	2173	0.396
2012–13	2119	0.333
2013–14	2533	0.324
2014–15	4340	0.531
2015–16	4772	0.562
2016–17	3366	0.376
2017–18	4907	0.562
2018–19	7160	0.861

Source: Authors, compiled from data in *All India Survey of Higher Education* (various years).

positions, formally or informally. Indian faculty in general, including faculty in engineering institutions, have very few research publications to their credit. The overall research productivity of faculty members in engineering education is quite low, with very few exceptions. Part of the problem lies with the utter absence of research environment. The lack of research-oriented teachers also results in students not participating in research activities. Loyalka et al. (2014) observed that only about one-sixth of students in India participated in at least one faculty research project. All students do not necessarily take up internships, and industry-institute collaborations are also limited. Students get motivated by inspiring high-quality teachers. A large number of private colleges do not have qualified high-quality faculty in required numbers, as the system itself is not producing them. Caught in this vicious cycle, India is facing the challenge of inadequate qualified faculty in the engineering education.

Excess Supply

We do not have estimates of requirements of engineering manpower integrated with educational planning. There are some projections with regard to the requirements of colleges and number of graduates, but these do not seem to have taken into account the growth of colleges and sanctioning of intake in those colleges. For example, AICTE has projected that the country would need 3400 engineering colleges with an intake of 500,000 by 2014–15. But in 2014–15, there were 3400 colleges with an intake of 17.05 lakh students (AICTE 2019). Thus, there is a huge excess supply of institutions and thereby graduates. In terms of enrolments versus intake, we find there is an excess supply of about 50 per cent.

The AICTE is ordering closure of colleges, and the reason for this action has nothing to do with such projections, and nor is it in response to the malpractices adopted by these colleges or the dubious quality of education they are offering, but rather it is because enrolments are falling. Several engineering colleges in the country do not find takers for their courses. The owners of these colleges face a tough situation, as they are unable to run their programmes with shrinking revenues. Many colleges close down on their own behalf. In a sense, the prevailing market forces compel colleges that have excess capacity, or underutilise their capacity, with admissions much below the approved intake, to shut down. The owners of these colleges then project themselves as victims of circumstances. During the last eight years (2012–13 to 2019–20), AICTE has approved the progressive closure of 778 colleges across India. In 2018–19 against the total intake capacity at undergraduate level of 14 lakhs, the total enrolment was 7.2 lakhs, just around 51 per cent. Thus, close to half of the approved student places (6.9 lakh) remained vacant without takers in engineering colleges in the country (Table 8.10).

Quality concerns in engineering education in India are incomplete without a reference to unemployment and the related issues that engineering graduates face. This is particularly important in the context of rapidly growing demand for engineering manpower as well as other conditions in the labour market in India and abroad. Technology is advancing at an unprecedented pace across the world and has transformed the global labour market. The adoption of exponential technologies is disrupting industries by creating new markets and transforming existing markets through product or business innovations. In the new age of automation and unprecedented technological advances, the nature

Table 8.10 Number of Vacant Student Places in Engineering/Technology Institutions in India

	Total vacant seats	% to total intake (All institutions)	% to total intake (Private institutions)
2012–13	5,84,255	37.64	39.66
2013–14	6,89,908	42.21	44.33
2014–15	8,30,203	48.68	51.21
2015–16	7,76,527	47.60	50.06
2016–17	7,71,556	49.55	52.40
2017–18	7,26,108	49.18	51.95
2018–19	6,87,203	48.92	52.12

Source: Authors, derived from AICTE database.

of job market in several economies is changing rapidly. Modern technology is altering the skills that employers seek, and therefore, the training imparted in the educational institutions needs to be revisited. In fact, many graduates are unsure about using the knowledge and skills obtained during their studies in today's dynamically changing labour markets. In the labour market, job roles are being drastically modified, redefined and changed altogether, and certain types of jobs are becoming redundant while new occupations with new roles are being created. Today, we are riding a new wave of uncertainty as the pace of innovation continues to accelerate and technology extensively influences the very basic characteristics of labour market (WDR 2019). It is important to analyse what it means to be an engineer in the twenty-first century and how the skills and training imparted in institutions might better prepare engineers of the future (Winberg et al. 2020).

Efforts should be made towards producing quality engineers – with character and values – who can be meaningfully employed in the labour market and contribute to the larger developmental goals of the society and country. Overall, engineering education in India has failed to establish a robust technical ecosystem that can produce quality graduates.

4. Conclusion

Based essentially on secondary data, this chapter has attempted to analyse the changing face of engineering education in India during the last half a century. Three major dimensions in engineering education are discussed in the study: changing trends and patterns of the growth, inequalities in growth, and quality of education.

India has experienced a massive expansion of engineering education during the last half century. The explosion in numbers is propelled by the private sector. We find that engineering education, along with rest of higher education in India, is heavily privatised, with about 90 per cent of the sector being in private hands. The private sector that is currently involved in engineering education operates more on commercial basis and less on philanthropic basis; it is also financially not supported much by the state. The dominance of the private sector in engineering education has resulted in several kinds of problems. The private sector has displaced the public sector almost completely. The recent data on several aspects of engineering education further show that this privatisation has resulted in disparities. For example, the private sector invested only in those places where it was rewarding which has led to regional inequalities. There is a significant growth in the number of engineering institutions as well as enrolment in southern and western regions as compared to northern and eastern regions. The participation of private sector has also widened inequalities by caste in terms of access to engineering education. However, inequality by gender has narrowed over the years. The increasing presence of the private sector in engineering and other technical and professional education studies has also led to disciplinary distortions, as the private providers are largely offering market-friendly and job-oriented programmes in those streams of engineering that help them to expand enrolment, generate revenues through student fees, improve financial status and, more importantly, increasing their profit margins.

This large-scale expansion has not been accompanied by an improvement in quality; in fact, it is plausible to argue that the expansion has taken place at the cost of quality of education. The quality-quantity trade-offs have become clear; democratic pressures coupled with economic constraints has resulted in quantity taking precedence over quality. With regard to quality improvement, it appears that the union government has been focusing only on a few high-quality institutions like the IITs, leaving quantitative expansion to the states, which, given the fiscal constraints, left the task to the private sector, and the private sector cared little for quality. With massive expansion of poor-quality engineering education, the employability of the graduates is greatly questioned in the labour market. Several surveys have shown that only about one-fourth of the graduates are employable as the rest do not possess the required skills that meet the labour market needs. It is argued that majority of the engineering graduates in India receive low-quality training in non-elite institutions while very few get high-quality training in elite institutions.

The brief analysis attempted here suggests that there is a need for major restructuring of the engineering education sector, specifically with a better understanding of the emerging market dynamics. Leaving all players in the market to operate freely in engineering education (as has been the case for the last three decades) may lead to a great distortion in the sector, which has already started with the devaluation of engineering degree. Therefore, there is an urgent need to discuss the critical changes that the engineering education sector has experienced (and continue to experience) in the recent years. These may include understanding the changing aspirations of parents when it comes to engineering education, revisiting the role of the private sector, searching for new strategies to cope up with the declining demand, and above all, effective intervention of the state (if any) to regulate and restructure the engineering education sector to address the recent challenges. The *National Education Policy 2020* (GoI 2020c) proposes revolutionary changes in technical education (and also in the entire education system). Apart from effective regulation, the policy requires all institutions including engineering colleges and universities to get transformed into multidisciplinary institutions, with focused inclusion of humanities and liberal arts, so that critical and interdisciplinary thinking can be developed among the graduates. Adding focus on post-graduate teaching and research programmes in engineering and technology, it also proposes major curricular reforms, which when implemented, will equip engineering graduates with a good amount of knowledge in cutting-edge areas of engineering and technology and prepare them well to face the challenges of the globalized world in the twenty first century.

Acknowledgement

The chapter partly draws from an ongoing study on 'Growth of Engineering Education in India', a research project funded by the Indian Council of Social Science Research, New Delhi, through its programme of National Fellows, awarded to the first author (Jandhyala B. G. Tilak).

9

Teachers and Students as Political Actors in Indian Higher Education

Aishna Sharma, Vanessa Chishti and Binay Kumar Pathak

1. Introduction

The two primary pragmatic objectives of any higher educational institution (HEI) are teaching and research. For the accomplishment of these tasks, academic freedom – allowing students and teachers the agency to work without arbitrary external constraints – is a necessary condition.[1] In higher education in India, this agency has been progressively shrinking over the past several years owing to the dominance of a neoliberal discourse in higher education policy and political interference. The democratic functioning of universities has been severely impacted with the exclusion of teachers and students from institutional decision-making, formal and informal curbs on the freedom to dissent as well as a culture of debate and intellectual openness. It is here that the role of unions and political associations of teachers and students in preserving this democratic nature of HEIs, publicness of higher education and the academic freedom of teachers and students gains importance.

The present chapter aims to address the following questions: (1) What is the role of dissent in a higher education system? (2) What is the role of teachers' and students' political organization in preserving democracy in a higher education system? (3) What is the role of these political organizations in protecting the academic freedom of faculty? (4) What is the role played by them in preserving the publicness of Indian higher education? We address these questions taking Indian higher education system as a case study. In this chapter, the case for teachers as political actors is studied through an analysis of the two pan-India

---

[1] Agency, here, refers to intrinsically active and proactive human will, where a person is seen as a doer and a judge (Marginson 2006).

teachers' associations – All India Federation of University and College Teachers' Organisation (AIFUCTO) and Federation of Central Universities Teachers' Association (FEDCUTA). Jawaharlal Nehru University (JNU), a central university, has been discussed as a special case study, and the experience of JNU is contrasted with that of two state universities. For our reflections on students as political actors, we discuss organized student political movements related to campus issues, which often articulate wider emancipatory political visions, as well as student participation in political agitations against the excesses of the regime. We look at a few case studies: JNU, Film and Television Institute of India (FTII), Central University of Hyderabad (HCU), Banaras Hindu University (BHU), Aligarh Muslim University (AMU) and Jamia Millia Islamia (JMI)– HEIs which have been witness to student movements in recent times.

The chapter is organized as following: Section 2 gives the background of the study. Section 3 gives the methods used in the chapter. Section 4 discusses the treatment of the teachers' and students' political organizations in higher education policy. Section 5 presents the role of teachers' organizations in Indian higher education system. Section 6 discusses the role of students' organizations in Indian higher education system. Section 7 provides concluding remarks.

2. Background

Transformation of the Indian Higher Education Space

We identify two broad changes in the landscape of higher education in India: neoliberal educational policy and political interference through nationalism discourse.

Neoliberal Discourse and Indian Higher Education

The years following 2010 witnessed a drastic transformation in Indian higher education. We observe changes of two types: endogenous privatization and exogenous privatization (Ball and Youdell 2007).[2] Exogenous privatization has manifested in the form of a growing number of private HEIs in the country after 2010. Eighty per cent of the state private universities existing today were

---

[2] Exogenous privatization is a type of privatization which involves opening up of public education services to private sector, and using the private sector to design, manage or deliver aspects of public education. Under endogenous privatization, ideas, techniques and practices from private sector are imported into public sector to make it more business-like (Ball and Youdell 2007).

established after 2010 (GoI 2019d). The endogenous privatization, which may also be described as the proliferation of new public management (NPM) practices, has restructured the public-funded HEIs in important ways. The beginning of this decade saw the institution of Performance-Based Appraisal System (PBAS), designed to 'measure' the performance of faculty across different universities and colleges using standardized yardsticks. We also had institution of National Institutional Ranking Framework (NIRF) in 2016, which assesses institutions on certain standard parameters. This neoliberal form of accountability has resulted in teachers' work being reduced solely to the number of teaching and supervision hours and the number of publications, systematically undervaluing and curbing autonomy to engage in research projects with long periods of gestation (Das and Chattopadhyay 2014).

Another major change has been a steady contraction in the state spending on publicly funded institutions. In 2017, the Indian government established the Higher Education Financing Agency (HEFA), which provided loans, rather than grants, to HEIs for infrastructure and R&D. HEIs have to repay loans through 'internal sources' leading to concerns about fee hikes in public-funded HEIs. In 2018, a regulation was introduced to provide 'graded autonomy' to HEIs on the basis of their 'performance', which could provide a regulatory freedom for HEIs performing well to start self-financed courses and decide on fee structure, sparking concerns over accessibility. We also saw that, in 2019, many HEIs hiked their fees, including JNU, FTII and Indian Institutes of Technology (IITs), to name a few. The higher education, which is ideally a public good, could take the form of a private commodity which can be acquired by those who can afford to pay higher fees; this, however, reduces diversity on university campuses. A lack of diversity would cause a lack of awareness among students of the different issues that the society faces at large.

The above neoliberal reforms, premised on market-led principles in Indian higher education, alter the very public good nature of education; education may become accessible to only those who can afford to pay. The courses on offer would get restricted to management or engineering programmes, which provide an assured return to the students; disciplines like humanities and social sciences get relegated as not only irrelevant but also seen as dangerous for being 'critical' and potentially subversive (Nair 2017). Not only this, the metrics of performance emphasize research over teaching. This not only affects the quality of teaching-learning outcomes in HEIs, but also encourages faculty to undertake applied/replicable research with shorter timelines, at the cost of basic research, which is considered risky.

Nationalism Discourse and Indian Higher Education

Teachers' and students' agency has also been implicated by the recent nationalism discourse in Indian higher education space. There has been an attempt to silence the expression of any alternative views. Some of the measures suggested by the government have been to install flag masts or having battle tanks placed in JNU to instil nationalism among the constituents of the university. The politics on JNU campus has been criticized in the Draft National Education Policy (DNEP). The army has also been pitted against intellectuals; intellectualism is being criticized, with little appreciation of imaginative speech today, whereas during the national movement, differences in thoughts, which were not just about nationalism, were appreciated (Nair 2017).

Both kinds of change, neoliberal economic reform and the assertion of an aggressive nationalism, have severely curtailed the academic freedom of the faculty and student alike, affecting the nature and quality of education. It is here that the teachers and students assume a crucial role as political actors to preserve this academic freedom.

We use the theses of Michel Foucault and Jürgen Habermas to situate the role of teachers and students in preserving the academic freedom and autonomy of institutions.

Subject Formation and Resistance: Implications for Academic Freedom

The neoliberal discourse not only changes what academics do, but also what they think of themselves. The discourse expects an academic to behave in a self-interested manner. Foucault (2008) understands a *homo economicus* man to be a subject of neoliberalism who can be governed through their self-interest. They are, therefore, a subject of their 'interests' (Foucault 2008: 269–74). They can be governed not by coercion, not through their love for neoliberalism but *through the love of what neoliberalism* puts at risk (Cannizzo 2015). In this case, the risk would be losing out in the race or appearing less productive as per the benchmarks established by neoliberal accountability. They, therefore, form a self which helps reproduce the logic of the larger discourse.

Thus, a subject is formed through their *will* and not coercion. We must note that this *will to govern oneself* as per the larger discourse could change into *will not to govern oneself like that*. It is here, in this very *will*, that the resistance could develop. As a result of these neoliberal measures, the academicians may develop conflicts inside themselves. The governance mechanism may place competing demands on the faculty like delivering output in a time-bound manner and maintaining quality at the same time. It might as well constrain the academic freedom of faculty. The resistance could develop due to different interfaces (or contexts) that teachers function with. We discuss these in an upcoming section.

This resistance to the policy discourse could pave the way for re-establishing/ establishing academic freedom and preserving the public good nature of higher education, and also has a potential to even overthrow the present discourse in favour of another one. As also argued by Kumar (2016), dissent is crucial in a university; it could lead to the generation of new socially relevant knowledge. Dissent can support the culture of questioning and thinking, a culture of academic freedom as well as democratic decision-making in the university.

Habermas' Public Sphere

Our thinking on education is informed by scholarship around Habermas's concept of the public sphere, in both a socio-theoretical and a normative sense. It is normative because we regard education, especially higher education, as a communicative process that ought to be democratic in access and in its organization, and critical in its social function (Calhoun 1992). In a social theoretical sense, education is inextricably embedded in and participating in a wider public sphere. Its constituents – teachers and students – are also part of radical counter-publics (Fraser 1990) seeking progressive social transformations, both by generating critical scholarly resources that find wider circulation and through direct political action. Education is a crucial institutional element in the maintenance of hegemony, where the 'incorporation' of the young as subjects who take for granted existing social arrangements, through various subtle and unsubtle means, takes place (Apple 2004). This institutional design can be contested, and in this respect, critical scholarship, critical pedagogy, organized political activity, democratic spaces for conversation and collective self-organized initiatives such as support groups are all necessary elements.

Higher education, then, is both a modality of social control and a fertile field for political radicalism. Fighting back against interventions on the campuses, participating in protests of wider import and contemplating alternatives of how collective life and institutions may be organized, teachers and students have emerged as important constituents of the radical counter-public that contests the regime's project of hegemony.

What Are the Universities for?

The essential function of the HEIs is not only to conduct teaching and learning but also to produce 'organic intellectuals', that is the individuals protecting the very foundations of our society. For an organic intellectual to exist, autonomy to think and speak is needed. In contrast, the privatization in the Indian higher education would rather lead to producing self-interested, self-seeking and socially insensitive individuals who are interested in only promoting their own careers (Patnaik 2017). For creation of organic individuals, the HEIs should act as public spheres; Habermas's public sphere consists of non-violent social integration which is based on discourse and not money or power (Marginson 2011). The HEIs provide space for criticism and challenge, which could provide ideas for even states to reform and renew themselves (Marginson 2011).

HEIs often become the first sights for many individuals where democracy is practised and understood. The dissenting voices often become the very foundation for ensuring democratic rights within the university. And later when these individuals go out to the larger society, their beliefs get transmitted to those places, be it their households, workplace or community.

To understand if there is a presence of democracy, one could look at two major features, as posited by Dewey (1923): one, mutual interest as a factor of control and two, freer interaction between social groups and continuous readjustment through meeting new situations produced by varied intercourse. Thus, it is a mode of associated living where individuals take into account the implications of their actions on to others and vice versa, breaking down the barriers of class, race and national territory (Dewey 1923: 93). Thus, in as much as it renders agency to the individuals, along with it is attached a sense of responsibility towards others. The democratic ideals need a voice to be raised; there should be a possibility of dissent, particularly against the forces which seek to curb the academic freedom of universities. HEIs should become such spaces. The teachers' and students' political organizations often pose as dissenting voice working towards democratic ideals.

3. Methods

For understanding the role of teachers' union organization, we conducted in-depth interviews with four faculty members from three universities: two from JNU and one each from the state universities in India. We also used secondary data from the websites of the major teachers' union organizations. JNU is a central university, located in Delhi, which gives it more ease of access to University Grants Commission (UGC) or Ministry of Human Resource Development (MHRD). On the contrary, the other two state universities have limited funds comparatively impacting their salaries and research culture. To understand the role of political organizations, we identify certain interfaces which could become potential points of resistance to preserve the democratic culture of universities and the publicness of higher education. Broadly these interfaces are discipline of the faculty, political affiliation of university-level political organizations, ownership of a university, university administration and lastly, the regulatory authorities like UGC/MHRD and the state. We discuss the implications of these interfaces in the analysis section.

For student political activity in HEIs, a small, albeit dated, qualitative literature has been consulted. These reflections are based on and informed by personal experiences (participant observations) of authors, conversations with former and current student activists and union members in a handful of different HEI campuses.

4. A Look at Policy

Policies and Teachers' Political Associations

The teachers' associations were considered important even in the early 1990s, when the Rastogi Committee suggested a revision of pay scale of universities teachers, after consulting with members of AIFUCTO and with other organizations and bodies. There has been neglect, over the years, of the teachers' demand for salaries and other service conditions in India. The National Knowledge Commission (GoI 2019a) expressed the need to improve the working conditions of teachers and raise their salaries in order to attract and retain high-quality teachers and also the need to provide academic autonomy to teachers to retain them. Much of this stems from the low priority accorded to teaching profession in the country.

But, over the years, the perspective towards the teacher' and students' politics has altered. The DNEP (GoI 2019b) intends to proscribe the union activities in the universities, calling it a distraction. It notes that the university is a place of learning and not a playground for tackling social issues, failing to recognize the link between universities, political activities within the universities and welfare of the larger society.

Policies and Students' Political Associations

The Radhakrishnan Commission, the first ever commission to reform higher education in post-independence India in 1948, strongly supported the university unions arguing that such organizations bolstered the intellectual development of the students. With respect to student unions, the commission highlighted that unions should be allowed to work without any interference from the university authorities.

We see a decline in the importance given by the policy to the student union organizations in more recent years. On the instruction of the Supreme Court of India dated 12 December 2005, the government of India constituted a committee under the chairmanship of former chief election commissioner, J. M. Lyngdoh, to investigate the question of whether a balance could be struck between campus democracy and academic life (GoI 2019d). Implicit in the setting up of the committee itself is the notion that student political activity has a fundamentally disruptive potential and is at odds with the conduct of the academic life at universities or colleges. As the report of the Lyngdoh Committee itself suggests, the committee seriously contemplated banning student political activism before settling for an arrangement that sought to strike some kind of balance. While on the one hand the committee asserted the importance of campus democracy for students, it recommended a series of measures to check 'politicization' and 'criminalization'. Under the reforms proposed by the committee, HEI administrations were empowered to decide whether unions would be appointed or elected, what would be the form of election, what would be the pool of candidates, how it would be conducted, and how any non-compliance with the protocol would be penalized.

The Lyngdoh Committee has been criticized on a number of counts like strengthening HEI administration against dissenting student voices and promoting oppositional political agendas in the name of checking the criminalization of student politics.[3] The conflation of 'politicization' with 'criminalization' has been criticized for confusing two distinct issues. While the consequences of the Lyngdoh reforms have not been measured quantitatively,

---

[3] http://indianexpress.com/article/opinion/columns/a-voice-under-35-a-difficult-moment-for-student-politics/.

the impression seems to be that the criminalization of politics has continued more or less unabated. The apparent failure of the reforms stems from a fundamental misapprehension of the relationship between campus democracy and disruptions of academic life.

5. Teachers' Political Associations in Indian Higher Education Institutions: A Snapshot

The AIFUCTO was formed in 1962. This body has an all-India presence, with over 5 lakh college and university teachers associated with it through more than 250 affiliates across the country.[4] For over five decades it has been holding consultations with successive governments, MHRD and UGC over issues relating to teachers' service conditions and higher education policies. The mode of communication includes writing letters to different ministers and also holding debates and discussions through seminars organized by the AIFUCTO.

The other major teachers' organization in the country is the FEDCUTA, which represents teachers' associations of the central government universities and works closely with AIFUCTO. FEDCUTA was created in 1987, after breaking off from AIFUCTO. The AIFUCTO and FEDCUTA focus on fighting for the teachers' rights and liberties and democratic functioning of universities, and they work towards retaining the publicness of the higher education (see Appendix 1 for their objectives). Both organizations work towards embracing democratic ideals – that is ensuring justice and equality for all and through democratic means like debates among themselves, dialogues with others, and discussions among the larger academic community.

In addition to this, the Delhi University Teachers' Association (DUTA) is another large body which is representative of lakhs of teachers working in the colleges affiliated to the University of Delhi. The DUTA is an associate of FEDCUTA and upholds the same mandate.

The Jawaharlal Nehru University Teachers' Association (JNUTA), established in 1971, works closely with AIFUCTO and FEDCUTA. It was initially called JNU Staff Association. However, after much deliberation a teachers' organization exclusively for the teachers of the university was formed called JNUTA; the first meeting of JNUTA took place on the 27 April 1973.[5]

---

[4] As on 12 June 2013; http://www.aifucto.org/.
[5] https://www.jnu.ac.in/jnuta.

Membership to this association is open to all the teachers and research staff of the university.[6] In addition to taking care of the service conditions as well as the rights and liberties of the teachers (as also mentioned under FEDCUTA), the association aims to secure harmony among teachers and promote objectives for which the university has been established (see Appendix 2 for detailed list of objectives).

We first present a theoretical framework of the interfaces to situate the resistance of teachers' political organization. These interfaces could change the *will to govern oneself* to the *will to not to govern oneself* as per the larger discourse.

The Interfaces with Teachers' Unions: A Theoretical Framework

The teachers' political organizations in India do not work in isolation. There are various interfaces in India which could come into play in determining the working conditions and thus the agency of the teachers' union in protecting their identities as teachers, the higher education system as a whole, and work for larger social welfare. These interfaces could pave a way for sprouting resistance to the larger discourse. Table 9.1 provides a summary of the possibilities of subject formation and the ensuing resistance and the reality of resistance of political organizations as informed by these interfaces using inferences drawn from Michel Foucault's thesis on the role of *will* in resistance.

Following this, we would understand the role played by each of the major organizations considered in the chapter.

We now look at how some of the teachers' union organizations have worked towards preserving the teachers' agency, safeguarding the publicness of higher education system as a whole and contributing to the larger society.

All India Federation of University and College Teachers' Organisation and Federation of Central Universities Teachers' Association

The two organizations have been trailblazing the teachers' movement in the country for protecting the teachers' rights and agency. Let us take the broad issues addressed by them one by one:

---

[6] Research staff includes research assistants, documentation officers and other such categories of members of research staff, which are subject to change by the general body of the association.

Table 9.1 Interfaces of Teachers' Political Organizations and Emergence of Resistance

Interface	Possibilities of subject formation/resistance	Resistance by political organization (insights from the interview and field)
Discipline	• The cultural aspects of a discipline are connected with the cognitive aspects of it (Becher 1994). • Subject matter of the study influences: The sciences are generally involved in issues pertaining to nature, machines, human biology, etc. The social sciences, on the other hand, is devoted to social issues, and work is organized outside the classroom as well. • Possibility of resistance through self-reflection is greater in social science faculty.	• Faculty from both sciences and social sciences discipline participate. However, due to the nature of their work, the faculty from sciences discipline tend to be more aloof than those from social sciences discipline.
Political affiliation	• Political parties could determine the agenda of the teachers' organizations through the *will* of the faculty who are a part of these organizations.	• The ruling political parties tend to dominate, which cause tensions. However, the resistance aims at bringing everyone together and work to improve the condition of teachers.
Ownership of a university	• Private universities: Students come from well-to-do families and the courses offered are also professional in nature and focused more on building skills as per the *will* of the market. • Public universities: Due to the subsidized education, students from varied backgrounds come and study in such institutions, and are aware of the ground reality the nation faces; hence greater possibility of resistance exists.	• The faculty of public universities are the members of these political organizations. Due to the diverse population in public universities and greater awareness about social issues, there emerges resistance to preserving democracy in universities.
University administration	• Some of the dimensions of bureaucratic form of organization, as mentioned by Weber (1947), which could pose as constraint in the agency of the university/college teachers include rules governing the behaviour of positional incumbent, procedural devices for work situation and hierarchy of authority. • Bureaucracy stresses rules and the teachers wish to do things per their convenience (Moodie and Eustace 1974: 162). • A *wilful subject* should follow administration to avoid conflicts. But they *will not be governed* if academic freedom gets curtailed and could create resistance.	• Resistance is usually aimed towards university administration decisions like a raise in fees, which affect the democratic culture of the universities.

Interface	Possibilities of subject formation/ resistance	Resistance by political organization (insights from the interview and field)
UGC/MHRD/ Government	• Policy measures may not be in sync with the mission of the university and impact the agency of faculty to function in the public sphere. • Policy measures could usher in privateness of higher education in place of publicness of higher education. • Policy measures could curb the democracy of the nation also. • Some faculty members may form themselves into *wilful* subjects by internalizing the fear of losing out or being touted as an outcaste. In contrast, due to the varying contexts, as listed above, some may develop the will to resist.	• There has been resistance against neoliberal policies such as introduction of PBAS and raise of fees, which curb the academic freedom of faculty. • The political organizations have peacefully protested against the Citizenship Amendment Act, 2019, and compilation of National Register of Citizens to preserve democracy in the country.

Source: Authors' conceptualization, in-depth interviews, field observations.

Teachers' Agency/Academic Freedom

The teachers' academic freedom has been trampled upon time and again by the various higher education policy prescriptions, as mentioned earlier. It is also challenged by bureaucratic nature of university administrations.

A similar concern was raised by a former leader of the JNUTA, who stated that the policy space has been in the hands of bureaucracy rather than that of the teachers. The introduction of JNU's admission policy, without consulting the academic council of the university, the highest governing body comprising the teachers of the university, is a case in point.[7]

Higher Education System as a Whole

With respect to the preserving the entire higher education system, these organizations have held peaceful agitations and various seminars and conferences over the years. The purpose of these conferences has been not only to discuss the issues and the higher education policy but also to make specific suggestions to the policymakers regarding changes, if any.

For instance, in August 2019 they organized a conference in association with Bombay University and College Teachers' Union (BUCTU) in University of Mumbai to discuss about the National Education Policy. Another conference

---

[7] http://www.duta-du.info/2017/04/fedcuta-press-release-09042017.html.

was organized to discuss education reforms in India. There were peaceful protests against growing privatization in higher education, introduction of graded autonomy in the universities, instituting HEFA as a funding agency for central institutions and a proposal to set up Higher Education Empowerment Regulatory Authority (HEERA) replacing the UGC and All India Council for Technical Education (AICTE).

Working Conditions of Teachers

University and college teachers face constant delays in implementation of the pay commission's recommendations. AIFUCTO, along with FEDCUTA, had time and again written letters to the central government and held peaceful agitations demanding the government to implement the 7th Pay Review Committee Recommendations. Similar action was taken requesting 100 per cent assistance from the central government to the state governments for the implementation of the 7th Pay Review Committee Recommendations in all state universities. The AIFUCTO and FEDCUTA (along with DUTA) organized a Court Arrest programme on 5 September, celebrated as Teachers' Day in India, and put forth all their demands, including revision of pay scales to the government. In the past, these organizations have also protested against institution of PBAS, with only a slight success in having amendments made to the regulation.

6. Teachers: Case Studies of Jawaharlal Nehru University and Two State Universities

Jawaharlal Nehru University

JNU was set up in 1969 under the JNU Act 1966. The mission of the university is to promote principles of national integration, social justice, secularism, democratic way of life, international standing and scientific approach to the problems of society. The university at the time of its inception was considered as a means to charting a new course of national integration, providing unlimited access to people from every area of the country (Batabyal 2014: 31–2). Not only this, an immense trust was placed on the teachers, who were thought to be building the very character of the university (Batabyal 2014: 40).

The very ideal on which the university is based is the creation of space for democratic thinking and practices. Such a culture has been sustained for over decades in the university despite burgeoning political interferences and neoliberal policies. A significant role in achieving these objectives has been played by the teacher union movements, student union movements and most importantly the unity among the two. Peaceful protests undertaken by these political associations not only seek to address the issues faced by higher education and nation as a whole, but also aim to broaden the horizon of scholarship and development of a critical self in teachers as well as students.

Teachers' Union in Jawaharlal Nehru University

The issues undertaken by faculty in JNUTA could be categorized broadly as intra-university issues and inter-university issues. The categorization has been done on the basis of the place-specificity, that is according to the place where the issue belongs. It needs a mention here that although an issue could be specific to a certain physical space, it could get manifested at a different place. The origin, however, remains the political or policy arena.

Intra-university issues. Intra-university issues would be understood as those concerning the universities directly. JNUTA has always stood against the standardization of performance assessment in higher education policy, against the new policy for admissions to MPhil and PhD programmes under the UGC regulations of 2016.[8] JNUTA also demanded the constitution of a committee to look into the possibility of academic reforms to institutionalize decentralization in decision making processes.[9] An example of curbing academic freedom was the sacking of a chairperson of a school for speaking against the unjust measures used by the selection committee of the university. JNUTA defended the faculty's right to question and dissent.[10]

The incident of 9 February 2016 following which the students were arrested challenged the democratic culture of the university. The university was pitted against the rhetoric of nationalism. JNUTA raised its voice against such an attack on the university by starting the campaign of 'Save JNU'. The movement caught on in other universities nationally and internationally who joined the protest for

---

[8] UGC had introduced interview as a sole criterion for admission to MPhil and PhD. Following resistance by students' and teachers' communities, the UGC relaxed the admission criteria, giving 70 per cent weightage to written entrance exam and 30 per cent to the oral examination. Another policy which received a lot of resistance was capping of supervisor-student ratio at the PhD level, which led to a dip in number of PhD seats in 2017.
[9] https://www.jnu.ac.in/sites/default/files/Bulletin022014-15.pdf.
[10] https://jnuta.wordpress.com/2017/09/19/jnuta-statement-on-the-removal-of-prof-nivedita-menon-as-chairperson-of-ccptsis/.

the need for freedom of expression and autonomy of academic institutions. The JNUTA with the support of other teachers of the university organized teach-ins at the administrative block to defend the tradition of intellectual debate and discussion in the campus, and explicated the meaning of nationalism (Azad et al. 2016).

Inter-university issues. Some of the issues pertain to other universities but have implications for the entire higher education system, where JNUTA has participated alongside FEDCUTA and AIFUCTO. These issues concern salary revision, four-year graduate programme of Delhi University, standardized performance assessment of faculty, the National Education Policy,[11] regulation on graded autonomy, Citizenship Amendment Act (2019), to name but a few. The senior leadership of JNUTA was responsible for creation of the Coordination Commission of Teachers' Association of Delhi (CCTAD) in 2014, a common forum for teachers of all the universities in Delhi.

University A

University A is a state university established in 1937, with over 150 affiliated colleges. The state where the university is situated has a vibrant culture of dissent. It has fourteen state universities, one central university and two deemed-to-be universities. All universities and colleges in the state have their own teachers' organizations and they are consolidated at a common platform called Federation of University Teachers' Association (FUTA). In-depth interviews of two faculty members who were associated with the teachers' union in the state were conducted in the context of protests which were taking place in University A. The objective was to understand the role of teachers' union vis-à-vis UGC policies and its impact on teachers' agency. One of interviewees was a retired faculty from University A who was serving as a dean in one of the departments, and he was also a member of the Academic Council of the university. At the time of interview, he was also a member of executive council of AIFUCTO and a member of FUTA, which was affiliated to AIFUCTO. He raised the issue of implementation of PBAS in the state, citing the difficulties faced by the college teachers. He noted that college teachers primarily engage in teaching with little time to do research. Also, with the exception of the University College (one the colleges affiliated to the University A), none of the colleges had research centres where faculty could guide MPhil and PhD students, thus hampering any

[11] https://www.jnu.ac.in/sites/default/files/Bulletin022014-15.pdf.

opportunity teachers have to score points as per the PBAS.[12] Another issue was the absence of teaching departments in a medical university and a technological university, both of which were oriented towards research. The AIFUCTO member was, therefore, against the standardization imposed by the central government. Since they did not receive funds from the centre, they did not feel accountable to them directly. The National Education Policy was criticized as well for being exclusionary in nature.

The other interviewee, who was a teaching faculty and part of the political union of University A, cited how the teachers' agency was being crumbled by the university administration, which was accepting all guidelines given by the UGC. On the issue of PBAS, despite the resistance by the faculty, who proposed changes to the assessment system, the suggestions of UGC were accepted by the administration. To sum up, a strong culture of critical thinking, and hence resistance to safeguard one's identity as a teacher, was found in the university; the faculty were aware of the movements against PBAS, which took place in other universities outside their state.

University B

University B is one among the oldest in the country, having been established in 1857. There are two major teacher union organizations in the university, of which one is an affiliate of AIFUCTO. As faculty members from the teachers' union could not be met with during the field survey, a faculty member who had been a part of the university for long, as a part of student movement prior to becoming an active faculty member, was interviewed. It was found that there was only limited political interference in the working of these associations; also, there was no agitation against PBAS. As per the experience of the faculty member, there was hardly any dissent and persistence on the part of teachers. However, in the past one year, one of the teachers' union organizations had become active due to change in the leadership, and it had raised issues related to teachers' promotion, allocation of teachers' accommodation and other injustice done to the teachers. Two reasons put forth by the faculty for lack of aggression so far: one was the presence of lobbies within the university based on various factors, like caste or ideology, which brought division amongst the faculty and

---

[12] Research centres are special centres installed within the college where there is a provision to supervise research students, in terms of equipment and faculty. Research students are enrolled in these research centres and are allotted supervisors from these centres.

the other was that there was a lack of collective consciousness of belonging to one group of teachers.

What Makes Jawaharlal Nehru University Different?

The uniqueness of JNU lies in its culture of dissent, to preserve not only democratic culture within the university but also outside the university. Based on the above analysis and field visits, we identify the following points of differentiation:

Teacher and Student Unity in Protecting the Higher Education

The unity has been sustained because of democratic culture within the classrooms, which are the starting points where teachers encourage students to speak their mind, without any inhibitions. These students come from varied backgrounds, facing the challenges related to language, confidence, caste, different academic orientations and syllabi. The classrooms in JNU become the starting point for students to begin thinking, not only academically but also for real-world scenarios. The university is primarily inclined towards interdisciplinary research, which provides students with a vast knowledge landscape. In JNU, the teachers are also well aware of the various issues confronting a student and try to seek solutions to students' problems. For instance, it was for this very reason that the teachers had protested against the administration's new admission policy of 2016 (mentioned earlier) because many students are not equipped with that cultural capital to be able to perform well in interviews.

The teacher-student unity is also effected by the research orientation of the university, as the association between the students and the teachers stretches to six years or more.[13] When this is coupled with the fact that it is primarily a residential university, where the students live in hostels in which the faculty members also act as wardens, ample opportunities for teacher-student interactions arise. Nair (2017) argues that in a residential university such as JNU which is a seat of transformative encounters with different forms of food cultures, living, religious and sexual practices, hostels become an important site of socialization.

---

[13] For the integrated MPhil/PhD programme.

Teachers' Perceptions of Student Activism

JNUTA has always supported student activism on campus. Faculty feel that real learning cannot take place only within classrooms. For them after dinner talks are equally important.[14] However, in the last couple of years, their show of support towards students has been criticized. Some of the faculty within the teachers' union who were against the student activism belonged mostly to the science disciplines. It was found that the disintegration between teachers and students has grown over time owing to an increase in the proportion of science faculty and due to the introduction of PBAS, leaving faculty with less time for students.

The teacher-student unity could be seen explicitly after the 9 February 2016 incident, following which teachers of JNU organized teach-ins to lecture on nationalism as a token of support extended to the student community. Similarly, the student union supported the protest movement against API raised by JNU teachers, along with teachers from other universities.

Revival of Teacher Associations by Jawaharlal Nehru University Teachers' Association's Leadership

The former president of JNUTA shared the role he played in reviving the FEDCUTA, which had become a defunct organization. Not only this, the JNUTA also revived the relationship between AIFUCTO and FEDCUTA by bringing FEDCUTA back to Delhi. Some of the important initiatives taken by him include setting up the CCTAD, as discussed above, and organizing a pan-India seminar on concerns in higher education in India for all teachers' associations. All these endeavours were undertaken keeping in mind the accountability one has as a teacher towards the larger society.

7. Students' Political Associations in Indian Higher Education Institutions

In pre-independence India, in the early to mid-twentieth century, a large numbers of students participated in anti-colonial mobilizations. This time period marked not only the first but also the last instance of a wide-ranging national

---

[14] The university organizes after dinner talks, inviting some special speakers, on varied issues related directly to higher education as well as to society or other policy initiatives taken up by the government. These talks are organized in the mess-room of a hostel and are open to all the students and teachers.

coordination among agitating students in modern India. After independence, the student movement rapidly lost its 'national' character, while the tendency towards close alignment with mainstream electoral parties continues. In the decade after independence, students participated in regional and linguistic-based movements, which prompted the passing of the States Reorganization Act of 1956. Students have been mobilized in large numbers by the left-wing and anti-caste movements in places such as Punjab, Maharashtra, Tamil Nadu, Kerala and Bengal. Students have, notably, agitated both for and against caste-based reservations in education and employment.

Presently, the student organizations that are able to act at a national level are those affiliated to important national parties. The two largest student organizations in India, namely, the Akhil Bhartiya Vidyarthi Parishad (ABVP) and the National Students' Union of India (NSUI), are affiliated with the largest national parties – Bhartiya Janata Party and Indian National Congress, respectively, although the Congress has contracted dramatically in influence in the past decade. The strength and agendas of these student organizations are closely tied to the fortunes of their parent parties. Despite their large membership and presence on several HEI campuses, coordinated actions on students' issues are unheard of, since the political agendas of these student wings are fully subservient to the parent party. They are animated by the dynamics of national, regional or local politics, and not by an understanding of students as a distinct interest group. None of these large student organizations has challenged the neoliberal consensus on education that their parent parties uphold. The organized voices against privatization have come from left-affiliated, feminist, anti-caste and other progressive student political groups.

A Question of Perspective

The past few years have witnessed a wave of renewed student activism that has been widely reported. This has prompted a pitched debate on the nature and desirability of student political activism with sharply articulated positions on both sides. Student activism is often seen as a disciplinary problem, a waste of time and resources, and many argue that students ought to be concerned solely with scholastic and professional achievement, both imagined as purely technical, apolitical questions. At the same time, some argue that student activism enriches the process of teaching and learning, enhances capacities for leadership and organization, and hence ought to be seen for what it is – an integral part of academic life. While in the first perspective students are seen as 'human resources' and bearers of skills that can be monetized in the formal economy, in the latter they are seen as political agents, as bearers of social identities and economic interests. Progressive student activism in India is undoubtedly part of a broader counter-public, where critical and democratic sensibilities are fashioned, and the transformation, or amelioration, of India's grossly unequal social structure is contemplated with seriousness.

It must be noted that student activism on HEI campuses is inevitable. Neither the student nor the university can be abstracted from the world around them; both are embedded in and deeply marked by definite social, political, economic and cultural contexts. Students carry class, gender, sexual, caste, religious, linguistic, and regional identities and concerns – none of which can remain external to institutions of higher education. From their physical location to curricula to the appointment of institutional heads and hiring of faculty – every aspect of the institutional life of a university or college is stamped with the imprint of social, political, economic and cultural hierarchies and cleavages. The notion that various articulations of interest can be expunged from campus life is implausible.

Who Is the Student?

This section focuses on the public university and college system because, as argued below, student political activism is more prevalent on these campuses than in private institutions, although more than half of enrolment of students in an undergraduate degree is in the private sector.[15] For many, being a student is a brief and transitory state in a person's lifetime, spanning for no more than between one and four years. This, of course, excludes India's proportionally small population of research students. As in most modern societies, formal education is seen as a means to economic and social mobility. Admission to public institutions, where the costs of education are relatively low, is fiercely competitive, both for subjects that promise lucrative careers (engineering, medicine) and for those that probably do not (the liberal arts). The opportunities and life chances of students can vary immensely based on their social location. Inequalities of class, caste, gender and status within student bodies continue to shape, quite powerfully, the experience of education and life chances beyond. The public university or college can very easily become a space

---

[15] http://www.ey.com/Publication/vwLUAssets/Private_sector_participation_in_Indian_higher_education/$FILE/Private_sector_participation_in_Indian_higher_education.pdf

of aspirations – equal parts optimistic and desperate – that are easily disappointed by the challenge of finding secure employment.

While many students take a pragmatic approach to their role on a HEI campus, acute perception of being in a precarious situation can make students responsive to political agendas that speak to their concerns. These differences find political expression in what we describe below as 'sectional' students' organizations, such as left-wing groups, women's groups, anti-caste groups, minority rights groups or community welfare groups. Such groups have been instrumental in making visible the many forms of exclusion, both overt and subtle, that continue to operate in higher education.

Classifying student Organizations

There is considerable variety among organized student groups in HEIs in India with respect to goals, political/ideological orientations and forms of organization. Students are likely to be organized in political, social and cultural groups which represent a particular section of students and not the student body as a whole. We will call these sectional students' organizations. Many (but not all) HEIs have a students' union which can either be elected by students or nominated by the administration. The students' union is supposed to represent the interests of the whole student body to the campus administration, and even more widely. The Jawaharlal Nehru University Students' Union (JNUSU) has for several years been dominated by left-affiliated student groups of various kinds and is known to take up ideological issues of very wide import.

Students' unions are, broadly speaking, likely to function in one of two ways. One we call the 'governance' or 'bridge' model, where the role of the union is to act as a link between the administration, faculty and students. Organized political groups are unusual (they come into their own in the second model of student union). The student union is envisioned by the stakeholders as a body that can assist in campus governance, deal with pragmatic questions such as organizing college or university festivals, assist in admissions, garner support for university policies among students and so on. The union might even be seen as part of the campus administration itself. Representative student bodies organized along these lines may receive institutional support and funds from the administration. The governance or bridge model is typically found in privately owned and managed HEIs, and public sector HEIs specializing in technical subjects such as engineering, medicine, management, statistics and the pure and applied sciences.

Though we suspect that appointed unions are easily more in number, a many of the HEI campuses have more politicized student unions, usually elected, what we are calling the political and/or ideological model, the student union of the second type. In this case, students are often organized into political groups and union representatives might continue to espouse explicit political/ideological leanings. The relationship between the union and the campus administration can be tense and can also depend to a larger extent on how close the two are to the ruling political dispensation. Student unions affiliated with mainstream political parties are likely to enjoy the patronage of heads of institutions, who are usually political appointees.

Sectional students' organization can be further divided into two types: political and non-political. By 'non-political', we mean student organizations that make no explicit or implicit claims to either support or challenge the existing distribution of power or resources in a particular society. This would include charity and social service organizations, cultural or religious student associations, and societies for co-curricular activities such as dance, drama, debating and so on. Religious or cultural associations with explicitly political agendas are obviously excluded by this definition.

The student organizations we classify as political are those that make explicit claims regarding the social and political order. These can further be divided into what we are calling affiliated and autonomous student organizations. Affiliated organizations are those that are affiliated to mainstream electoral political parties; these are as diverse as India's multiparty electoral system and can be for or against the ruling dispensation depending on their particular affiliation. Where sectional students' groups exist and compete for union posts, affiliated political organizations usually have the most significant presence owing to their large numbers, support from campus and local administrations as well as the resources they are able to mobilize owing to their affiliation – including, in some instances, considerable wealth, strongmen and deadly weapons. The category of autonomous political organizations pertains to groups that make explicit claims regarding the social and political order, but remain unaffiliated to any mainstream electoral parties. Their ideological orientation can be either conservative or progressive, though the latter appears to be the case more often. This includes unaffiliated left, feminist, queer and anti-caste groups. Such groups flourish most commonly in public HEIs dedicated to the study of law, humanities and social sciences.

Student Activism: Stakes and Stakeholders

As noted above, the period after the 1990s has seen a decline in ideological politics and the rise of campus politics. This change can reasonably be attributed to, among other things, the liberalization of India's economy. Liberalization of the economy brought in its wake not just pro-market policies, such as the relative withdrawal of the state from the provision of welfare services, but also a change in political and ideological dispensations, new habits of body and mind, such as the growing legitimacy of consumer lifestyles and possessive individualism. This has produced not just a different set of social relations, but also dramatically different subjectivities. The rise of pragmatic and localized 'campus politics' as opposed to the grander, more ambitious 'ideological' politics of the 1940s to 1970s period is symptomatic of this shift. Ideological politics of the kind espoused by left groups, whether affiliated or autonomous, has a significant presence on a handful of university campuses and is decidedly marginal elsewhere, if present at all. The implication is, quite simply, that the public university or college is almost entirely the theatre of progressive student activism in India.

The attitude of different campus stakeholders towards student activism merits a brief comment. Established structures of privilege are reproduced through informal networks, preferential treatment, non-implementation of caste-based reservation quotas and deep lacunae in pedagogy and research. Access to HEI-related jobs (even low-paying, low-prestige jobs) in India is regulated by class, caste, religious, linguistic, ethnic and kinship networks. The politicization of appointments to public office, including administrative and faculty posts in HEIs, is standard practice all over the country. HEI campuses can end up becoming very specific constellations of caste and community power; this applies also to the students. Therefore, to think of students, administration, faculty, administrative staff and service staff as the stakeholders in HEIs is only one way of slicing it. It is, for instance, possible to think of different caste lobbies (predominantly upper caste) as stakeholders in HEIs cutting across the occupational categories listed here.

Faculty attitudes to student politics vary quite widely. In Central Universities like Delhi University, JNU and HCU, teachers may be supportive of student activism and may actively participate in student agitations. For most HEIs, however, the faculty members are either indifferent or hostile to student political activity. To understand this one must keep in mind the fact the student-teacher equation in most places continues to be one of hierarchy and social distance. The non-teaching or administrative/clerical staffs in HEIs also stay away from student politics. The influence of service staff, usually marked off from other categories in the HEI by differences of caste as well as social class, is very marginal to the political life of most institutions. The absence of links between various stakeholders is also due to the contractualization of university and college jobs, which has meant precarious employment for all three categories mentioned here and the consequent decline in organized union activity.

8. Students: Case Studies of Higher Education Institutions

Where unions are elected, and union representatives are politically or ideologically motivated, student demands will often be framed around questions such as infrastructure, curricular reform, academic policies and discriminatory treatment. In recent times, two much broader questions have taken centre stage: access and dissent. In the past few years, a number of HEIs have seen pitched battles between administrations and anti-establishment and dissident student groups, with faculty being very involved in some instances. Through the following case studies, we aim to show both the concerted attack on subversive political opinion and activity among students, and the resistance offered by student groups.

Film and Television Institute of India

The students of prestigious Film and Television Institute of India (FTII), under the leadership of the FTII Students' Association (FSA), commenced a strike in the year 2015 that lasted 139 days. The strike was motivated by the students' unease with the politically motivated appointment of a former actor. The FSA also objected to the reconstitution of the FTII governing panel with ideological appointments.

After several rounds of negotiation, the FSA called off the strike citing government indifference and fatigue among students. The heavy-handed government response drew considerable criticism from progressive film-makers and academics who saw the interventions in FTII as political interference in education and the erosion of artistic freedom.

Central University of Hyderabad

Rohith Vemula, a PhD student at the HCU and an activist of the Ambedkar Students' Association (ASA) committed suicide on 17 January 2016. The proximate reason for Rohith's suicide, his friends and comrades contend, was that the university stopped paying him his monthly fellowship to punish him for his involvement in ASA's activities. This was described as the 'institutional murder' of a bright, articulate, politically conscious student. A student agitation raged in HCU, drawing wide solidarity from across the country and creating awareness among others.

Banaras Hindu University

In the winter of 2017, women students at BHU started a mass political agitation against sexual harassment and sexual assault on campus. The agitation won public support and captured the attention of the media. Representatives of the university administration could not defend themselves in media debates. Despite the initially patronizing, dismissive and repressive handling of the protests by the administration, they had to yield, resulting in the chief proctor and the vice chancellor being replaced.

This incident is important because BHU does not have an elected student union. Moreover, the protest was not led by any political association, rather it was organized and led by 'ordinary' students who may not participate in politics usually. In a university which has a history of criminalized student politics, this issue-based agitation indicates the evolution of a new kind of student politics.

Jawaharlal Nehru University

JNU has been in news for one reason or other since the present political dispensation at the centre assumed power. The events of 9 February 2016 leading to the arrest of students are mentioned above. Following that, JNU students and faculty have been targets of vicious attacks by the media, and a concerted blitz of disinformation on social media. JNU students and teachers, and politically active campuses in general, have been caricatured as 'anti-nationals': thankless maliciously motivated political subversives, growing fat on state subsidies, and criticizing the regime. Student activists have been ridiculed as grifters and socially undesirables. In response, student groups in JNU (and elsewhere) have refused to limit themselves to the pragmatic grievances of students, imagined as consumers, and continue to advance an expansive conception of students as bearers of potentially critical political subjectivities.

JNUSU includes a variety of groups organizing on caste, gender and sexuality, and minority issues. The JNUSU has led student movements at the national level, and in JNU, it has successfully fought for measures such as gender sensitization and an effective anti-sexual harassment committee, various kinds of scholarships, subsidized food in the hostels, irregularities in admissions as well as the establishment of academic centres dedicated to the study of discrimination and inclusion (Karat 1975; Batabyal 2014). These groups have been vehement critics of neoliberal education policies, of the myriad ways in which social exclusion operates in HEIs and of successive regimes.

In January of 2020, the JNUSU was leading students in an agitation against a proposed fee hike and demanding the removal of the vice chancellor. After a round of unsatisfactory talks with the government, students announced their intention to continue agitating. On the 5 January, a large group of masked individuals, armed with rods, sticks, glass bottles and clubs, went on a rampage for three hours attacking students in their rooms. Over twenty-eight people were seriously injured, and several women reported instances of sexual harassment. Police were present in large numbers outside the campus, and their refusal to stop the attack has fuelled speculations that the university administration and police were complicit in the attack.[16]

Jamia Millia Islamia and Aligarh Muslim University

On the 11 December 2019, the Indian Parliament passed the Citizenship Amendment Act (CAA), designed to ease the naturalization process for non-Muslim migrants from neighbouring Afghanistan, Pakistan and Bangladesh. The unprecedented introduction of a religious criterion for citizenship, as many fear, will be used alongside the proposed National Register of Citizens (NRC) to diminish or deny citizenship rights to India's 200 million Muslims. On the same day, Muslim women began a sit-in at Shaheen Bagh which sparked a non-violent mass resistance in defence of India's secular constitution, with sit-ins commencing at several sites across the country. Students participated in the sit-ins in large numbers, and organized protests of their own.

JMI and AMU are both minority institutions; the latter is the largest in India. Home to large numbers of non-Muslim students as well, both campuses were witness to days of anti-CAA/NRC protests by students. On the 15 December, students on both campuses, whether or not they were participating in the protests, were the target of violent police action.[17] Similar scenes were repeated in AMU. A year on, no one has been held responsible for the violence.[18]

---

[16] https://time.com/5760597/what-happened-during-jnu-attack-india/.
[17] https://thewire.in/government/jamia-police-attack-report.
[18] https://thewire.in/rights/nhrc-investigation-police-violence-jamia-milia-islamia-aligarh-muslim-university.

9. Conclusion

HEIs in India have been facing challenges in various forms. These include paralyzing their functioning through neoliberal onslaught manifested in the form of endogenous and exogenous privatization; restricting academic freedom through regulations such as indicators for academic performances and institutional ranking; and defaming institutions for dissenting views of students and teachers against policies and dominant discourses. There have been attempts to implicate students and teachers in legal and criminal cases including sedition charges. Such attempts to dissuade students and teachers from social and political activities have gone to the extent of physical attacks on campuses. Despite such pillory, HEIs in India have not given up being active public spheres and protecting their academic freedom. Their endeavours to contribute to wider social, economic and political life can be observed from the support to and participation of students and teachers in public movements like protests against CAA/NRC and the recent farmers' agitation against three controversial acts favouring corporatization of agriculture. The number of students and teachers extending their support to such causes and participating in protests would appear small in comparison to the higher education system of the country, but these small numbers are encouraging from the perspective of public movements and democracy.

While international agencies like the UNESCO and schemes such as Unnat Bharat Abhiyan tend to advocate social responsibility of HEIs, recent National Education Policy (NEP) (2020) recommends limited political activities by students and teachers. Such attempts to dissociate political activities from higher education received attention on social media and newspapers in the wake of the Lyngdoh Committee Recommendations and the 9 February 2016 incident at JNU. Facing these discourses, associations and unions of students and teachers are struggling hard to fulfil their objectives of being forums for safeguarding rights of their members and preserving the ethos of higher education. AIFUCTO and FEDCUTA have been successful in mobilizing their members and showcasing their dissent through different democratic means but they have not found much success in influencing policymakers to accept their demands. Among the unions of teachers, JNUTA has been leading the teachers' movements with their non-relenting struggles on all possible forums, from protests to fighting legal battles. As noted by the former president of JNUTA, who had worked extensively with other pan-India associations, teachers' associations in most of the places are not active because the role of the teacher is not clear to the very teachers of universities. Against this backdrop, it needs to be asked as to how the culture of JNU or the JNUTA can be replicated in other universities to sensitize teachers more of their role as a teacher and towards the society.

While there are student movements in almost every corner of the country, JNUSU stands out owing to its coordinated struggle with JNUTA and other students' unions. The JNUSU leads the way in demonstrating how teachers ought to be treated as guides or companions and in quashing the general perception that teachers' and students' bodies share antagonistic relationships. As most of student organizations are affiliates of political parties, they tend to follow the parent organization. The glorious past of student movements from the days of independence struggle has been replaced by allegations of wastage of resources in the name of struggle for social, economic and political rights. A coordinated approach by students might help to regain their right to act as political actors.

Appendix 1: Objectives of FEDCUTA

The objectives of FEDCUTA are as follows:

(i) To advocate, secure, maintain and safeguard the rights and liberties of the teachers and to help the teachers to fulfil their academic and social obligations.
(ii) To suggest, initiate and work for suitable legislation affecting educational policy with special reference to rights and responsibilities of teachers.
(iii) To promote democratic functioning of the Central Universities, especially in terms of elected teachers' participation in decision-making process.
(iv) To take necessary steps to improve the conditions of service of teachers of the Central Universities.
(v) To promote studies and discussion of academic matters.

Appendix 2: Objectives of JNUTA

The objectives of JNUTA are as follows:[1]

a) To promote democratic functioning of the University specially in terms of teachers' participation in decision-making processes;
b) To promote studies and discussion on academic matters;
c) To advocate, secure, maintain and safeguard the rights and liberties of teachers and to help the teachers to fulfil their academic obligations;
d) To take necessary steps to improve the conditions of service of the teachers of the University;
e) To suggest, initiate and work for suitable legislation affecting educational policy with special reference to rights and responsibilities of teachers;
f) To organize and administer and/or help in the administration of social security for teachers;
g) To promote social harmony amongst the teachers of the University and to organize recreational activities for their benefits;
h) To promote harmonious relations and cooperation between the teachers of the University and other sections of the University Community; and
i) To promote the objectives for which the University has been established.

---

[1] https://www.jnu.ac.in/jnuta-constitution.

References

Agarwal, P. (2006), 'Higher Education in India: The Need for Change', Working Paper, No. 180, New Delhi: ICRIER.

Agarwal, P. (2007a), 'Higher Education in India: Growth, Concerns and Change Agenda', *Higher Education Quarterly*, 61 (2): 197–207.

Agarwal, P. (2007b), *Private Higher Education in India: Status and Prospects*, London: Observatory of Borderless Higher Education (OBHE).

Agarwal, P. (2009), *Indian Higher Education Envisioning the Future*, New Delhi: Sage.

All India Council for Technical Education (AICTE) (1994), *Report of the High-Power Committee for Mobilisation of Additional Resources for Technical Education (Swaminathan Committee Report)*, New Delhi: AICTE.

All India Council for Technical Education (AICTE) (2019), 'AICTE Approved Institutes for the Academic Year: 2019–2020'. Available online: https://facilities.aicte-india.org/dashboard/pages/dashboardaicte.php (accessed 20 May 2020).

Altbach, P. G. (2004), 'Globalisation and the University: Myths and Realities in an Unequal World', *Tertiary Education and Management*, 10 (1): 3–25.

Altbach, P. G. (2005), 'The Rise of the Pseudouniversity', in P. G. Altbach and D. C. Levy (eds), *Private Higher Education: A Global Revolution*, 23–7, Rotterdam: Sense Publishers.

Altbach, P. G. (2018), 'Indian Higher Education Twenty-first Century Challenges', in K. Kumar (ed.), *Routledge Handbook of Education in India*, 205–15, Abingdon: Routledge.

Anandakrishnan, M. (2007), 'Higher Education II: A Critique of Knowledge Commission', *Economic and Political Weekly*, 42 (7), 557–60 (17 February).

Anandakrishnan, M. (2010), 'Accountability and Transparency in University Governance', *University News*, 8–14 November, 48 (45), 18–23.

Anandakrishnan, M. (2016), 'State Councils of Higher Education: Expectations and Experiences', in N. V. Varghese and G. Malik (eds), *India Higher Education Report 2015*, 399–411, Abingdon: Routledge.

Apple, M. W. (2004), *Ideology and Curriculum*, New York: Routledge Falmer.

Arum, R., A. Gamoran and Y. Shavit (2007), 'More Inclusion Than Diversion: Expansion, Differentiation, and Structure of Higher Education', in Y. Shavit, R. Arum and A. Gamoran (eds), *Stratification in Higher Education: A Comparative Study*, 1–38, Stanford, CA: Stanford University Press.

Association of Indian Universities (AIU) (2012), *Foreign Educational Providers in India, 2010*, New Delhi: AIU.

Austin, G. (1999), *The Indian Constitution: Cornerstone of a Nation*, Oxford: Oxford University Press.

Ayyar, R. V. V. (2015), 'Unfashionable Thoughts: An Ex-policymaker's Perspective on Regulation in Education', Visakhapatnam: Centre for Policy Studies. Available online: http://www.aprasannakumar.org/pdf%20files/unfashionable-thoughts.pdf (accessed 29 June 2021).

Ayyar, R. V. V. (2016), 'Regulation of Higher Education: Why and Whitherto', in N. V. Varghese and G. Malik (eds), *India Higher Education Report 2015*, 377–98, Abingdon: Routledge.

Azad, R., J. Nair, M. Singh and M. S. Roy (eds) (2016), *What the National Really Needs to Know. The JNU Nationalism Lectures*, New Delhi: HarperCollins.

Ball, S. and D. Youdell (2007), *Hidden Privatisation in Public Education*, London: Institute of Education, University of London.

Banerjee, R. and V. P. Muley (2008), *Engineering Education in India*, Mumbai: Observer Research Foundation.

Banya, K. and Jt. Elu (2001), 'The World Bank and Financing Higher Education in Sub-Saharan Africa', *Higher Education*, 42 (1): 1–34.

Batabyal, R. (2014), *JNU: The Making of a University*, New Delhi: Harper Collins.

Becher, T. (1994), 'The Significance of Disciplinary Differences', *Studies in Higher Education*, 94 (9): 151–63.

Becker, G. S. (1993 [1964]), *Human Capital: A Theoretical and Empirical Analysis with Special Reference to Education*, Chicago: University of Chicago Press.

Bent, E., J. Hill, J. Rose and L. P. Tikly (2012), *Making the Difference – Ethnicity and Achievement in Bristol Schools*, Bristol: University of Bristol Press.

Bhasin, N. (2017), 'Centre-State Financial Relations: A Study on the Role of Finance Commission', *VISION: Journal of Indian Taxation*, 4 (1): 68–78.

Bhushan, S. (2009), *Restructuring Higher Education in India*, Jaipur: Rawat Publications.

Bhushan, S. (2010), *Public Financing and Deregulated Fees in Indian Higher Education*, New Delhi: Bookwell.

Bhushan, S. (2016), 'Institutional Autonomy and Leadership in Higher Education', in N. V. Varghese and G. Malik (eds), *India Higher Education Report 2015*, 412–28, Abingdon: Routledge.

Bhushan, S. (2019), 'Future of Higher Education Financing and Governance', in B. Sudhanshu (ed.), *The Future of Higher Education in India*, 133–46, Singapore: Springer.

Bjarnason, S., K. Cheng, J. Fielden, M. Lemaitre, D. Levy and N. V. Varghese (2009), *A New Dynamic: Private Higher Education*, Paris: UNESCO.

Black, S. E. and P. J. Devereux (2010), 'Recent Developments in Intergenerational Mobility', NBER Working Papers, No. 15889, Cambridge, MA: National Bureau of Economic Research.

Borooah, V. K. (2017), *The Progress of Education in India: A Quantitative Analysis of Challenges and Opportunities*, London: Palgrave Macmillan.

Borooah, V. K. and N. S. Sabharwal (2017), 'English as a Medium of Instruction in Indian Education: Inequality of Access to Educational Opportunities', CPRHE Research Papers, No. 7, New Delhi: Centre for Policy Research in Higher Education, National University of Educational Planning and Administration.

Bothwell, E. (2020), 'India Overtakes Germany Research Output', *Times Higher Education World University Ranking*, 20 October. Available online: https://www.timeshighereducation.com/news/india-overtakes-germany-research-output.

British Council (2014), *Understanding India: The Future of Higher Education and Opportunities for International Cooperation*, London: British Council.

British Council India (2020), 'UKIERI Objectives and Key Achievements'. Available online: https://www.britishcouncil.in/programmes/higher-education/ukieri/ukieri-objectives-and-key-achievements (accessed 24 November 2020).

Calhoun, C. (1992), 'Introduction', in C. Calhoun (ed.), *Habermas and the Public Sphere*, 1–48, Cambridge, MA: MIT Press.

Cannizzo, F. (2015), 'Academic Subjectivities: Governmentality and Self-Development in Higher Education', *Foucault Studies*, 20: 199–217.

Cantwell, B., S. Marginson and A. Smolentseva, eds (2018), *High Participation Systems of Higher Education*, Oxford: Oxford University Press.

Cao, Y. and D. Levy (2015), 'China's Private Higher Education: The Impact of Public-Sector Privatization', *International Higher Education*, 41: 14–15.

Carnoy, M. and R. Dossani (2011), 'The Changing Governance of Higher Education in India', Working Paper, Stanford, CA: Stanford University Press. Available online: https://aparc.fsi.stanford.edu/publications/the_changing_governance_of_higher_education_in_india (accessed 23 January 2021).

Carnoy, M. and R. Dossani (2013), 'Goals and Governance of Higher Education in India', *Higher Education*, 65 (5): 595–612.

Cemmell, J. (2002), 'Public vs. Private Higher Education – Public Good, Equity, Access: Is Higher Education a Public Good?', Paper presented at the First Global Forum on International Quality Assurance, Accreditation and the Recognition of Quality in Higher Education, Paris: UNESCO, 17–18 October.

Chakrabarti, A. and R. Joglekar (2006), 'Determinants of Expenditure on Education: An Empirical Analysis Using State-Level Data', *Economic and Political Weekly*, 41 (15) (15 April): 1465–72.

Chakrabarty, K. C. (2010), 'Betting on Young India', Speech delivered at the 4th International Finance and Banking Conference on 25 November 2009 in Mumbai, *Money Today*, 10 February.

Chakraborty, P. and M. Gupta (2016), 'Evolving Centre-State Financial Relations', *Economic and Political Weekly*, 1 (16): 43–6.

Chanana, K. (2012), 'Higher Education and Gender Issues in Knowledge Economy: Who Studies What, Why and Where', in D. Neubauer (ed.), *The Emergent Knowledge Society and Future of Higher Education: Asian Perspectives*, 177–93, Abingdon: Routledge.

Chancel, L. and T. P. Piketty (2017), 'Indian Income Inequality, 1922–2014: From British Raj to Billionaire Raj?', WID, World Working Paper Series, No. 2017/11. Available online: https://wid.world/document/chancelpiketty2017widworld/ (accessed 28 June 2021).

Chanda, R. (2016), 'Internationalization of Higher Education: Student and Institutional Mobility', in N. V. Varghese and G. Malik (eds), *The Indian Higher Education Report 2015*, 431–58, Abingdon: Routledge.

Chandra, P. (2017), *Building Universities that Matter: Where are Indian Institutions Going Wrong?*, Hyderabad: Orient BlackSwan.

Chapman, B., L. Dearden and D. Doan (2020), 'Global Higher Education Financing: The Income-Contingent Loans Revolution', in C. Callender, W. Locke and S. Marginson (eds), *Changing Higher Education for a Changing World*, 87–100, London: Bloomsbury Academic.

Chattopadhyay, S. (2007), 'Exploring Alternative Sources of Financing Higher Education', *Economic and Political Weekly*, 42 (42) (20 October): 4251–9.

Chattopadhyay, S. (2009), 'The Market in Higher Education: Concern for Equity and Quality', *Economic and Political Weekly*, 44 (29) (18 July): 53–61.

Chattopadhyay, S. (2010), 'An Elitist and Flawed Approach to Higher Education', *Economic and Political Weekly*, 45 (18) (1 May): 15–17.

Chattopadhyay, S. (2012), *Education and Economics: Disciplinary Evolution and Policy Discourse*, New Delhi: Oxford University Press.

Chattopadhyay, S. (2016), 'New Modes of Financing Higher Education: Cost Recovery, Private Financing and Education Loans', in N. V. Varghese and G. Malik (eds), *India Higher Education Report 2015*, 333–52, Abingdon: Routledge.

Chattopadhyay, S. (2020), 'NEP 2020: An Uncertain Future for Indian Higher Education', *Economic and Political Weekly*, 55 (46) (21 November): 23–7.

Choudhury, P. K. (2016), 'Growth of Engineering Education in India: Status, Issues and Challenges', *Higher Education for the Future*, 3 (1): 93–107.

Choudhury, P. K. (2019), 'Student Assessment of Quality of Engineering Education in India: Evidence from a Field Survey', *Quality Assurance in Education*, 27 (1): 103–26.

Clancy, P. and G. Goastellec (2007), 'Exploring Access and Equity in Higher Education: Policy and Performance in a Comparative Perspective', *Higher Education Quarterly*, 61 (2): 136–54.

Clark, B. R. (1983), *The Higher Education System: Academic Organization in Cross-national Perspective*, Berkeley, CA: University of California Press.

Clarke, B. (1998), *Creating Entrepreneurial Universities*, Paris and Oxford: IAU and Elsevier Science.

The Constitution of India (1950), Available online: https://www.refworld.org/docid/3ae6b5e20.html (accessed 12 December 2020).

Credit Suisse (2021), *Global Wealth Report*. Available online: https://www.credit-suisse.com/about-us/en/reports-research/global-wealth-report.html (accessed 28 June 2021).

Cross-Border Education Research Team (2020), *International Campus Survey hosted at University of New York at Albany*. Available online: http://cbert.org/resources-data/intl-campus/ (accessed 1 December 2020).

Dandekar, V. M. (1991), 'Reform of Higher Education', *Economic and Political Weekly*, 26 (46): 2631–7.

Das, D. and S. Chattopadhyay (2014), 'Academic Performance Indicators: Straightjacketing Higher Education', *Economic and Political Weekly*, 49 (50): 68–71.

Das, M. and T. Ray (2019), 'Student Mortgage Loans *vis a vis* Income-Contingent Loans: Problems and Prospects', in N. V. Varghese and J. Panigrahi (eds), *India Higher Education Report 2018*, 267–307, New Delhi: Sage.

Deshpande, J. V. (2000), 'AICTE as Politicians' Handmaiden', *Economic and Political Weekly*, 35 (49): 4307–8.

Deshpande, S. and U. Zacharias (2013), *Beyond Inclusion: The Practice of Equal Access in Higher Education*, New Delhi: Routledge.

Dewey, J. (1923), *Democracy and Education: An Introduction to the Philosophy of Education*, New York: Macmillan.

Dubey, A., A. Mehndiratta, M. Sagar and S. Kashiramka (2019), 'Reforms in Technical Education Sector: Evidence from World Bank-Assisted Technical Education Quality Improvement Programme in India', *Higher Education*, 78 (2): 273–99.

Dubey, S. (2019), 'Impact of Public Education Expenditure across Different Levels on Higher Education Access in India: A Panel Data Study', in S. Bhushan (ed.), *The Future of Higher Education in India*, 181–94, Singapore: Springer.

The Economic Times (2020), 'Education Ministry Seeks Extension of Loan-Based Funding', 31 October. Available online: https://economictimes.indiatimes.com/news/politics-and-nation/education-ministry-seeks-extension-of-loan-based-funding/articleshow/78959712.cms.

Fernandes, L. (2006), *India's New Middle Class: Democratic Politics in An Era of Economic Reform*, Minneapolis: University of Minnesota Press.

Foucault, M. (2008), *Birth of Biopolitics: Lectures at the College de France 1978–79*, New York: Palgrave Macmillan.

Fraser, N. (1990), 'Rethinking the Public Sphere: A Contribution to the Critique of Actually Existing Democracy', *Social Text*, 25/26: 56–80.

Friedman, M. (1962), *Capitalism and Freedom*, Chicago: Chicago University Press.

Froumin, I. and O. Leshukov (2018), 'The Russian Federation: Pragmatic Centralism in a Large and Heterogeneous Country', in M. Carnoy, I. Froumin, O. Leshukov and S. Marginson (eds), *Higher Education in Federal Countries*, 354–99, London: Sage.

Geetha Rani, P. (2015), 'Interstate Disparities in Interest Subsidies on Education Loans in India: Why and How Does It Persist?', *University News*, 53 (48): 74–85.

Geetha Rani, P. (2019), 'Shifts in the Financing of Higher Education', in S. Bhushan (ed.), *The Future of Higher Education in India*, 147–65, Singapore: Springer.

Geetha Rani, P. (2011), *Economic Reforms and Financing Higher Education in India*. Available online: http://www.aiiserver.com/glf/wp-content/uploads/2011/03/

ECONOMICREFORMS-AND-FINANCING-HIGHER-EDUCATION-IN-INDIA. pdf.

Geetha Rani, P. (2016), 'Financing Higher Education and Education Loans in India: Trends and Troubles', *Journal of Social Sciences*, 12 (4): 182–200.

Ghuman, R. S., S. Singh and J. S. Brar (2009), *Professional Education in Punjab: Exclusion of Rural Students*, Patiala: Publication Bureau, Punjabi University.

Glennerster, H. (1991), 'Quasi-markets for Education?', *Economic Journal*, 101 (408): 1268–76.

Gnanam, A. (2008), 'The Private Higher Education in the Current Indian Context in Gupta', in D. C. Levy and K. B. Powar (eds), *Private Higher Education Global Trends and Indian Perspectives*, 104–14, New Delhi: Shipra Publications.

Goastellec, G. (2006), 'Accès et Admission à l'Enseignement Supérieur: Contraintes Globales, Réponses Locales?', *Cahiers de la Recherche sur l', Education et les Savoirs*, 5: 15–36.

Government of India (GoI) (1956), *The University Grants Commission Act*, Government of India. Available online: https://www.ugc.ac.in/oldpdf/ugc_act.pdf (accessed 28 June 2021).

Government of India (GoI) (1986), *National Policy on Education*, New Delhi: Ministry of Human Resources Development, Government of India.

Government of India (GoI) (1993), *Funding of Institutions of Higher Education (Report of Justice Dr. K. Punnayya Committee 1992–93)*, New Delhi: UGC. Available online: https://www.ugc.ac.in/oldpdf/pub/report/9.pdf (accessed 28 June 2021).

Government of India (GoI) (2000), *Report on a Policy Framework for Reform in Education*, New Delhi: Prime Minister's Council on Trade and Industry, Government of India (Reprinted in *Journal of Indian School of Political Economy* (October–December 2003): 840–5). Available on: https://ispepune.org.in/PDF%20ISSUE/2003/JISPE403/2038DOCU-3.PDF.

Government of India (GoI) (2004), *Central Government Subsidies in India: A Report*, New Delhi: Department of Economic Affairs, Ministry of Finance. Available online: https://finmin.nic.in/sites/default/files/cgsi-2004.pdf (accessed 28 June 2021).

Government of India (GoI) (2009a), *National Knowledge Commission Report to the Nation 2006–2009*, New Delhi: National Knowledge Commission. Available online: https://www.aicte-india.org/downloads/nkc.pdf (accessed 28 June 2021).

Government of India (GoI) (2009b), *Report of 'The Committee to Advise on Renovation and Rejuvenation of Higher Education' under the Chairpersonship of Prof Yash Pal*. Available online: https://www.aicte-india.org/downloads/Yashpal-committee-report.pdf (accessed 28 June 2021).

Government of India (GoI) (2013), *Twelfth Five Year Plan (2012–17)*, New Delhi. Available online: https://niti.gov.in/planningcommission.gov.in/docs/plans/planrel/fiveyr/12th/pdf/12fyp_vol3.pdf (accessed 28 June 2021).

Government of India (GoI) (2016), *Report of the Committee for Evaluation of the New Education Policy*, New Delhi: MHRD.

Government of India (GoI) (2017a), *The Central Goods and Services Act, 2017*, New Delhi: Government of India. Available online: http:// gstcouncil.gov.in/sites/default/files/CGST.pdf (accessed 28 June 2021).

Government of India (GoI) (2017b), 'University Grants Commission (Institutions of Eminence Deemed to Be Universities) Regulations 2017', *The Gazette of India*, 337 (4) (30 August 2017): Part III, Section 4. Available online: https://www.ugc.ac.in/pdfnews/5403862_Gazette-Institutions-of-Eminence-Deemed-to-be-Universities.pdf (accessed 28 June 2021).

Government of India (GoI) (2017c) University Grants Commission (Open and Distance Learning) Regulations, 2017. Available online: https://deb.ugc.ac.in/pdf/ODLRegulations2017.pdf (accessed 28 June 2021).

Government of India (GoI) (2018a), 'Ministry of Human Resource Development UGC (Categorisation of Universities (only) for Grant of Graded Autonomy) Regulations', *The Gazette of India* (12 February 2018): Part III, Section 4. Available online: https://www.ugc.ac.in/pdfnews/1435338_182728.pdf (accessed 28 June 2021).

Government of India (GoI) (2018b), *UGC (Minimum Qualifications for Appointment of Teachers and Other Academic Staff in Universities and Colleges and Measures for the Maintenance of Standards in Higher Education)*, New Delhi: UGC. Available online: https://www.ugc.ac.in/pdfnews/4033931_UGC-Regulation_min_Qualification_Jul2018.pdf (accessed 28 June 2021).

Government of India (GoI) (2018c), *UGC (Promotion of Academic Integrity and Prevention of Plagiarism) Regulations 2018*. Available online: https://www.ugc.ac.in/pdfnews/7771545_academic-integrity-Regulation2018.pdf (accessed 28 June 2021).

Government of India (GoI) (2019a), *Analysis of Budgeted Expenditure on Education 2015-16 to 2017-18*, New Delhi: Ministry of Education. Available online: https://www.education.gov.in/sites/upload_files/mhrd/files/statistics-new/Budget%20Exp%202017-18%20-27-6-2020.pdf (accessed 27 June 2021).

Government of India (GoI) (2019b), *Draft National Education Policy 2019*, New Delhi: Ministry of Education. Available online: https://www.education.gov.in/sites/upload_files/mhrd/files/Draft_NEP_2019_EN_Revised.pdf (accessed 11 August 2020).

Government of India (GoI) (2019c), *Public Notice. CARE: Reference List of Quality Journals, University Grants Commission (UGC)* Available online: https://www.ugc.ac.in/pdfnews/8378640_Public-Notice-CARE-14-01-2019.pdf (accessed 28 June 2021).

Government of India (2019d), *Annual Report 2018–19*. New Delhi: University Grants Commission.

Government of India (GoI) (2020a), Notes on Demand for Grants 2020–21, Department of Higher Education, MHRD, Union Budget 2020–21, Ministry of Finance, Budget Division, Available online: https://www.indiabudget.gov.in/budget2020-21/doc/eb/sbe59.pdf (accessed 28 June 2021).

Government of India (GoI) (2020b), *Budget Speech of Finance Minister for Union Budget 2020–21*. Available online: https://www.indiabudget.gov.in/doc/budget_speech.pdf (accessed 28 June 2021).

Government of India (GoI) (2020c), *The National Education Policy 2020*, New Delhi: Ministry of Education. Available online: https://www.mhrd.gov.in/sites/upload_files/mhrd/files/NEP_Final_English.pdf (accessed 11 August 2020).

Government of India (GoI) (2020d), *National Institution for Transforming India (NITI) Aayog Annual Report 2019–20*, New Delhi: NITI Aayog. Available online: https://niti.gov.in/sites/default/files/2020-02/Annual_Report_2019-20.pdf (accessed 28 June 2021).

Government of India (GoI) (2020e), *National Institutional Ranking Framework*, NIRF booklet_2020_printing.cdr Available online: https://www.nirfindia.org/nirfpdfcdn/2020/pdf/Report/IR2020_Report.pdf (accessed 28 June 2021).

Government of India (GoI) (2020f), *Public Notice: Expression of Interest (UG Course Mapping/ SWAYAM) dated 31.07.2020*, New Delhi: UGC. Available online: https://www.ugc.ac.in/pdfnews/ 4981711_ Public-Notice-EOI.pdf (accessed 11 August 2020).

Government of India (GoI) (2020g), *Union Budget of India 2020–21 Expenditure profile 2020-21*. Available online: https://www.indiabudget.gov.in/budget2020-21/doc/eb/stat3a.pdf (accessed 29 June 2021).

Government of India (GoI) (2020h) *All India Survey on Higher Education 2018–19*, New Delhi: Ministry of Human Resource Development.

Government of India (GoI) (2021a), Notes of Demand for Grants 2021–22, Ministry of Education, Department of Higher Education, Union Budget 2021–22, Ministry of Finance, Budget Division, available online https://www.indiabudget.gov.in/doc/eb/sbe25.pdf (accessed 27 July 2021).

Government of India (GoI) (2021b), *UGC (Institutions of Eminence Deemed to Be Universities (Amendments) Regulations 2021*. Available online: https://www.ugc.ac.in/pdfnews/1789815_IoE-Regulation (Deemed)-Jan2021.pdf (accessed 27 January 2021).

Government of India (GoI) (2021c). University Grants Commission's Consolidated List of All Universities as on 18 June 2021. Available online: https://www.ugc.ac.in/oldpdf/Consolidated%20list%20of%20All%20Universities.pdf (accessed 29 June 2021).

Government of India (GoI) (2021d) *All India Survey on Higher Education 2019–20*, New Delhi: Ministry of Education. Available online: https://www.aishe.gov.in/aishe/viewDocument.action?documentId=276 (accessed 29 June 2021)

Gudo, C. (2014), 'Financing Higher Education in Kenya: Public-Private Partnership Approach', *International Journal of Educational Policy Research and Review*, 1 (1): 1–5.

Gupta, A. (2005), 'International Trends in Private Higher Education and the Indian Scenario', Research and Occasional Paper Series CSHE, No. 11.05, Berkeley: University of California Press.

Gupta, A. (2008), 'Judicial Interventions and Private Higher Education in India', in A. Gupta, D. C. Levy and K. B. Powar (eds), *Private Higher Education Global Trends and Indian Perspectives*, 239–52, New Delhi: Shipra Publications.

Gupta, A. (2016), 'Emerging Trends in Private Higher Education in India', in N. V. Varghese and G. Malik (eds), *India Higher Education Report 2015*, 355–74, Abingdon: Routledge.

Hallak, J. and M. Poisson (2007), *Corrupt Schools, Corrupt Universities: What Can Be Done?*, Paris: IIEP-UNESCO.

Hatakenaka, S. (2017), 'What Is the Point of Multidisciplinary Research Universities in India? Lessons from International Experience', in D. Kapur, and P. B. Mehta (eds), *Navigating the Labyrinth: Perspectives on India's Higher Education*, 70–99, Hyderabad: Orient BlackSwan.

Hatekar, N. (2009), 'Changing Higher Education Scenario in India', *Economic and Political Weekly*, 44 (38): 22–3.

Henry, O. and M. Ferry (2017), 'When Cracking the JEE Is Not Enough', *South Asia Multidisciplinary Academic Journal*, 15: 1–28.

Hurtado, S. (1994), 'Graduate School Racial Climates and Academic Self-Concept among Minority Graduate Students in the 1970s', *American Journal of Education*, 102 (3): 330–51.

The Indian Express (2020), '20 Years on, Where Are the Board Toppers?', 27 December, cover page. Available online (video): https://www.youtube.com/watch?v=-w5kp-iBfnk.

International Facts and Figures (2020), *Universities UK International*. Available online: https://www.universitiesuk.ac.uk/policy-and-analysis/reports/Pages/international-facts-figures-2020.aspx (accessed 1 December 2020).

Jayaram, N. (2006), 'India, in Forest', in J. F. James and P. G. Altbach (eds), *International Handbook of Higher Education, Part Two: Regions and Countries*, 747–67, Dordrecht: Springer.

Jongbloed, B. (2004), 'Regulation and Competition in Higher Education', in P. Teixeira, B. Jongbloed, D. Dill and A. Amaral (eds), *Markets in Higher Education: Rhetoric or Reality?*, 87–111. Dordrecht: Kluwer Academic Publishers.

Jongbloed, B. (2007), 'Creating Public-Private Dynamics in Higher Education Funding: A Discussion of Three Options', in J. Enders and B. Jongbloed (eds), *Public-Private Dynamics in Higher Education: Expectations, Developments and Outcomes*, 113–38, Bielefeld: Transaction Publishers.

Kannan, K. P. (2019), 'India's Social Inequality as Durable Inequality: Dalits and Adivasis at the Bottom of an Increasingly Unequal Hierarchical Society', Centre for Development Studies Working Paper, No. 488, Trivandrum: Centre for Development Studies.

Kapur, D. and M. Khosla (2017), 'The Supreme Court and Private Higher Education: Litigations Patterns and Judicial Trends', in K. Devesh and P. B. Mehta (eds), *Navigating the Labyrinth: Perspectives on India's Higher Education*, Hyderabad: Orient BlackSwan.

Kapur, D. and P. B. Mehta (2004), 'Indian Higher Education Reform: From Half-Baked Socialism to Half-Baked Capitalism', Center for International Development at Harvard University, Working Paper, No. 103, Cambridge, MA: Harvard University.

Kapur, D. and P. B. Mehta (2017), 'Introduction', in D. Kapur and P. B. Mehta (eds), *Navigating the Labyrinth Perspectives on India's Higher Education*, Hyderabad: Orient BlackSwan.

Karabel, J. (1999), 'The Rise and Fall of Affirmative Action at the University of California', *Journal of Blacks in Higher Education*, 25: 109–12.

Karat, P. (1975), 'Student Movement at Jawaharlal Nehru University', *Social Scientist*, 3 (10): 47–54.

Karram, G. (2011), 'Africa: Rapid Growth in Private Religious Universities', *University World News*, No. 197, 13 November.

Kaul, S. (2006), 'Higher Education in India: Seizing the Opportunity', Indian Council for Research on International Economic Relations Publication, Working Paper, No. 180, New Delhi: Indian Council for Research on International Economic Relations. Available online: http://www.icrier.org/pdf/WP_179.pdf (accessed 28 June 2021).

Kezar, A. J., T. C. Chambers and J. C. Burkhardt (2005), *Higher Education for Public Good: Emerging Voices from National Movement*, San Francisco: Jossey-Bass.

Khadria, B. (2016), 'Higher Education and International Migration', in N. V. Varghese and G. Malik (eds), *The Indian Higher Education Report 2015*, 275–304, Abingdon: Routledge.

Krishnan, K. P. (2017), 'Financing of Higher Education in India: The Way Forward', in D. Kapur and P. B. Mehta (eds), *Navigating the Labyrinth Perspectives on India's Higher Education*, Hyderabad: Orient BlackSwan.

Kulandaiswamy, V. C. (2005), 'Reconstruction of Higher Education in India', *The Hindu*, 18 May. Available online: Available on http://kulandaiswamy.com/downloads/National_Knowledge_Commission.pdf (accessed 11 August 2020).

Kumar, A. (1999), *The Black Economy in India*, New Delhi: Penguin India.

Kumar, A. (2013), *The Indian Economy Since Independence: Persisting Colonial Disruption*, New Delhi: Vision Books.

Kumar, A. (2016), 'Nurture Dissent in the Universities', *Tribune*, 14 April. Available online: http://www.tribuneindia.com/news/comment/nurture-dissent-in-the-universities/221966.html.

Levy, D. C. (1986), *Higher Education and the State in Latin America: Private Challenges to Public Dominance*, Chicago: University of Chicago Press.

Levy, D. C. (2005), 'Private Higher Education's Surprise Roles', in P. G. Altbach and D. C. Levy (eds), *Private Higher Education: A Global Revolution*, 33–6, Rotterdam: Sense Publishers.

Levy, D. C. (2006), 'The Unanticipated Explosion: Private Higher Education's Global Surge', *Comparative Education Review*, 50 (2): 218–40.

Locatelli, R. (2018), 'Education as a Public and Common Good: Reframing the Governance of Education in A Changing Context', UNESCO Education Research and Foresight Working Papers, No. 22, February. Paris: UNESCO. Available online: http://unesdoc.unesco.org/images/0026/002616/261614E.pdf (accessed 28 June 2021).

Loyalka P., M. Carnoy, I. Froumin, R. Dossani, J. B. G. Tilak and P. Yang (2014), 'Factors Affecting the Quality of Engineering Education in the Four Largest Emerging Economies', *Higher Education*, 68 (6): 977–1004.

Madheswari, S. P. and S. D. Mageswari (2020), 'Changing Paradigms of Engineering Education – An Indian Perspective', *Procedia Computer Science*, 172: 215–24.

Maitra, S. (2019), 'Self-financing Courses in Public Institutions', in N. V. Varghese and J. Panigrahi (eds), *India Higher Education Report 2018*, New Delhi: Sage.

Malik, G. (2020), 'Governance and Autonomy: A Study of Central and State Universities', in N. V. Varghese and M. Garima (eds), *Governance and Management of Higher Education in India*, 152–73, New Delhi: Sage.

Malish, C. M. and P. V. Ilavarasan (2011), 'Social Exclusion in Information Capitalism: A Study of Online Recruitment Advertisements of the Indian Software Industry', in K. Nicolopoulou, M. Karatas-Ozkan, A. Tatli and J. Taylor (eds), *Global Knowledge Workers: Diversity and Relational Perspectives*, 114–39, Cheltenham, UK: Edward Elgar.

Malish, C. M. and P. V. Ilavarasan (2016), 'Higher Education, Reservation and Scheduled Castes: Exploring Institutional Habitus of Professional Engineering Colleges in Kerala', *Higher Education*, 72 (5): 603–17.

Mani, S. and M. Arun (2012), 'Liberalisation of Technical Education in Kerala: Has Higher Enrolment Led to a Larger Supply of Engineers', *Economic and Political Weekly*, 52 (21): 63–73.

Marginson, S. (2006), 'Hayekian Neo-liberalism and Academic Freedom', Keynote address to Philosophy of Education Society of Australia Women's College, University of Sydney, Sydney, 23 November.

Marginson, S. (2011), 'Higher Education and Public Good', *Higher Education Quarterly*, 65 (4): 411–33.

Marginson, S. (2016), *Higher Education and the Common Good*, Melbourne: Melbourne University Publishing.

Marginson, S. (2018), 'Private/Public in Higher Education: A Synthesis of Economic and Political Approaches', *Studies in Higher Education*, 43 (2): 322–37.

Marginson, S. (2020a), 'Public and Common Goods: Key Concepts in Mapping the Contributions of Higher Education', in C. Callender, W. Locke and S. Marginson (eds), *Changing Higher Education for a Changing World*, 249–64, London: Bloomsbury Academic.

Marginson, S. (2020b), 'The World Research System: Expansion, Diversification, Network and Hierarchy', in C. Callender, W. Locke and S. Marginson (eds), *Changing Higher Education for a Changing World*, 35–51, London: Bloomsbury Academic.

Marginson, S. and M. van der Wende (2007), 'Globalization and Higher Education', Education Working Paper, No. 8, Paris: Directorate of Education, OECD.

Marginson, S. and X. Xu (2021), 'Moving Beyond Centre-Periphery Science to Philosophy of Education Society of Australia: Towards an Ecology of Knowledge', *Centre for Global Higher Education Working Paper* No. 63, Oxford: ESRC/OFSRE Centre for Global Higher Education. Available online: https://www.researchcghe.org/publications/working-paper/moving-beyond-centre-periphery-science-towards-an-ecology-of-knowledge/ (accessed 29 June 2021)

Marks, S. P. (2017), 'Challenges for Knowledge Creation for Indian Universities', in C. Raj Kumar (ed.), *The Future of Indian Universities: Comparative and International Perspectives*, Oxford: Oxford University Press.

McDonough, P. M. (1997), *Choosing Colleges: How Social Class and Schools Structure Opportunity*, Albany: State University of New York Press.

McMahon, W. (2009), *Higher Learning Greater Good*, Baltimore, MD: Johns Hopkins University Press.

Middlehurst, R. and J. Fielden (2011), *Private Providers in UK Higher Education: Some Policy Options*, Oxford: Higher Education Policy Institute (HEPI).

Ministry of Education (MoE) (2013), *Rashtriya Uchchatar Shiksha Abhiyan (National Higher Education Mission)*, Ministry of Human Resource Development in collaboration with the Tata Institute of Social Sciences. Available online: https://www.education.gov.in/sites/upload_files/mhrd/files/RUSA_final090913.pdf (accessed 29 June 2021).

Ministry of Education (MoE) (2015), *All India Survey of Higher Education*, New Delhi: Department of Higher Education, MoE.

Ministry of Education (MoE) (2018), *Analysis of Budgeted Expenditure on Education-2017–18*, New Delhi: MHRD, Government of India.

Ministry of Education (MoE) (2019), *All India Survey of Higher Education*, New Delhi: Department of Higher Education, MoE.

Ministry of Human Resource Development (MHRD) (2005a), *All India Survey of Higher Education*, New Delhi: Department of Higher Education, MHRD.

Ministry of Human Resources Development (MHRD) (2005b), *Selected Educational Statistics*, New Delhi: MHRD.

Ministry of Human Resources Development (MHRD) (2008), *Selected Educational Statistics*, New Delhi: MHRD.

Ministry of Human Resource Development (MHRD) (2011a), *All India Survey on Higher Education (2010–11)*, New Delhi: Department of Higher Education, Government of India.

Ministry of Human Resources Development (MHRD) (2011b), *Selected Educational Statistics*, New Delhi: MHRD.

Ministry of Human Resource Development (MHRD) (2016), *All India Survey of Higher Education (2014–15)*, New Delhi: Department of Higher Education, Government of India.

Ministry of Human Resources Development (MHRD) (2017), *All India Survey on Higher Education (2015–16)*, New Delhi: Department of Higher Education, Government of India.

Ministry of Human Resource Development (MHRD) (2018), *All India Survey of Higher Education (2017–18)*, New Delhi: Department of Higher Education, Government of India.

Ministry of Human Resource Development (MHRD) (2019), *All India Survey of Higher Education (2018–2019)*, New Delhi: Department of Higher Education, Government of India.

Ministry of Human Resource Development (MHRD) (2020), *National Education Policy*, New Delhi: Department of Higher Education, Government of India.

Mishra, A. (2011), 'INDIA: Degrees Replace Dowries for Educated Classes', *University World News*. Available online: https://www.universityworldnews.com/post.php?story=20111125211736183 (accessed 15 September 2020).

Misra, A. (2011), 'India: Regulation Lags Private Higher Education Growth', *University World News*, No. 197, 13 November.

Moodie, G. C. and R. Eustace (1974), *Power and Authority in British Universities*, London: George Allen & Unwin.

Nair, J. (2017), 'The Provocations of the Public University', *Economic and Political Weekly*, 52 (37): 34–41.

National Sample Survey Office (NSSO) (1995), *India-Participation and Expenditure in Education, 1995–96, 52nd Round*, New Delhi: Ministry of Statistics and Programme Implementation, Government of India.

National Sample Survey Office (NSSO) (2007–8), *India – Participation and Expenditure in Education, 64th Round*, New Delhi: Ministry of Statistics and Programme Implementation, Government of India.

National Sample Survey Office (NSSO) (2014a), *Employment and Unemployment Situation in India, NSS 68th Round*, New Delhi: Ministry of Statistics and Programme Implementation, Government of India.

National Sample Survey Office (NSSO) (2014b), *India: Social Consumption-Education Survey 2014, NSS 71st Round*, New Delhi: Ministry of Statistics and Programme Implementation, Government of India.

National Sample Survey Office (NSSO) (2018), *Household Social Consumption on Education in India, 75th Round (June 2017–July 2018)*, New Delhi: National Statistical Organisation, Ministry of Statistics and Programme Implementation, Government of India.

Nayyar, D. (2007), 'Globalisation What Does It Mean for Higher Education?', *Economic and Political Weekly*, 42 (50) (15 December): 30–5.

NSB (National Science Board) (2020), *Science and Engineering Indicators*. Available online: https://ncses.nsf.gov/pubs/nsb20201.

Oketch, M. O. (2004), 'The Emergence of Private University Education in Kenya: Trends, Prospects, and Challenges', *International Journal of Educational Development*, 24 (2): 119–36.

Organisation for Economic Co-operation and Development (OECD) (1996), *Knowledge-based Economy (Document for General Distribution)*, Paris: OECD.

Organisation for Economic Cooperation and Development (OECD) (2008), *Growing Unequal? Income Distribution and Poverty in OECD Countries*, Paris: OECD.

Organisation for Economic Co-operation and Development (OECD) (2017), *Education Spending (Indicator)*. Paris: OECD. Available online: http://doi: 10.1787/ca274bac-en (accessed 19 September 2017).

Ostrom, E. (1990), *Governing the Commons: The Evolution of Institutions for Collective Action*, Cambridge: Cambridge University Press.

Ovichegan, S. (2013), 'Social Exclusion, Social Inclusion and Passing: The Experience of Dalit Students at one Elite Indian University', *International Journal of Inclusive Education*, 18 (4): 359–78.

Panigrahi, J. (2010), 'Determinants of Educational Loan by Commercial Banks in India: Evidence and Implications Based on a Sample Survey', *Journal of Educational Planning and Administration*, 24 (4): 379–400.

Panigrahi, J. (2017), 'Resource Allocation and Innovative Methods of Financing Higher Education in India', CPRHE Research Paper, No. 6, New Delhi: NIEPA.

Panigrahi, J. (2019), 'Institutional Strategies to Overcome Declining Public Funding in Higher Education', in N. V. Varghese and J. Panigrahi (eds), *India Higher Education Report 2018: Financing of Higher Education*, 139–64, New Delhi: Sage.

Patnaik, P. (2017), 'Funding Education', *People's Democracy*, 41 (38): 1–4. Available online: http://peoplesdemocracy.in/2017/0723_pd/financing-education.

Paul, S. (2009), 'Internationalization of Higher Education: Strategic Implications', *Economic and Political Weekly*, 44 (9), February: 36–41.

Peterson, P. M. (2020), 'Public Trust and the Public Good', *International Higher Education*, 100: 9–10.

Planning Commission (1952), *The First Five Year Plan (1951–1956)*, New Delhi: Government of India.

Planning Commission (1956), *Second Five Year Plan (1956–1961)*, New Delhi: Government of India.

Planning Commission (1961), *Third Five Year Plan (1961–1966)*, New Delhi: Government of India.

Planning Commission (1969), *Fourth Five Year Plan (1969–1974)*, New Delhi: Government of India.

Planning Commission (1976), *Fifth Five Year Plan (1974–1979)*, New Delhi: Government of India.

Planning Commission (1981), *Sixth Five Year Plan (1980–1985)*, New Delhi: Government of India.

Planning Commission (1985), *Seventh Five Year Plan (1985–1990): Sectoral Programmes of Development*, Vol. II, New Delhi: Government of India.

Planning Commission (1992), *Eighth Five Year Plan (1992–1997): Sectoral Programmes of Development*, Vol. II, New Delhi: Government of India.

Planning Commission (1997), *Ninth Five Year Plan (1997–2002): Thematic Issues and Sectoral Programmes*, Vol. II, New Delhi: Government of India.

Planning Commission (2002), *Tenth Five Year Plan (2002–2007): Sectoral Policies and Programmes*, Vol. II, New Delhi: Government of India.

Planning Commission (2008a), *Eleventh Five Year Plan (2007–2012), Vol. I: Inclusive Growth*, New Delhi: Government of India.

Planning Commission (2008b), *Eleventh Five Year Plan (2007–2012), Vol. II: Social Sector*, New Delhi: Government of India.

Planning Commission (2008c), *Eleventh Five Year Plan (2007–2012), Vol. III: Agriculture, Rural Development, Industry, Services and Physical Infrastructure*, New Delhi: Government of India.

Planning Commission (2013a), *Twelfth Five Year Plan (2012–2017), Vol. II: Economic Sectors*, New Delhi: Government of India.

Planning Commission (2013b), *Twelfth Five Year Plan (2012–2017), Vol. III: Social Sectors*, New Delhi: Government of India.

Prabhu, B. V. and A. S. Kudva (2016), 'Success of Student Internship in Engineering Industry: A Faculty Perspective', *Higher Education for the Future*, 3 (2): 1–19.

Prakash, V. (2007), 'Trends in Growth and Financing of Higher Education in India', *Economic and Political Weekly*, 42 (31): 3249–58.

QS World University Ranking (2020), Available online: https://www.topuniversities.com/university-rankings/world-university-rankings/2020 (accessed 28 June 2021).

Raina, D. (2015), 'Transformation in the World of Higher Learning: Changing Norms and Values of Universities and Research Institutes in India', in R. S. Raina (ed.), *Science Technology and Development in India: Encountering Values*, 104–18, Hyderabad: Orient Blackswan.

Rajagopal, S. (2012), 'Engineering Students Afflicted with "Back Paper Syndrome"', *The Hindu*, 25 February. Available online: http://www.thehindu.com/todays-paper/tp-national/tp-kerala/engineering-students-afflicted-with-back-paper-syndrome/article2930905.ece (accessed 20 September 2017).

Ramaswamy, R. (2020), 'Science in the Public Sphere: Obligations and Responsibility', *Economic and Political Weekly*, 55 (47) (28 November): 33–6.

Rao, M. G. and N. Singh (2001), 'Federalism in India: Political Economy and Reforms', UCSC Economics Working Paper, No. 484. Available online: http://dx.doi.org/10.2139/ssrn.288352.

Rao, S. S. (2006), 'Engineering and Technology Education in India: Uneven Spread, Quality and Social Coverage', *Journal of Educational Planning and Administration*, 20 (2): 205–25.

Rao, S. S. (2007), 'Neglected Terrain in the Quest for Equality: Women in Elite Engineering and Technology Education', in J. B. G. Tilak (ed.), *Women's Education and Development*, 187–212, New Delhi: Gyan Publishing House.

Rao, U. R. (2003), *Revitalising Technical Education, AICTE Review Report*, New Delhi: All-India Council for Technical Education.

Reserve Bank of India (RBI) (2019), *State Finances: A Study of Budgets of 2019–20*, New Delhi: Reserve Bank of India. Available online: https://rbidocs.rbi.org.in/rdocs/

Publications/PDFs/STATEFINANCE201920E15C4A9A916D4F4B8BF01608933FF0BB.PDF.

Roach, E. (2007), 'Engineering Education in India: A Story of Contrasts', *World Education News and Reviews* (World Education Service, New York), 1 January. Available online: https://wenr.wes.org/2007/01/wenr-january-2007-engineering-education-in-india-a-story-of-contrasts (accessed 15 November 2020).

Roemer, J. E. (1998), *Equality of Opportunity*, Cambridge, MA: Harvard University Press.

Sabharwal, N. S. and C. M. Malish (2016a), *Diversity and Discrimination in Higher Education: A Study of Institutions in Selected States of India* (Research Report), New Delhi: CPRHE/NIEPA.

Sabharwal, N. S. and C. M. Malish (2016b), 'Student Diversity and Civic Learning in Higher Education in India', CPRHE/NIEPA Research Paper, No. 3, New Delhi: CPRHE/NIEPA.

Sabharwal, N. S. and C. M. Malish (2018), 'Student Diversity and Social Inclusion: An Empirical Analysis of Higher Education Institutions in India', CPRHE/NIEPA Research Paper, No. 10, New Delhi: CPRHE/NIEPA.

Sabharwal, N. S., S. Thorat, T. Balasubrahmanyam and D. G. Diwakar (2014), 'Diversity, Academic Performance and Discrimination: A Case Study of a Higher Educational Institution', IIDS Working Paper, New Delhi: Indian Institute of Dalit Studies.

Salim, A. A. (2008), 'Opportunities for Higher Education: An Enquiry into Entry Barriers', in K. N. Nair and P. R. G. Nair (eds), *Higher Education in Kerala: Micro Level Perspective*, 49–88, New Delhi: Danish Books.

Salmi, J. (2009), *The Challenge of Establishing World-Class Universities*, Washington, DC: World Bank.

Samuelson, P. (1954), 'The Pure Theory of Public Expenditure', *Review of Economics and Statistics*, 36 (4): 387–9.

Santiago, P., K. Trembly, E. Basri and E. Arnal (2008), *Tertiary Education for the Knowledge Society*, Vol. 2, Paris: OECD.

Sarkar, N. (2020), 'Has the Covid-19 Pandemic Accentuated Inequality in the Higher Education Sector? Evidence from India', Webinar presentation for *the ESRC/OFSRE Centre for Global Higher Education*, 24 November. Available online: https://www.researchcghe.org/events/cghe-seminar/has-the-covid-19-pandemic-accentuated-inequality-in-the-higher-education-sector-evidence-from-india/.

Sen, A. (1999), *Development as Freedom*, Oxford: Oxford University Press.

Shanghai Ranking (2020), '2020 Academic Ranking of World Universities' (ARWU). Available online: http://www.shanghairanking.com/World-University-Rankings-2020/India.html.

Shavit, Y. A. and A. R. Gamoran (2007), *Stratification in Higher Education: A Comparative Study*, Stanford, CA: Stanford University Press.

Singh, A. (2004), *Fifty Years of Higher Education in India: The Role of the University Grants Commission*, New Delhi: Sage.

Singh, L. C. and S. Misra (2008), 'Self-financing Higher Education: Issues and Concerns', in A. Gupta, D. C. Levy and K. B. Powar (eds), *Private Higher Education Global Trends and Indian Perspectives*, 126–33, New Delhi: Shipra Publishers.

Sirowy, L. and A. Inkeles (1990), 'The Effects of Democracy on Economic Growth and Inequality: A Review', *Comparative International Development*, 25 (1): 126–57.

Sivasankaran, C. J. and P. K. Raveendran (2004), 'An Investigation in to the Problem of Wastage in the Engineering Colleges in Kerala', *Report Submitted to Kerala Research Programme on Local Development*, Trivandrum: Centre for Development Studies.

Slantcheva, S. and D. C. Levy, eds (2007), *Private Higher Education in Post-communist Europe: In Search of Legitimacy*, New York: Palgrave Macmillan.

Smolicz, J. J. (1999), 'Privatization of Higher Education: Emerging Commonalities and Diverse Educational Perspectives in the Philippines, Australia, Poland and Iran', *Development and Society*, 28 (2): 205–28.

Srivastava, A. and N. Koshal (2018), 'What About Provincial Institutions in Higher Education Policy in India?', *International Higher Education*, 95, 26–8.

Srivastava, D. K., T. K. Sen, H. Mukhopadhyay, C. Bhujanga Rao and H. K. Amar Nath (1997), *Government Subsidies in India*, New Delhi: National Institute of Public Finance and Policy.

Stiglitz, J. E. (1999), 'Knowledge as a Global Public Good', in I. Kaul, I. Grunberg and M. Stern (eds), *Global Public Goods: International Cooperation in the 21st Century*, 308–32, New York: Oxford University Press.

Stiglitz, J. E. (2015), *The Great Divide: Unequal Societies and What We Can Do about Them*, New York: W. W. Norton.

Teichler, U. (2015), 'The Future of Higher Education: A View Reflecting the State and the Tasks of Higher Education Research', in P. Zgaga, U. Teichler, H. G. Schuetze and A. Wolter (eds), *Higher Education Reform: Looking Back – Looking Forward*, 29–48, Frankfurt am main: Peter Lang.

Thorat, S. (2016), 'Higher Education Policy in India: Emerging Issues and Approaches', in N. V. Varghese and G. Malik (eds), *India Higher Education Report 2015*, 15–40, Abingdon: Routledge.

Thorat, S. and P. Attewell (2007), 'The Legacy of Social Exclusion: A Correspondence Study of Job Discrimination in India', *Economic and Political Weekly*, 42 (41): 4141–5.

Tilak, J. B. G. (1992), 'Student Loans in Financing Higher Education in India', *Higher Education*, 23 (4): 389–404.

Tilak, J. B. G. (1989), 'Center-State Relations in Financing Education in India', *Comparative Education Review*, 33 (4): 450–80. Available online: http://www.jstor.org/stable/1188449.

Tilak, J. B. G. (1994), 'The Pests Are Here to Stay: Capitation Fee in Disguise', *Economic and Political Weekly*, 29 (7): 348–50.

Tilak, J. B. G. (2004), 'Public Subsidies in Education in India', *Economic and Political Weekly*, 39 (4): 343–59.

Tilak, J. B. G. (2007), 'Student Loans and Financing of Higher Education in India', *Journal of Educational Planning and Administration*, 21 (3): 231–56.

Tilak, J. B. G. (2008), 'Higher Education: A Public Good or a Commodity for Trade? Commitment to Higher Education or Commitment of Higher Education to Trade', *Prospects*, 38: 449–66.

Tilak, J. B. G. (2015), 'How Inclusive Is Higher Education in India?', *Social Change*, 45 (2): 185–223.

Tilak, J. B. G. (2016), 'A Decade of Ups and Downs in Public Expenditure on Higher Education in India', in N. V. Varghese and G. Malik (eds), *India Higher Education Report 2015*, 307–32, Abingdon: Routledge.

Tilak, J. B. G. (2017), 'Union-State Relations in India's Higher Education', NUEPA Occasional Paper, No. 50, New Delhi: NUEPA.

Tilak, J. B. G. (2018), 'Private Higher Education in India', in J. B. G. Tilak (ed.), *Education and Development in India*, 535–51, Singapore: Palgrave Macmillan.

Tilak, J. B. G. and Rani, G. (2000), *University Finances in India: A Profile. Mimeograph*, New Delhi: NIEPA.

Tilly, C. (2007), 'Poverty and the Politics of Exclusion', in D. Narayan and P. Petesch (eds), *Moving Out of Poverty: Vol. 1. Cross-Disciplinary Perspectives on Mobility*, 45–76, Washington, DC: World Bank.

Times Higher Education World University Ranking (2020), Available online: https://www.topuniversities.com/university-rankings/world-university-rankings/2020.

Tinto, V. (1975), 'Dropout from Higher Education: A Theoretical Synthesis of Recent Research', *Review of Educational Research*, 45 (1): 89–125.

Trow, M. (1973), *Problems in the Transition from Elite to Mass Higher Education*, Berkeley, CA: Carnegie Commission on Higher Education.

Trow, M. (2006), 'Reflections on the Transition from Elite to Mass to Universal Access: Forms and Phases of Higher Education in Modern Societies Since WWII', in J. F. Forest and P. G. Altbach (eds), *International Handbook of Higher Education*, 243–80, Dordrecht: Springer.

Umarji, V. (2011), 'B-schools Fail to Write off Empty Classroom Worries', *Business Standard*, 23 July.

United Nations, Department of Economic and Social Affairs, Population Division (UNDESA) (2018), *World Urbanization Prospects: The 2018 Revision*, Online Edition. Available online: https://population.un.org/wup/.

UNESCO (2010), *Engineering: Issues, Challenges and Opportunities for Development*, Paris: UNESCO.

UNESCO (2017), *Education for Sustainable Development Goals: Learning Objectives*, Paris: UNESCO.

UNESCO (2020), *Global Flow of Tertiary-Level Students*, Paris: UNESCO Institute of Statistics. Available online: http://uis.unesco.org/en/uis-student-flow (accessed 26 November 2020).

UNESCO (2021), *UNESCO Institute of Statistics data*. Available online: http://data.uis.unesco.org/#.

United States-India Educational Foundation (USIEF) (2020), *Study in India*. Available online: http://www.usief.org.in/Study-in-India.aspx (accessed 28 January 2021).

University Grants Commission (UGC) (2003a), *Higher Education in India: Issues Concerns and New Directions*, New Delhi: UGC.

University Grants Commission (UGC) (2003b), *UGC (Establishment of and Maintenance of Standards in Private Universities) Regulations, 2003*, New Delhi: UGC.

Upadhya, C. (2007), 'Employment, Exclusion and Merit in the Indian IT Industry', *Economic and Political Weekly*, 42 (20): 1863–9.

Varghese, N. V. (2001), 'Higher Education and Distributional Equity', *Perspectives in Education*, 17: 95–108.

Varghese, N. V., ed. (2004), *Private Higher Education: Country Experiences*, Paris: IIEP.

Varghese, N. V., ed. (2006), *Growth and Expansion of Private Higher Education in Africa*, Paris: IIEP/UNESCO.

Varghese, N. V. (2008), 'Private Sector: Partner in Higher Education Development in Africa', *IIEP-ADEA-AAU Policy Brief*, Accra: AAU.

Varghese, N. V. (2011), *Expanding Higher Education with Equity*, Paris: IIEP/UNESCO.

Varghese, N. V. (2013), 'Private Higher Education: The Global Surge and Indian Concerns', in IDFC Foundation (ed.), *India Infrastructure Report 2012: Private Sector in Education*, 145–56, London and New Delhi: Routledge Taylor and Francis Group and IDFC.

Varghese, N. V. (2015a), 'Challenges of Massification of Higher Education in India', CPRHE Research Papers, No. 1, New Delhi: NUEPA.

Varghese, N. V. (2015b), 'Reshaping of Higher Education in Asia: The Role of Private Sector', THF Working Papers Series, No. 10, Singapore: THF.

Varghese, N. V. (2019), 'Education and Economic Inequalities: What Indian Evidence Tells Us', *Journal of Educational Planning and Administration*, 33 (3): 175–92.

Varghese, N. V. (2020a), 'Internationalization and Cross-Border Mobility in Indian Higher Education', *International Journal of African Higher Education*, 7 (2): 123–39.

Varghese, N. V. (2020b), 'Internationalization of Higher Education: Global Trends and Indian Initiatives', in P. Mittal and S. R. D. Pani (eds), *Reimagining Indian Universities*, 1–11, New Delhi: Association of Indian Universities.

Varghese, N. V. and G. Malik, eds (2016), *India Higher Education Report 2015*, Abingdon: Routledge.

Varghese, N. V. and J. Panigrahi (2019), 'Financing of Higher Education: An Introduction', in N. V. Varghese and J. Panigrahi (eds), *India Higher Education Report 2018*, New York: Sage.

Varghese, N. V., J. Panigrahi and A. Rohatgi (2018), 'Concentration of Higher Education Institutions in India: A Regional Analysis', CPRHE Research Paper, No. 11, New

Delhi: Centre for Policy Research in Higher Education, National University of Educational Planning and Administration.

Varghese, N. V., N. S. Sabharwal and C. M. Malish, eds (2018), *India Higher Education Report 2016: Equity*, New Delhi: Sage.

Varma, R. and D. Kapur (2010), 'Access, Satisfaction, and Future: Undergraduate Education at the Indian Institutes of Technology', *Higher Education*, 59 (6): 703–17.

Wadhwa, R. (2019), 'Pathways to Internationalization in Indian Higher Education: Reflections on Policy Options', in S. Bhushan (ed.), *The Future of Higher Education in India*, 307–28, Singapore: Springer.

Wallerstein, I. (1974), 'The Rise and Future Demise of the World Capitalist System: Concepts for Comparative Analysis', *Comparative Studies in Society and History*, 16 (4): 387–415.

Weber, M. (1947), *The Theory of Social and Economic Organisation*, trans. A. M. Henderson and T. Parsons, New York: Free Press.

Winberg, C., M. Bramhall, D. Greenfield, P. Johnson, P. Rowlett, O. Lewis, J. Waldock and K. Wolff (2020), 'Developing Employability in Engineering Education: A Systematic Review of the Literature', *European Journal of Engineering Education*, 45 (2): 165–80.

World Bank (1986), *Financing Education in Developing Countries: An Exploration of Policy Options*, Washington, DC: World Bank.

World Bank (2019), *World Development Report: The Changing Nature of Work*, Washington, DC: World Bank.

World Bank (2021), 'Indicators'. Available online: https://data.worldbank.org/indicator.

Websites

http://www.aifucto.org/
http://www.duta-du.info/2014/02/historic-march-by-students-and-teachers.html
http://www.duta-du.info/2017/04/fedcuta-press-release-09042017.html
http://www.ey.com/Publication/vwLUAssets/Private_sector_participation_in_Indian_higher_education/$FILE/Private_sector_participation_in_Indian_higher_education.pdf
http://www.firstpost.com/india/jnu-jamia-teachers-agitate-against-the-new-ugc-teacher-academic-performance-criteria-2816004.html
http://indianexpress.com/article/opinion/columns/a-voice-under-35-a-difficult-moment-for-student-politics/
https://www.jnu.ac.in/jnuta
https://www.jnu.ac.in/jnuta-fedcuta
https://www.jnu.ac.in/sites/default/files/Bulletin022014-15.pdf

https://www.jnu.ac.in/sites/default/files/JNUTA_Press%20Release_11_January%20
    2017.pdf
https://jnuta.wordpress.com/2017/09/19/
    jnuta-statement-on-the-removal-of-prof-nivedita-menon-as-chairperson-of-ccptsis/
http://www.livemint.com/Politics/JXOYq7baWCd4WxdbuVUqRK/DU-rolls-back-
    FYUP-reverts-to-threeyear-structure.html
https://thewire.in/136259/panchgavya-svarop-iit-csir-cow-urine/
https://thewire.in/26566/post-jnu-we-need-a-fresh-debate-on-higher-education/
https://thewire.in/government/jamia-police-attack-report
https://thewire.in/rights/nhrc-investigation-police-violence-jamia-milia-islamia-
    aligarh-muslim-university
https://time.com/5760597/what-happened-during-jnu-attack-india/
https://www.telegraphindia.com/1170904/jsp/nation/story_170729.jsp

Index

Note: There are no index listings for the Government of India, and the relevant ministries, which are referenced throughout the book, but there are listings for the public agencies most active in higher education, such as the University Grants Commission.

access to higher education. *See under* equality and equity in higher education
accreditation 36, 44, 139, 147, 156. *See also* National Assessment and Accreditation Council
agriculture in higher education 8, 26, 83–4, 161–4
AICTE. *See under* All India Council for Technical Education
aid for higher education 13, 42
All India Council for Technical Education 26, 36, 38, 56, 59–60, 104–5, 116–17, 124, 145–6, 149, 150, 151–2, 188, 191, 194, 195–6, 198, 205, 206, 207, 223
autonomy of institutions 38, 39, 45, 59, 64–5, 133, 143, 151, 154–5, 158–9, 159–60, 166, 178–80, 213, 225
arts programmes in higher education 33, 51, 161–4

business studies 33, 83–5, 119, 161–4

China 2, 6, 19, 42, 168, 172, 186
Clark, Burton, triangle of coordination 158–9
classification of universities. *See under* system design and organisation in higher education
colonialism and the colonial legacy 14, 41
commerce programmes in higher education. *See under* business studies
common good and higher education 2, 18–19, 24, 68. *See also* public good and higher education

Constitution of India and higher education. *See under* regulation and governance
COVID-19 pandemic 2, 11–14, 167
and the economy 11–13, 47, 64
in higher education 12–14

democratic function of higher education. *See under* higher education, role and mission
diversity in India, regional and cultural-linguistic 14
doctoral education (PhDs) and research degrees 8, 10, 28–9, 152, 173–4, 205–6

East Asia 2, 18–19, 99, 186
economic and social inequalities 14, 68–73, 73, 81–2, 109–11, 115. *See also* equality and equity in higher education
economy and higher education. *See under* higher education, role and mission
education as a field of study in higher education 33, 37–8, 84–5, 161–4
emerging ('developing') countries and higher education 2, 14, 95, 98–101
engineering 8, 21, 29, 30, 83–5, 87, 103, 117, 119, 161–4, 187–210
sub-disciplinary balance of enrolments 202–4
equality and equity in higher education 2, 7, 12, 18–19, 20–1, 31–5, 46, 48–9, 58, 61, 67–93, 109–15, 134, 195, 230
disabled students 79

gender and Gender Parity Index
  (GPI) 14, 33–4, 74–6, 77, 78, 79, 81,
  81–2, 82–4, 86–8, 109, 111, 115, 188,
  195, 199–201, 235
  language 34–5, 87–8, 90, 93, 110
  practices inside institutions 78–9,
  89–90, 93
  religion 81–2, 86, 236
  rural and remote students 7, 32, 74–6,
  78, 80, 82, 83, 87–8, 129–34
  scheduled tribe (ST) and scheduled
  caste (SC) students 7, 31, 32–3, 35,
  37, 73, 74–6, 77, 79, 81–2, 82–4, 86,
  88, 108–10, 115, 188, 200–1, 229
  socio-economic status 34, 67–93,
  109–11, 115, 118, 200–2
  state and regional inequalities 15,
  31–2, 85–6, 87–8, 112–15, 121–42,
  188, 195–9
ethical and unethical practices 18–19, 65,
  120, 147, 150, 151–2, 153
externalities. *See under* public good and
  higher education

foreign aid. *See under* aid for higher
  education
foreign campuses and foreign investment
  in higher education in India 15, 42,
  62–3, 160, 176–7, 184
foreign students. *See under* international
  students
Foucault, Michel 214, 220
funding and financing of higher education
  4–6, 13, 17, 20, 29–30, 39, 40–1, 45,
  47–65, 97–8, 101–3, 110–15, 118,
  122–4, 125, 127–34, 135–8, 139,
  141–2, 148, 156–7, 179, 187, 194, 213
  higher education and GDP 40, 46,
  53, 55, 65
  public-private partnerships 60–1
  student loans 41, 47, 49, 52, 57–9, 65,
  75–6, 98, 117–19, 202, 213
  student scholarships 74–6, 77, 181
  tuition fees 40, 52, 60, 65, 77, 98, 103,
  116, 202, 213, 236

gender issues in higher education. *See
  under* equality and equity

GER. *See under* Gross (Tertiary)
  Enrolment Ratio
globalization (economic
  globalization) 97, 166–7, 171–7, 184
governance. *See under* regulation and
  governance
graduate employment and
  unemployment 1, 4, 35, 91–2, 120,
  150, 188, 193–4, 206–9
Gross (Tertiary) Enrolment Ratio 3–4,
  25–6, 27–8, 43, 80, 80–1, 83, 101,
  119, 129–30, 150
growth of higher education 3–5, 67, 95,
  97
  in India 3–7, 24–30, 33, 43, 45–6,
  101–2, 107–15, 119–20, 150, 187–8,
  188–95, 208–9

Habermas, Jurgen 214–16
HEFA. *See under* Higher Education
  Financing Agency
higher education, role and mission 1–2,
  23, 64–5, 68–73, 152, 216
  and civic virtues such as solidarity,
  community, tolerance 1–2, 17–19
  and democracy 1–2, 22, 31, 45, 51, 64,
  68–73, 211–39
  and the economy 1–2, 3, 4, 23, 25–6, 51,
  64–5, 69, 187–8, 191, 193–4
  and modernisation 2, 5–7, 68, 187
  and social equality 2, 35, 67–93
  See also common good and higher
  education, public good and higher
  education
Higher Education Financing Agency 40–1,
  46, 52, 61–2, 213, 223
humanities 33, 51, 84–5, 161–4

Institution of Excellence 30, 36, 64, 155,
  159, 176, 178–81. *See also* ranking of
  universities, stratification, world class
  university
IoE. *See under* Institution of Excellence
internationalization 21, 40–2, 165–86
  Indian (branch) campuses abroad 42,
  167–8, 175–6
  international collaboration 42, 154,
  168–9, 182, 183, 185

inward student mobility 42, 155, 166, 172–4, 181
outward student mobility 171–4
See also foreign campuses and foreign investment in higher education in India
international students. See under inward student mobility

leadership in higher education 19, 236
learning support programmes 78–9

management education 30, 84–5, 119, 120, 161–4
management in higher education 37–9. See also leadership, regulation and governance
markets in higher education 16–17, 23–4, 29–30, 32, 34, 37, 45, 50, 63, 96–7, 144–5, 153, 158–9, 209, 213. See also private sector, privatization
massification in higher and tertiary education 3–5, 10, 23–46, 59, 68, 70, 72–3, 80, 95, 96, 98, 101, 119, 187. See also Trow, Martin
Massive Online Open Course. See under open learning
medical sciences 8, 26, 29, 30, 33, 37, 45, 83–5, 103, 119, 124, 145, 146, 161–4

NAAC. See under National Assessment and Accreditation Council
National Assessment and Accreditation Council 36, 142, 145, 146, 154, 178
National Education Plan 5, 9, 11, 20, 24, 25, 43–5, 64, 65, 148, 155–7, 158–9, 176
national political culture 14–19
nationalist (ultra-nationalist) politics 214, 235–7
NEP. See under National Education Plan
Nordic Europe 2, 17

OECD. See under Organisation for Economic Cooperation and Development
online provision of higher education 6, 12, 14, 44, 63, 157, 167, 175

open learning 28, 42, 63, 157, 161–2, 175, 181
Organisation for Economic Cooperation and Development 19, 43, 68, 72, 98

policy challenges for higher education in India 2, 14, 17–19, 19–20, 187
political activity on campuses 22, 211–39
positional (status) goods in higher education 17, 160
private education in India 21, 26–30, 32, 34–5, 37, 39, 44, 46, 56, 57, 80, 87, 95–120, 127, 147, 149–51, 192, 194, 196, 208–10, 221
and COVID-19 pandemic 12
regulation of private education 18, 46, 106, 116–17, 120, 123, 134–5, 143, 149–51
privatization of higher education 95–120
in other higher education systems 97–101
private sector 5, 21, 23–4, 53, 96–7, 104, 105–7, 107–15, 117–19, 126, 129–30, 134–5, 139, 189, 191–5, 212–13, 237
privatization of public institutions 26, 29, 47, 52, 59–64, 97–8, 104–5, 212–13, 237
public good and higher education 1–2, 14–19, 24, 48–50, 64, 68, 69–70, 95–6, 211–39
and knowledge 49, 70, 96, 166, 227
See also common good and higher education

quality in higher education, and quality assurance 35–7, 44, 46, 50, 61, 116–17, 120, 121, 123, 127, 134, 139, 147, 148, 153, 158, 195, 204–8, 213
quasi-public good
See under public good and higher education

rankings of universities 8–9, 14–15, 35–6, 44, 144–5, 154, 166, 169–71, 179–80
regulation and governance in higher education 21, 37–9, 44–5, 121–42, 143–64, 179, 188, 214–15

Constitutional provisions for equity in higher education 73, 77
performance-based regulation 147, 152, 213, 237
research in India 8–11, 36, 38, 41, 161–4, 168–9, 206, 213
autonomy of researchers 11, 152–3, 211, 213, 237
and National Education Plan 10
national investment and funding 10, 49, 51, 56, 59
research publications 8–10, 15, 153, 161–4, 168–9, 179, 181, 185, 206
See also doctoral education, international collaboration
rural sector 2, 32, 44, 59, 78, 115

Samuelson, Paul 16, 48, 96
schooling 32, 35, 40, 43, 52–3, 55, 71–2, 90
sciences 8, 51, 84–5, 90, 119, 221
science, technology, engineering and mathematics 3, 76, 78, 82–5, 87–8, 187–210
Sen, Amartya 3
social demand for higher education 2, 4–5, 23, 70, 150
See also growth of higher education, massification
social inequality. See under economic and social inequality; see also equality and equity in higher education
social sciences 8, 11, 33, 51, 90, 161–4, 221
Standards. See under quality and quality assurance
states in higher education 39, 40, 43, 52, 53–5, 56, 85–6, 106, 112–15, 116–17, 121–42, 143–64, 191–3, 195–9
horizontal imbalances 122–3, 129–34, 134–5, 136–8, 141
State Higher Education Councils 138–41
See also union-state relations
STEM. See under science, technology, engineering and mathematics
students as agents in higher education 50, 159, 211–39

students' organisations and unions 212–39
student loans. See under funding and financing of higher education
system design and organisation in higher education 10–11, 15, 24, 26, 27, 43–4, 102
stratification 10, 17, 37, 64–5, 72–3, 83, 121, 159–60, 178–80

teachers in higher education 37, 64, 143, 152–3, 158, 161–4, 204–5, 211–39
teachers' organisations and unions 211, 212–39
teaching and learning in higher education 2, 36, 89–90, 181, 213, 227
teacher-student relations 227–8
teaching and research nexus 10–11, 133, 148
Trow, Martin 5, 24
tuition fees. See under funding and financing of higher education

union-state relations in India 21, 37, 54–5, 121–42, 147, 148, 149–51
vertical imbalances 122–3, 134–5, 141
urbanisation 3, 6–7
urban sector 32, 115
UGC. See under University Grants Commission
UNESCO. See under United Nations Educational, Social and Cultural Organisation
United Nations Educational, Social and Cultural Organisation 12, 18, 187, 237
United States of America 6, 18, 24, 26, 31, 42, 98, 99, 168, 173, 182–3, 185
University Grants Commission 8, 25, 38, 56, 106, 124, 126, 127, 128, 138, 145, 146, 149, 150, 151, 152–3, 154–5, 161, 166, 177, 188, 217

WCU. See under world class universities 178–80
world class universities 15, 36, 43, 155, 178–80. See also Institutions of Eminence, ranking of universities, stratification

www.ingramcontent.com/pod-product-compliance
Lightning Source LLC
Chambersburg PA
LVW052215300426
825CB00011B/1700